Imperfect XML

PAUL DOUGHERTY
23-APR-2005

Imperfect XML

Rants, Raves, Tips, and Tricks . . . from an Insider

David Megginson

♦Addison-Wesley

Upper Saddle River, NJ • Boston • Indianapolis • San Francisco
New York • Toronto • Montreal • London • Munich • Paris • Madrid
Capetown • Sydney • Tokyo • Singapore • Mexico City

Many of the designations used by manufacturers and sellers to distinguish their products are claimed as trademarks. Where those designations appear in this book, and Addison-Wesley was aware of a trademark claim, the designations have been printed with initial capital letters or in all capitals.

The author and publisher have taken care in the preparation of this book, but make no expressed or implied warranty of any kind and assume no responsibility for errors or omissions. No liability is assumed for incidental or consequential damages in connection with or arising out of the use of the information or programs contained herein.

The publisher offers excellent discounts on this book when ordered in quantity for bulk purchases or special sales, which may include electronic versions and/or custom covers and content particular to your business, training goals, marketing focus, and branding interests. For more information, please contact:

U. S. Corporate and Government Sales
(800) 382-3419
corpsales@pearsontechgroup.com

For sales outside the U.S., please contact:

International Sales
international@pearsoned.com

Visit us on the Web: www.awprofessional.com

Library of Congress Cataloging-in-Publication Data:

Megginson, David (David Paul), 1964–
   Imperfect XML : rants, raves, tips, and tricks from an insider / David Megginson.
      p. cm.
   Includes bibliographical references and index.
   ISBN 0-13-145349-1 (pbk. : alk. paper)
   1. XML (Document markup language) I. Title.
   QA76.76.H94M439 2004
   006.7'4—dc22   2004021752

Copyright © 2005 Pearson Education, Inc.

All rights reserved. Printed in the United States of America. This publication is protected by copyright, and permission must be obtained from the publisher prior to any prohibited reproduction, storage in a retrieval system, or transmission in any form or by any means, electronic, mechanical, photocopying, recording, or likewise. For information regarding permissions, write to:

Pearson Education, Inc.
Rights and Contracts Department
One Lake Street
Upper Saddle River, NJ 07458

ISBN 0-13-145349-1
Text printed in the United States on recycled paper at Courier in Stoughton, Massachusetts.
First printing, December 2004

Contents

List of Tables	xi
List of Figures	xiii
Preface	xv

PART ONE	**XML Decision Making**	**1**
Chapter 1	**The Standards Maze**	**3**
1.1	The Advantages of Standardization	4
	1.1.1 Interoperability	5
	1.1.2 Reuse	6
	1.1.3 Abstraction	6
1.2	The Disadvantages of Standardization	7
	1.2.1 FUD	8
	1.2.2 Monoculture	8
	1.2.3 Square Pegs	9
	1.2.4 Abstraction	10
1.3	XML Standards Players	10
	1.3.1 ISO	11
	1.3.2 W3C	12
	1.3.3 OASIS	13
	1.3.4 WS-I	14
	1.3.5 IDEAlliance	14
	1.3.6 RosettaNet	15
	1.3.7 Ad Hoc Groups	15
	1.3.8 Specialist Groups	16
1.4	XML-Related Specifications	17
	1.4.1 Core Specifications	18
	1.4.2 Embeddable Specifications	19
	1.4.3 Utility Specifications	21
	1.4.4 Application Specifications	24
1.5	Special Topics	26
	1.5.1 *De Facto* versus *De Jure* Standards	26
	1.5.2 Consistency and Compatibility	27
1.6	Final Words on Standards	29
Chapter 2	**Planning an XML Project**	**33**
2.1	Components of an XML Project	33
	2.1.1 Creation	35
	2.1.2 Storage and Archiving	36

	2.1.3	Search and Retrieval	36
	2.1.4	Transformation	37
	2.1.5	Rendering	38
	2.1.6	Transport	38
2.2	XML Project Pitfalls		38
	2.2.1	Unspoken Expectations	39
	2.2.2	Unrealistic Expectations	39
	2.2.3	Resistance to Change	40
2.3	How XML Projects Can Succeed		41
	2.3.1	Winning Friends and Influencing Users	42
	2.3.2	Successful XML Technology	44
2.4	Final Words on Planning		47

PART TWO   XML Implementation   49

Chapter 3   XML Documents   51

3.1	Advantages of XML for Documents		53
	3.1.1	Single-Source Publishing	53
	3.1.2	Hybrid Data Publishing	55
	3.1.3	Custom Publishing	56
	3.1.4	Reuse	57
	3.1.5	Knowledge Preservation	58
3.2	Disadvantages of XML for Documents		59
	3.2.1	People and Software	60
	3.2.2	Layout Control	61
3.3	Formatting and Production		62
	3.3.1	Change Markup	62
	3.3.2	Looseleaf Publishing	66
	3.3.3	Multiple Text Flows	67
3.4	Special Topics		69
	3.4.1	Client-Side XML	69
	3.4.2	Reuse	70
	3.4.3	Idioms	72
	3.4.4	Content Management	74
3.5	Final Words on Documents		76

Chapter 4   XML Data   77

4.1	The Advantages of XML Data		78
	4.1.1	Platform and Storage Independence	78
	4.1.2	Self-Documentation	79
	4.1.3	Reusability	79
	4.1.4	Verification	79
	4.1.5	Archiving and Auditing	80

4.2	The Disadvantages of XML Data		80
	4.2.1	Interoperability	80
	4.2.2	Abstraction	81
	4.2.3	Resources	81
4.3	Common Data Styles		81
	4.3.1	The Tabular Style	82
	4.3.2	The Graph Style	85
	4.3.3	The Hierarchical Style	90
4.4	Markup Issues		93
	4.4.1	Whitespace Handling	93
	4.4.2	Non-XML Content	95
4.5	Special Topics		97
	4.5.1	Identification	98
	4.5.2	Transactions	103
	4.5.3	Data Typing	105
	4.5.4	Data Binding	109
4.6	Final Words on XML Data		111

Chapter 5 **XML Networking**   113

5.1	Advantages of XML Networking		114
	5.1.1	Internationalization	114
	5.1.2	Transparency	114
	5.1.3	Extensibility	114
	5.1.4	Compatibility	115
	5.1.5	Network Resources	116
5.2	Disadvantages of XML Networking		117
	5.2.1	Performance	117
	5.2.2	Security	117
	5.2.3	State	118
5.3	XML Networking Styles		118
	5.3.1	RPC	121
	5.3.2	Asynchronous Messaging	126
	5.3.3	Web Services	127
	5.3.4	Grid Computing	131
	5.3.5	Syndication	132
	5.3.6	Other Styles	134
5.4	Special Topics		136
	5.4.1	Layering	136
	5.4.2	Switching and Routing	138
5.5	Final Words on XML Networking		139

PART THREE Special Issues 141

Chapter 6 XML Searching 143
- 6.1 The Advantages of XML Searching 143
  - 6.1.1 Context 143
  - 6.1.2 Correlation 145
- 6.2 The Disadvantages of XML Searching 147
  - 6.2.1 Usability 147
  - 6.2.2 Trust 149
  - 6.2.3 Interoperability 150
- 6.3 Markup Considerations 151
  - 6.3.1 In-Line Markup 151
  - 6.3.2 External Metadata 154
  - 6.3.3 Namespaces, Schemas, and the Semantic Web 159
- 6.4 Final Words on XML Searching 164

Chapter 7 XML and Legacy Information 167
- 7.1 Advantages of XML for Legacy Information 168
  - 7.1.1 Interfaces 168
  - 7.1.2 Transparency 170
  - 7.1.3 Code Reduction 172
  - 7.1.4 Network Effect 172
- 7.2 Disadvantages of XML for Legacy Information 173
  - 7.2.1 Analysis 173
  - 7.2.2 Granularity Mismatch 174
  - 7.2.3 Bloat 175
  - 7.2.4 Growth and Versioning 176
- 7.3 Special Topics 177
  - 7.3.1 Conversion Strategies 177
  - 7.3.2 Virtual XML 180
  - 7.3.3 Metadata 182
- 7.4 Final Words on XML and Legacy Information 184

Chapter 8 XML Performance and Size 185
- 8.1 Advantages of XML for Size and Performance 185
  - 8.1.1 Space Efficiency 186
  - 8.1.2 Software and Hardware Support 187
- 8.2 Disadvantages of XML for Size and Performance 188
  - 8.2.1 Repetition 188
  - 8.2.2 Encoding 189
  - 8.2.3 External References 189

Contents

	8.3	Processing Performance	190
		8.3.1 Parsing Interfaces	190
		8.3.2 Queries	191
		8.3.3 Transformations	194
		8.3.4 Pipelines	196
	8.4	Size	197
		8.4.1 Unicode and Character Size	197
		8.4.2 Internalization	198
		8.4.3 Compression	199
	8.5	Final Words on Performance and Size	199

Chapter 9 **Final Words** — 201

Glossary — 203
Bibliography — 207
Index — 215

List of Tables

1-1.	Element Names for a Book Title	29
4-1.	Simple Data Table	82
4-2.	Messy Data Table	82
4-3.	Employee Names and Titles (Relational)	86
4-4.	Employee Skills (Relational)	86
4-5.	Employee Units (Relational)	86
5-1.	XML Networking Styles	120
8-1.	A Binary Node	187

List of Figures

2-1.	Components of an XML project	34
3-1.	Single-source publishing	54
5-1.	Request/response versus publish/subscribe	120
5-2.	Stock quotes using RPC	132
5-3.	Stock quotes, using syndication	133
6-1.	External metadata for searching	159
7-1.	Communication using legacy interfaces	169
7-2.	Common facades over legacy interfaces	169
7-3.	Tree of DOM nodes	180
8-1.	XML processing in a pipeline	196
8-2.	XML processing without a pipeline	197

Preface

Welcome to your *second* book about the Extensible Markup Language [XML]. This may in fact be your third or twentieth XML book, but I did not design it to be your first. This book does not introduce the basics of XML syntax, explain how popular APIs and tools work, or offer design patterns or recipes for writing XML applications—many other XML books do an excellent job of that. Instead this book is about XML planning and decision making. Everyone involved with an XML project has to make decisions of some kind: whether to support XML at all, how to plan and schedule a project, what kind of goals to set, what standards to support, or what technical approaches to take. The best standards and libraries available will not help you at all if you try to use XML the wrong way or if XML is not the right technology for your project.

XML and its family of related specifications can be a complex and disruptive technology. The business success or failure of many XML projects hinges on the tiniest technical details, such as the choice of a parsing API; the technical success or failure of many XML projects depends on human factors, such as human resources and office politics. These responsibilities are usually divided between technologists and managers, but that division does not work as well for XML: A manager needs to master an unusually large number of technical details to plan and run an XML-related project, and a technologist needs to spend much more time than usual thinking about business needs and people skills to build effective systems.

As a result, this book deliberately takes a *middle-level* view of XML decision making, concentrating on the gray area between low-level technical issues and high-level management issues, the area that most technical books ignore. This book has many simple examples of XML markup and some source code listings, but nothing too complicated; there are many basic references of costs and benefits but little hard-core business theory and few case studies—and not a *single* pie chart—guaranteed. This is a book of XML rants, raves, tips, and tricks.

Together with facts, such as descriptions of specifications, this book contains many of my personal opinions, such as statements about the success or failure of individual specifications. I trust that you will be capable of distinguishing the two and that even when you disagree with the opinions, you will find them useful for identifying areas where other people are likely to disagree. In particular, unlike most XML-related books, this book tries not to overhype the technology.

The Idea of XML

Some of us inside the XML community believe that the technology is very useful but that it has been oversold. When XML first emerged in the late 1990s, the World Wide Web Consortium [W3C] and others promoted it not only as a technology but also as a social idea. Technically, XML was a simpler replacement for the older, complicated Standard Generalized Markup Language [SGML]. Socially, it was supposed to be the next logical step past the Hypertext Markup

Language [HTML] and the Web, ending the browser wars and enabling users to do new kinds of things on the Web, such as using software agents to analyze structured online information and perform such tasks as finding the lowest price for a pair of jeans. A common early description of XML, "SGML for the Web," touches on both ideas.

Technically, the core XML standard has been a runaway success. Several years on, there is little doubt that XML has replaced SGML: Vendors do not release new SGML products, and nearly all markup conferences have dropped *SGML* from their titles. People do not start new SGML projects, and the number of older SGML projects still being maintained shrinks every year. As a technology, XML has met and surpassed its technical goal of providing a simpler alternative to SGML. XML is easier than SGML ever was: For example, I spent six fruitless months of spare evenings trying to implement even a skeletal SGML parser in Java; I had the first prototype of the AElfred XML parser running after a few hours' work. SGML documents were almost never perfectly portable across systems, because all parsers supported different entity-resolution mechanisms and different SGML declarations; XML documents move seamlessly from parser to parser, XSLT engine to XSLT engine. XML is not without its own warts, but it has done well enough that it has infected many areas that SGML barely touched, such as save formats and configuration files for desktop applications. It has come to the point that developers feel that they have to justify *not* using XML as the basis for any new file format.

Socially, however, XML has not done nearly so well. Technical superiority is not enough: New technologies, such as the Internet, railroads, or vaccination, succeed because of a strong, contagious social message. Parents convince other parents to have their children inoculated; friends get their friends to use e-mail or text messaging so that they can communicate; small towns once competed with one another to have railroads pass through them to avoid being left behind by the new economy.

Most people do not care that XML is cleaner and easier to implement than other file formats: People want to know what XML will let them do and why they should do that. If XML does not capture people's imaginations—if it does not, at least in some small way, change their lives—it will stay just another tool in a technologist's toolbox, like Unicode or structured programming. If that happens, all the people who have invested heavily in XML start-ups and products are going to be very disappointed.

To date, XML in general has not managed to affect people's lives the way peer-to-peer file transfer, cell phones, video games, text messaging, or automated teller machines have. XML came out in 1998; today, one compelling social trend—Web logs, or *blogs*—happens to use XML, but more general XML applications have not yet succeeded. In 2004, despite the continuing hype, XML lacks momentum.

That lack of momentum matters a lot to anyone planning an XML project: An XML implementer has to start almost from scratch each time, convincing yet another small group of managers and users that XML is a good idea for them and working with their strengths and weaknesses to integrate XML into their small social group. If the project is successful, it ends up as an XML island, with little or no connection to other small XML islands.

Preface

If XML is not *the* answer, however, it may be *part* of it. Many quiet but critical infrastructure technologies—ASCII [ASCII], Unicode [UNICODE], the Internet Protocol [IP], and the Transmission Control Protocol [TCP]—provide a firm foundation for higher-level successes, such as the Web. As mentioned earlier, XML is already the foundation of the Web log movement, and that movement has significantly transformed the Web. XML did not make that transformation happen but provided a basic technology that made it easier for bloggers to share information, and provided software, libraries, and best practices to help them do it.

Structure of the Book

This book consists of three major parts.

1. Part One (Chapters 1 and 2) deals with making initial high-level decisions about XML, concentrating on standards support and project planning.
2. Part Two (Chapters 3–5) introduces the three major areas of XML work—documents, data, and networking—together with detailed discussions of the advantages, disadvantages, and special issues involved in making design and implementation decisions for each one.
3. Part Three (Chapters 6–8) concentrates on special issues that affect all areas of XML and require more detailed discussion: searching, working with legacy, or non-XML data, and XML performance and size.

You do not need to read the chapters in order: Each one is designed as a free-standing essay or article on a major XML topic, with only occasional cross-references. It would probably be a good idea, however, to start by reading Chapter 1, on XML standards and specifications, as a knowledge of XML specifications is useful background information for any XML reading.

If you are looking for information on specific topics, the glossary, bibliography, and index make excellent starting points. Use the glossary to find definitions of unfamiliar terms or concepts, and then use the index to find where the book discusses them.

Thanks

Many people have helped out with advice and suggestions for this book, although it is important to note that they do not necessarily agree with all, or even very much, of what I have written here. Thanks first to Mark Taub, my editor. I had a good experience working with Mark during the writing of my first book, *Structuring XML Documents,* so he was the obvious person to turn to when my judgment lapsed to the point that I was considering writing a second one. As before, Mark has been patient and helpful.

Ron Daniel, Neil Bradley, and Marc Hadley reviewed the initial book proposal and offered helpful comments and criticism. Ken Holman and Ron reviewed parts of the manuscript as I was writing it, providing useful feedback, both positive and negative. Ron, Eric Raymond, and Priscilla Walmsley all read the complete manuscript and offered extremely useful comments and criticism. Chanda Leary-Coutu came up with the perfect title for this book in minutes, after Mark Taub and I had spent nearly a year going from one stinker to another. Thanks also to Evelyn Pyle for her friendly, effective copy editing, making my prose read much better without ever losing the sense or style of it, and to Elizabeth Ryan for shepherding the book through production calmly and efficiently.

Finally, of course, thanks to my family—Tess, Emma, and Bonnie—for putting up with my being far too busy and far too grumpy for far too long while writing this book.

PART ONE

XML Decision Making

Fortunately, the era of waterfall design is coming to a close. These days, project managers are unlikely to lock in all the design decisions before implementation begins but instead allow their teams to work incrementally, going through iteration after iteration as they refine both the design and the implementation, discovering new requirements, new problems, and new solutions as they go. One result of this change is that strategic decision making becomes part of every stage of a project rather than simply the early planning stage. Everyone involved in an XML project—managers, engineers, documentation specialists, marketing and sales, and customers—needs to be able to participate in strategic decision making in some capacity.

Chapter 1 looks at the enormous number of XML-related technical specifications available. It surveys both the standards and the bodies that produce them, in order to help you make intelligent decisions about which specifications to follow and which to postpone or ignore.

Chapter 2 steps through some of the major issues in planning an XML project, pointing out common pitfalls and possible workarounds. Much of the advice in this chapter is based on my own experience as an SGML and XML consultant over the past decade on projects that succeeded, as well as those that people would rather forget.

CHAPTER 1

The Standards Maze

Technologists disagree about how to use the word *standard*. Some argue that the term can apply only to a document produced by an established international standards body, such as the International Organization for Standardization [ISO]; others allow the term for documents produced by vendor consortiums, such as the World Wide Web Consortium [W3C]; and yet others use the word to refer to any widely implemented specification.[1]

To help keep tempers down, this chapter avoids the term *standard* as often as possible in favor of the more neutral term *specification*; however, where *standard* does appear, the word refers to a specification that is widely implemented, regardless of its origin.[2] When the chapter needs to make more precise distinctions among specifications or standards, it adds a qualifier, such as *international, consortium, Internet, ad hoc,* or *de facto.*

This chapter begins with a frank look at both the advantages and the disadvantages of standardization. Shared specifications can bring enormous cost reductions and productivity improvements but can also drag a project to its death. The key is to know exactly what you hope to gain from following a public specification and how much it will cost you—in time, money, and lost functionality—to do so. Like laws and treaties, public specifications are the result of processes, negotiations, and political maneuvering. Knowing about the organizations and the people who publish XML specifications will help you to understand why a specification is the way it is and how it might change in the future. Before introducing the specifications themselves, then, the chapter surveys the players in the XML standards world.

Finally, the chapter examines the XML-related specifications themselves, organized not according to who wrote them but according to how you can use them. With a little practice, people working on XML projects can learn to sort out the live specifications from the duds.

---

[1] Dictionary definitions are little help, for two reasons: The definitions are typically too general, and dictionaries are written to reflect how people *use* (or used) words, not how they *should* use them.

[2] That usage is familiar to the general population: People call *Summertime* a *jazz standard*, for example, not because George and Ira Gershwin wrote it but because many jazz musicians perform it and record it.

1.1 The Advantages of Standardization

With standardization, three good things happen:

1. *Interoperability.* Things work together predictably, allowing people to spend less time solving unnecessary problems and more time doing what they want or need to do.
2. *Reuse.* The market is bigger, so more standard software components are available for less money; and
3. *Abstraction.* Once they agree on a standard way of doing things, people no longer have to worry about the minor details and can concentrate on higher-level problems.

The North American railroad system provides an excellent, pre-Internet example of how standardization works. By the middle of the nineteenth century, North American railroads were using many different common wide-rail gauges—the distance between the iron rails—and the variety of gauges caused problems. For example, when freight moved from southern New York to New Jersey, handlers had to unload the cargo from the freight cars designed for a 6 ft. gauge and reload it onto freight cars designed for New Jersey's 4 ft. 10 in. gauge.[3] Some railroads were incompatible by accident, whereas others chose unusual gauges deliberately to get what they hoped would be a competitive advantage. At first, railroads were mostly local, so the problems were not severe. However, the problem became particularly nasty during the second part of the nineteenth century when railroads started to interconnect into a national grid and, at the same time, smaller railroads started to merge into larger, regional or national companies. As Canada and the United States became industrialized and freight moved farther and farther by rail, the number of transshipment points increased until companies found themselves spending more and more time and money to do unnecessary work, unloading and reloading cargo that had already been loaded once or more. What the original, short-sighted companies had thought would be a competitive advantage turned into a money pit. There was increasing pressure to standardize on a single rail gauge so that a freight car loaded at its origin would not have to be unloaded until its destination, even if the destination were half way across the continent.

Standardization was a long, messy affair, but all but the narrow-gauge railroads—which had special challenges, such as tight turns in mountainous terrain—eventually standardized on the 4 ft. 8.5 in. gauge originally used by George Stephenson for the British Liverpool & Manchester Railway in the 1820s. Conversion must have been expensive for the railroads using the nonstandard gauges, as they had to rip up and relay many tens of thousands of kilometers of rail, but the demand for cheaper and easier transportation eventually forced those railroads to either standardize or be left out of the grid. From that point, the customers of North American railroads enjoyed a network effect: A freight car could be loaded in New York and delivered seamlessly to St. Louis or New Orleans, even if it passed over the tracks of many different railroads. Other

---

[3] For an excellent discussion of this topic, see *The Standarization of Track Gauge on North American Railways, 1830–1890* (http://www.vwl.uni-muenchen.de/ls_komlos/northam.pdf).

1.1 The Advantages of Standardization

forms of transportation, such as canal barges, were unable to compete and fell into steep decline. Despite the large distances between its cities, a cheap and effective transportation grid allowed the United States to grow from a rural backwater into the world's largest industrial power by the end of the nineteenth century.

The same pattern appears over and over again in the history of successful standards: the English *Magna Carta* mandated a standard systems of weights and measures so that tavern keepers could not shortchange their ale drinkers. Like the railroads, the earliest phone companies also tried to lock in customers by using incompatible systems, but the marketplace forced them to develop standards so that a customer of any company could phone a customer of any other company. As late as the mid-1990s, Microsoft original MSN (Microsoft Networks) was an incompatible, proprietary network designed to draw users away from the Internet, but all Microsoft's power and money failed to hold back standardization, so MSN became simply another Internet provider. North American 911 (emergency phone) service requires that a city standardize its addresses, assigning each dwelling a unique number and removing any duplicate street names, so that emergency vehicles can find their way more easily. At the time of writing, cellular phone users in the United States have only now gained the ability to keep the same phone number when they change service providers.

1.1.1 Interoperability

The first major advantage of standardization is interoperability, or allowing things to work together, just as standardization allowed any freight car to run on any railroad's tracks. Modern industrialized societies take interoperability for granted in numerous areas.

- We expect a new set of tires to fit our car whether the tires come from from Michelin, Pirelli, or Goodyear.
- We expect a Phillips #2 screwdriver to work with a Phillips #2 screw head whether the screwdriver comes from Snap-On, Mastercraft, or Black & Decker.
- In any given country—but not, obviously, around the world—we expect any given electrical plug to fit into any appropriate outlet.

It would be easy, of course, to extend the list to the length of this book or beyond; the point is that it is important not to take any of this for granted. It is all the result of standards work.

Interoperability is, of course, the foundation of the Internet. You can use a Microsoft browser to view a Web page delivered to you from an Apache server on a Dell box running Linux through a Cisco router across some Nortel fiber-optic equipment on through a Lucent switch and a Terayon cable modem into your local Linksys firewall and your 3COM Ethernet card without any concern about how the whole network fits together. As long as all the manufacturers follow the same standards, everything works.

Unfortunately, this level of interoperability is normal at the *protocol* level, but does not always appear at the *format* level. The Web page can get to your browser with no problem, but if the page itself was optimized for another browser, such as Mozilla, it might not display properly in yours. The browser-compatibility problem is minor today—the main browsers all do a reasonable job following standards—but it was very serious in the mid-1990s, when work began on XML. In fact, one of XML's main goals was to find a way to make information formats as reliably interoperable as Internet protocols, so that you wouldn't have to worry about what browser you use any more than you do about what brand of TCP/IP switch your internet service provider uses.

1.1.2 Reuse

The second major advantage of standardization is reuse. Once the rail gauges were standardized, Pullman and other companies could manufacture a standard set of coaches that would run on any tracks. That meant that the set-up costs were spread among many more customers, and prices fell. Something similar has happened with modular phone jacks: instead of renting a telephone from the phone company, people can now buy phones from any manufacturer and simply plug them in. Once the market opened up, many new manufacturers entered and created innovations, such as cordless phones, and drove down consumer prices.

In the technology world, reuse typically shows up in the form of libraries or software components. For example, because XML itself is standardized, software developers can use parsing and validation libraries from many different sources—commercial or free—rather than paying for expensive custom development or tying themselves to a single vendor. Authors creating information for a new XML-based data format can use off-the-shelf XML editing tools, databases can provide special XML import, export, and storage features useful to any project, and hardware manufacturers can create special devices for simplifying or accelerating XML processing. The more people use XML, the cheaper these tools get—or, in the case of free software, the better they get—because more people share the development time and cost.

1.1.3 Abstraction

The third advantage of standardization, abstraction, is not as well known as the other two but can sometimes be more important. Standardization allows people to ignore low-level details and to concentrate on higher-level issues that add more value. For example, most C++ programmers do not have to worry about CPU register use, most Java programmers do not have to worry about memory management, and most spreadsheet users do not have to worry about procedural code at all. It was not always this way: Problems that people solve themselves with spreadsheets today once required an expensive team of programmers writing low-level code customized for each job.

Slowly, the technology community is abstracting away lower-level problems for information management as people standardize on transmission protocols (TCP/IP and HTTP), storage (hard disk and CD-ROM), character encoding (Unicode), and now low-level structure (XML). A multi-million-dollar technology project 10 or 15 years ago might have spent many months of planning just to decide on these low-level issues; as the issues are now, effectively, decided for them, the project team can concentrate on higher-level problems that add more value to their work. Today's

1.2 The Disadvantages of Standardization

software is cheaper, more sophisticated, *and* easier to use precisely because good standards—formal or informal—help designers and programmers to avoid distractions and delays.

When it is successful, standardization pays enormous dividends; the disadvantages, spread among many users, become smaller and smaller. At the same time, those users become more productive as it gets easier and easier for them to work together.

Still, for every ultimately successful standardization effort, there are many failures, and even the successful specifications produce losers as well as winners (consider the railroads that had to rip up all their track). Leaving aside vendors with proprietary interests, however, four main areas of standards, or the attempt to create standards, can hurt people instead of helping them:

1. *FUD.* The existence of a real or proposed standard, or even the announcement of a plan to create one, can throw an entire industry into fear, uncertainty, and doubt.
2. *Monoculture.* Standardization discourages diversity, which is the best defense against design flaws and security vulnerabilities.
3. *Square pegs.* When a standard is successful, the pressure to apply it in inappropriate places, where its disadvantages far outweigh its benefits, can be enormous.
4. *Abstraction.* Although abstraction is sometimes helpful, ignoring lower-level issues can sometimes lead to large inefficiencies or even rule out simpler and better solutions to problems.

All the successful standards efforts mentioned earlier in this chapter have something in common: They dealt with things that people were already doing and solved problems that people had actually experienced. First, tavern keepers sold ale, and then people discovered that it was difficult to compare prices, so they solved the problem with standardization. First, companies built railroads, and then customers discovered that it was expensive to continually unload and reload cargo for long-distance shipping, so they solved that problem with standardization. First, companies built phone systems, and then people demanded the ability to call a telephone connected to any company's exchange, so they solved that problem with standardization.

It is difficult not to draw a lesson from these examples: Standardization pays. Unfortunately, it is also easy to draw the wrong lesson and to try to short-circuit the standardization cycle by writing standards before the fact. A quick glance over the XML standards family will show that almost none of the XML-related standards and specifications fits into the same pattern as the successful standards of the past. Instead of starting with implementation, discovering where the real problems are, and then solving those problems with standardization, many committees propose standards for things that do not even exist, in the hope that implementation will follow and that the problems people discover will happen to be the same ones they anticipated while writing their specification.

For example, some industry groups are designing voluminous public XML specifications for information interchange, when in fact, the companies in the industry have little experience sharing information in any format or medium, much less using XML. Various groups are frantically writing new high-level specifications for Web Services before anyone has even implemented the basic parts. In fact, it has come to the point that the most common complaint about XML is that there are too many specifications and standards for anyone to absorb. For example, Robin Cover lists nearly 600 XML-related specifications on his XML-related Web site,[4] not including separate versions of the same specification, and there are likely hundreds more that he has not stumbled on yet.

1.2.1 FUD

The first major drawback of standardization is FUD (fear, uncertainty, and doubt). Many industries have had experiences like those of the nineteenth-century railroads that had to tear up and relay their tracks after the change to standard rail gauge. Once a standard is well established, any company that does not support it risks serious economic penalties.

To try to avoid these problems, industries often form consortia to develop standards together in advance or develop standards through international standards bodies. Sometimes, a standards committee will have representation from only a few major companies, but the mere announcement of the committee's formation may be enough to freeze or at least slow down any other development in the area among both vendors and users creating their own systems. For example, as long as a W3C committee is working on an unfinished XML query language, companies and other large organizations will be hesitant to build systems that query XML documents; a successful query standard could make their work obsolete.

The value of a successful standard can easily outweigh the harm done by FUD, but the problem is that most standards efforts are *not* successful; in other words, before a specification fails, it manages to stifle the free experimentation that could have led to a successful standard. Sometimes, this effect is even deliberate: A few large companies will join together and announce a new standards effort—or convince an existing organization to announce one—simply to wrong-foot their competitors.

This problem has no simple solution. Companies are responsible for their shareholders' money, and governments are responsible for their taxpayers' money; neither can afford to risk money on systems that may soon be obsolete. This structural problem falls out from trying to build standards before the fact instead of basing them on real experience. Users have to evaluate specifications carefully to judge how successful they're likely to be and then take measured risks, where appropriate.

1.2.2 Monoculture

FUD is a danger mainly of unsuccessful attempts at standardization, but standardization sometimes causes harm by its own success. For example, standardizing on the potato helped reduce the Irish hunger problem in the eighteenth century and allowed the Irish population to grow. But once

---

[4] The Cover Pages (http://xml.coverpages.org/).

1.2 The Disadvantages of Standardization

the potato was virtually the only crop in the country, a single infection—*phytophthora infestans,* or potato blight—was able to destroy the country's ability to feed itself, killing more than half a million people and forcing many more to leave the country.

Technological monocultures can create similar problems. In 1988, the Morris Internet worm, transmitted through the Simple Mail Transfer Protocol [SMTP] between send-mail implementations, virtually shut down the entire Internet. From the mid-1990s on, the dominance of Microsoft's desktop applications has allowed first macro viruses and then e-mail viruses to shut down corporate intranets and sometimes entire Internet service providers over and over again, the same way that the potato blight kept devastating Ireland's crops.

In these cases, the problem was a software monoculture rather than a standards monoculture: Using a different SMTP server application—several alternatives, such as exim, are now available—word processor, or mail reader provides immunity to a worm or a virus. A standards monoculture, on the other hand, poses a much more serious threat because a design flaw or a security problem in a standard can affect all software that implements that standard, not only a single application.

The only good defense against viruses or serious technical problems is diversity, in both software and specifications, and standardization explicitly discourages that diversity. In effect, if we take standardization too far, we are back to planting nothing but potatoes.

1.2.3 Square Pegs

Like monoculture, the square-peg problem occurs mainly with successful standards. Once a standard is or appears to be successful, people will flock to it, soon resulting in pressure to apply the standard in areas where it was not intended to go. That pressure is not always a bad thing; for example, the telephone system was not designed to carry images, but FAX machines were a successful innovation. In fact, many technologies fail in their original application area and succeed somewhere else: Java never made much progress on the desktop but is now the technology of choice for server-side development. The Hypertext Markup Language [HTML] was not originally intended to be interactive, but early experiments with forms and server-side scripts led to the Web's ultimate success.

Nonetheless, despite the fact that a popular specification is a poor fit, technologists will continue to use it, because of either coercion from management or simple ignorance. For example, XSL Transformations [XSLT] was originally designed for publishing, but has become so well known that people often try to use it for data transformation in high-speed environments, usually resulting in dismal performance (see Chapter 8, XML performance and size for more details). Despite the best efforts of designers of the VRML (Virtual Reality Markup Language) [VRML], the Web simply turned out not to be a popular platform for delivering 3D graphics. The ease of use of JavaServer Pages (JSPs) led many developers to mix code and presentation to the point that Web sites became unmaintainable: The developers couldn't understand the presentational markup, and the graphic designers couldn't understand the Java code.

1.2.4 Abstraction

Abstraction, the fourth advantage of standardization, is also a disadvantage. Abstraction is a powerful technique, allowing a general to command tens of thousands of soldiers by delegating smaller details to subordinates, who then delegate even smaller details to their subordinates, and so on, so that the general can move all those people with a single command. Abstraction allows people to write networking applications without having to worry about the hardware details or even the lower-level network protocols, and it allows programmers to write XML applications without worrying about the details of character encoding.

On the other hand, abstraction can hide serious inefficiencies. Armies often blunder around because of weak communication along the chain of command; subordinates avoid taking responsibility for problems and do not pass on information that might harm them. Using HyperText Transfer Protocol [HTTP] libraries for high-speed network messaging may cause excessive buffer copying and network traffic. Java applications can still leak memory, and when the leaks do occur, they are more difficult to find.

XML markup itself is a relatively low level of abstraction, whereas the specifications built on top of XML are at an increasingly higher level and thus more abstract. Until high-level specifications like those for the Resource Description Framework [RDF] and Web Services, for example, get widespread deployment in production-grade systems, it is difficult to know what their hidden disadvantages might be. Will there be serious performance problems, deadlocks, security leaks? We do not know yet, and if these problems do occur, abstraction will make them more difficult to track down. Abstraction helps people avoid worrying about low-level details, but it can also prevent them from paying attention to low-level problems.

1.3 XML Standards Players

The organizations that write specifications are never quite sure how they want people to think about their work.

- On the one hand, they want to promote their specifications as independent creations that can stand and succeed on their on merits, outside of any context, such as people, places, politics, or specific moments in time. ("This isn't only an IBM and Microsoft specification.")
- On the other hand, however, the same groups want their specifications to share the authority and credibility of the people, companies, and organizations that created them. ("IBM and Microsoft are backing this specification.")

In reality, technical specifications do have context, both good and bad. Standardization is a social process, and specifications are social documents, capturing the result of human egos, negotiation, cooperation, and political maneuvering at specific places and times. To help provide some of that context, this section introduces some of the most important groups that create XML-related specifications.

1.3 XML Standards Players

1.3.1 ISO

The world's best-known standards body is likely the Geneva-based International Organization for Standardization [ISO], which developed XML's predecessor, Standard Generalized Markup Language [SGML]. ISO includes one member organization from each country, such as ANSI (American National Standards Institute), SAI (Standards Australia International), and BIS (Bureau of Indian Standards). Through ISO, these national groups share their requirements, work out their differences, and develop specifications to improve business worldwide.

ISO specifications cover such areas as railway engineering, agriculture, quality control, rubber and plastics, and just about anything that touches business and industry. The ISO 9000 series of specifications, for example, is widely accepted as the measure of quality control in business. In the computer technology world, the ISO specifications covering country-code abbreviations (ISO 3166), currency abbreviations (ISO 4217), and language abbreviations (ISO 639) are ubiquitous: anyone who has worked with business data for any amount of time is familiar with such abbreviations `de-CH` for the Swiss dialect of German or `JPY` for Japanese yen. The ISO 8859 specifications for character encoding are still popular, although slowly losing ground to Unicode, and ISO's American member organization, ANSI, developed the current specifications for the C and C++ programming languages.

There can be some confusion about ISO specifications, however. In addition to its own work and that of its member bodies, ISO often republishes work created and maintained by other organizations. For example, ISO publishes its own versions of the Unicode specification [UNICODE], developed and maintained by the Unicode Consortium, and of the RelaxNG XML schema specification [RELAXNG], developed and maintained by OASIS. Some governmental organizations have policies limiting them to specifications published by recognized international standards bodies, such as ISO. Stamping ISO's trademark on the covers of these specifications helps them to get past those barriers, but most technical specialists would not think of Unicode or RelaxNG as primarily ISO specifications.

As XML's predecessor, SGML, was an ISO specification, why did XML's creators not turn to ISO as well?[5] XML seems like an excellent candidate for an international standard, as it is a critical part of business infrastructure and requires a high amount of interoperability. In fact, aside from a few popular specifications, ISO has not played a prominent role in computer technology during the past decade or so. Technology specialists are quick to suggest reasons why ISO does so well with industrial standards but stumbles with high tech.

- ISO's formal processes are too slow and cumbersome for a fast-changing, networked world.
- ISO is dominated by Europeans, whereas high tech is dominated by North Americans.
- ISO specifications are not published freely online, discouraging early adopters.

---

[5] Note that ISO did revise SGML to include all the features of XML.

In fact, it is unlikely that any of these is the primary problem, although the last one certainly does ISO's specifications significant harm. The less formal standards bodies and consortia described later in this chapter can be just as slow and process heavy as ISO, and they often contain just as much or more non-U.S. participation. Rather, it is ISO's very structure that holds it back. The assumption that standards can be developed by negotiation among countries is a good one for dealing with transportation and smokestack industries. Manufacturing plants in any single country will have a lot in common with one another, as they operate under the same environmental regulations, trade rules, tax laws, and so on; finding common ground through a national standards body can make sense in these situations.

In information technology, however, the situation is entirely different because often, borders scarcely exist at all. A Web site in Israel or Egypt may serve primarily the U.S. market; a single programming team for a product may be scattered across several continents. The World Wide Web, Web logs, text messaging, e-mail, and Internet relay chat (IRC) enable direct, informal connections among users and developers worldwide. In an environment like this, ISO's emphasis on national bodies puts it at a severe disadvantage over bodies structured around communities of interest rather than political borders, because ISO brings the wrong parties to the table. A new XML-related specification is not a matter for negotiation among, say, Sudan, Indonesia, and the United States but rather among the people and organizations that will use the specification.

Although ISO does develop XML-relevant standards, such as the language codes mentioned earlier, it has become at best a minor player in the XML standards world. The ISO trademark on the cover of an XML-related specification is no guarantee of the specification's success; unfortunately, in many cases, it may even be an impediment. XML technologists and technology companies look elsewhere for authoritative XML-related specifications, starting with XML's own creator: the W3C.

1.3.2 W3C

The World Wide Web Consortium [W3C] was formed to develop and manage Web formats, such as Hypertext Markup Language [HTML], serving as counterpart to the IETF (Internet Engineering Task Force) [IETF],[6] which develops and maintains specifications for Internet protocols, such as the HyperText Transfer Protocol [HTTP]. The W3C originally concentrated on HTML and related specifications, such as Cascading Style Sheets [CSS], and on proof-of-concept Web software, such as the Amaya browser. HTML's syntax is heavily influenced by ISO's Standard Generalized Markup Language [SGML], however, and the W3C eventually redefined HTML as a proper SGML document type. By the mid-1990s, there was interest in a simplified version of SGML for the Web, not limited to the HTML tag set. Through the W3C—and mostly under the radar—a small group set out to develop what eventually became XML. As XML progressed, it started to attract attention both inside and outside the W3C, and people began to consider how

---

[6] Sir Tim Berners-Lee, HTML's creator, originally brought the HTML specification to the IETF; he founded the W3C only after the IETF HTML process bogged down. The two groups now coexist amicably, although they are set up very differently.

1.3 XML Standards Players

generic markup might work on the Web. The W3C formed more working groups to fill in what its members believed would be the missing pieces for building an XML-based Web:

- A standard programming interface, in the Document Object Model [DOM]
- A style sheet language for browser-based rendering in the XML Stylesheet Language [XSLT] and [XSL-FO]
- A way to link and point into documents in the XML Linking Language [XLINK] and XML Pointer Language [XPOINTER] specifications

Eventually, the W3C adopted XML as the base syntax for most of its Web specifications, from privacy to metadata and from vector graphics to mathematics.

People find some aspects of the W3C objectionable. Unlike ISO, the W3C does make its specifications freely redistributable: You can download them for free, republish them in your book, and so on. However, participation in W3C working groups is nominally limited to its members, both individual members and employees of member companies. Many XML specialists are self-employed or employees of nonmembers and resent being excluded from the committees developing XML-related standards and the associated closed mailing lists. In practice, nonmembers do serve on W3C working groups as *invited experts,* but, as the name implies, they serve by invitation only.

The W3C's position as custodian of XML and other core specifications gives it an immense amount of respectability in the XML standards world: Most other groups are delighted to have their work taken over by the W3C or even to publish it under the W3C logo as a W3C Note. At the same time, the W3C has struggled and failed to reproduce its original success with XML. The W3C created its original suite of XML-related specifications for its core competency, browsers and the Web. Like Java, however, XML has found its real success behind the firewall and inside the enterprise, areas outside the W3C's expertise.

The W3C has continued to flesh out the XML core with specifications for XML Namespaces [NAMESPACES] and a data model [INFOSET] and has continued to update its existing specifications, but its newer XML-related initiatives, such as the Semantic Web [SEMANTIC-WEB] have generated considerably less interest than the early XML work. Nevertheless, some of the W3C's latest specifications, especially those related to security, XML forms, and XML querying, may eventually form an important part of the XML infrastructure.

1.3.3 OASIS

For most of its existence, the Organization for Advancement of Structured Information Standards [OASIS]—originally called SGML Open—was the also-ran of the markup world, concentrating first on the scraps of SGML too small to interest ISO, such as entity catalogs, then on the scraps of XML too small to interest the W3C.

Over time, however, OASIS attracted a large number of XML specialists who were disenchanted with the W3C, and the organization has begun to define itself more distinctly. For example, OASIS took over the popular DocBook specification [DOCBOOK], originally developed by a separate consortium, and merged two earlier specifications into the RelaxNG schema language [RELAXNG], creating a serious competitor to the W3C's controversial XML Schema Language [XML-SCHEMA].

OASIS's first attempt at a big breakaway, however, came with ebXML [EBXML], a cooperative venture with the United Nations Centre for Trade Facilitation and Electronic Business [UN-CEFACT], which maintains some current non-XML standards for electronic data interchange (EDI). Especially inside governmental organizations, ebXML gained some press and a lot of interest, but the initiative was soon eclipsed by the new idea of *Web Services* (see Section 5.3.3). OASIS then worked to reposition ebXML inside Web Services and began developing new utility specifications for the Web Services world, covering such areas as Web Services Security (WSS) and Web Services Reliable Messaging (WSRM). So far, the effort has been moderately successful; the press treats OASIS as one of the major players in the Web Services world, an area in which the W3C, which maintains some core specifications, such as SOAP [SOAP], generally rates only a polite mention.

OASIS raises fewer barriers to starting new initiatives than the W3C does; essentially, all that is required is to find enough OASIS members interested, and a new *technical committee* (TC) springs into existence. Individual memberships are relatively inexpensive, and non-members are allowed to participate in developing specifications, but not to start new groups. As a result, OASIS does not have the same exclusionist reputation as the W3C but does have a large number of working groups focused on perhaps too many different areas.

1.3.4 WS-I

The Web Services Interoperability Organization [WS-I] is not a regular standards or specifications body; instead of writing specifications, its working groups create *profiles,* using existing specifications from other sources, together with sample implementations and implementation guidelines. At the beginning, the WS-I looked like one of two hostile camps in the Web Services world, appearing to represent mainly the interests of IBM and Microsoft—two of its founding members—whereas OASIS seemed to represent mainly the interests of Sun Microsystems and BEA, two of its major backers. In fact, WS-I and OASIS do have several Web Service–related specifications in direct competition, but the hostility is not as fierce as it might seem; many companies work with both organizations, and Sun now has a seat on the WS-I board of directors. In fact, Microsoft's backing of the WS-I is more of an attack on the W3C than on OASIS, as Microsoft very publicly abandoned the W3C Web Services choreography working group.

The WS-I lacks OASIS's depth—WS-I deals only with Web Services, not other areas of XML—but the large companies involved can commit significant time and money to developing and implementing profiles. It is unclear what will happen to competing specifications, but it appears that the future direction for Web Services will come mainly from the WS-I and OASIS, not the W3C.

1.3.5 IDEAlliance

IDEAlliance [IDEALLIANCE], formerly known as the Graphic Communications Association, plays an important role in the XML community by organizing the industry's major

1.3 XML Standards Players

conferences. IDEAlliance has also adopted several XML-related specifications that it now develops and promotes. Of these, the best known are the Publishing Requirements for Industry Standard Metadata [PRISM] and Information and Content Exchange [ICE].

Both of these specifications attracted attention when first released: PRISM, for distributing information in the magazine industry; ICE, for automating information delivery using XML. Both PRISM and ICE have since been overshadowed by other, more popular specifications. Nevertheless, they have much of interest in them, and their lessons may be useful in future specifications.

In particular, PRISM uses a clean, layered design: Instead of building an isolated stovepipe design from low-level XML—or XML and namespaces—on up, as most application specifications do, PRISM uses RDF as a data layer and the Dublin Core as a basic semantic layer, then adds information on top of those, which makes for a relatively thin specification that does not contain unnecessary duplication. Although PRISM itself is not widely implemented, any RDF processor will be able to read and manipulate PRISM files, and any software with built-in knowledge of the Dublin Core will be able to extract useful information. As a result, a specification built like PRISM is much more interoperable than most XML-based file formats and can reuse a much wider range of off-the-shelf software.

1.3.6 RosettaNet

RosettaNet [ROSETTANET] was an early industry consortium for developing electronic business standards in XML. As Web Services gained attention, RosettaNet was forced to recast its work as a higher-level layer on top of Web Services, in much the same way that OASIS did with ebXML.

In addition to the usual technical information, RosettaNet's existing specifications contain a lot of higher-level business information; for example, RosettaNet has standards in such areas as inventory management, service and support, and product information, whereas other organizations are concentrating on Web Services infrastructure, such as security and quality of service. RosettaNet's supporters hope, obviously, that they will be able to reuse much of this work as high-level processes for using Web Services, although the group receives little attention.

1.3.7 Ad Hoc Groups

ISO, the W3C, OASIS, WS-I, IDEAlliance, and RosettaNet are all formal organizations; although their processes differ, they all have paid staff available to support standards efforts that pass through some kind of official, well-defined process. Not all XML-related specifications develop that way, however. Some popular XML-related specifications have grown up outside the standards bodies and consortia, including the Simple API for XML [SAX], the Resource Directory Description Language [RDDL], and RSS[7] [RSS].

SAX, developed initially by the author of this book, stands out as the least formalized of all the efforts. I simply published a proposed Java-related specification and then led an informal

---

[7] RSS is a syndication format that exists in different versions from different sources; there is not even a generally agreed-on expansion for the abbreviation. Nevertheless, the versions are similar enough that software writers manage to support all of them without too much trouble.

e-mail discussion on the `xml-dev` mailing list on how to improve it. When people had spent long enough suggesting changes and fixing bugs, I released SAX 1.0 and later, SAX 2.0. Every major XML vendor quickly supported SAX for Java, and versions soon showed up in other major programming languages. Eventually, the term *SAX interface* or *SAX-like interface,* became a generic word in XML circles for any event-based parsing library.

RDDL, pronounced *riddle,* is only scarcely more formal than SAX, consisting of, at least, a properly written specification. Like SAX, RDDL grew out of discussions on the `xml-dev` mailing list, this time concerning what kind of resource an XML Namespaces URI should point to. RDDL is not as widely adopted as SAX or RSS and is not a *standard* by this chapter's definition, but RDDL is nonetheless a well-liked and simple specification filling an important role.

RSS started as a Netscape specification for sharing data with its mynetscape.com site, a community-based competitor to Yahoo's Web index. When Netscape lost interest in RSS and stopped maintaining the specification, various parties attempted to take it over and have been releasing competing—and incompatible—specifications called *RSS* ever since (see Section 5.3.5 for details). Nevertheless, the RSS specifications are the only XML standards to have had a major impact on the world at large, through their use as the foundation for the Web log, or *blog,* movement.

Genuine, community-based ad hoc specifications—rather than simply vendor proposals—have some significant advantages over formal specifications, advantages they share with the open-source software movement.

- Successful ad hoc specifications appear quickly. (Even a relatively lightweight organization, such as OASIS or the W3C, can take years to develop a specification.)
- Successful ad hoc specifications address real needs; otherwise, no one will pay attention to them.
- Successful ad hoc specifications succeed entirely on their own merits; they cannot coast on the reputation and authority of a sponsoring body, such as the W3C or WS-I.
- Successful ad hoc specifications are usually developed in the open, without the back-room horse trading that can take place in more formal organizations.

To balance these advantages, however, there are some disadvantages. In particular, without a formal organization and staff, there may not be continuity; the original maintainer may lose interest, Web sites may go out of date, or domain names may lapse. Furthermore, without clear ownership, confusion can emerge, as in the case of RSS. Still, it appears that the speed and transparency of ad hoc specifications—when they truly come from a community effort rather than a single vendor with a hidden agenda—often outweigh their disadvantages.

1.3.8 Specialist Groups

For the most part, the organizations and people described in the rest of Section 1.3 create specifications for basic XML infrastructure. However, XML's true value does not appear until someone applies it to a problem area outside itself; these are called *XML applications,* not to be confused with software. The people or organizations most qualified to publish specifications for

XML applications are not XML-specific standards organization but rather specialists in the application field.

There are, literally, hundreds of these bodies. Some are well-established standards bodies for their industries, some are long-running academic research projects, and others are ad hoc groups put together solely for the purpose of creating and maintaining an XML-related specification. Here are some examples:

- The International Press Telecommunications Council [IPTC] produces XML specifications for news content and syndication.
- The American Iron and Steel Institute publishes XML specifications for steel trading transactions.
- The Text Encoding Initiative publishes XML specifications for academic textual research.
- Health Level Seven [HL7] publishes XML specifications for medical patient records.
- The Mozilla Project [MOZILLA] publishes an XML specification for user interfaces.
- The U.S. Patent and Trademark Office [USPTO] publishes XML specifications for electronic intellectual-property filing and correspondence.
- XBRL International publishes XML specifications for business reports, such as balance sheets.

For a comprehensive list, see the XML applications section of Robin Cover's Cover Pages [http://xml.coverpages.org/xmlApplications.html].

Many criteria can be used to evaluate groups like these. For example, are they informal collections of individuals, mouthpieces for a single large vendor and its junior partners, or true industry consortia with wide representation? How committed are the members to implementing the specification when it is finished? Do they appear to have the technical expertise to do the work? Are they working to replace older specifications for existing technical and business processes, or are they trying to convince people to do something entirely new?

Even those questions are no substitute for research in the industry or subject area. Many companies and government organizations ask employees to get involved with XML specification groups as a sort of insurance, to make sure that the company is not left behind if anything significant emerges. Their commitment, however, can be very shallow: A company's name on the front of a specification is no guarantee that the company is even considering the specification seriously, much less planning to implement it.

1.4 XML-Related Specifications

Many specifications touch on XML in some way. Listing them all is far beyond the scope of this book; in any case, the list would be badly out of date by the time you read this book.

The specifications have noticeable differences, however. Some specifications are so tied up with XML that they seem to be almost a part of it; some are building blocks for creating higher-level, more abstract specifications; some specify how to work with XML documents instead of what goes into them; and most simply happen to use XML to represent information. The four categories used in this section are:

1. Core specifications
2. Embeddable specifications
3. Utility specifications
4. Application specifications

The last category is the largest but gets the least attention here; most of what people need to know about application specifications comes from the application field, not from XML itself. We begin with the core, XML, and the specifications that are so integral that they are almost a part of it.

1.4.1 Core Specifications

The core specifications are the lowest layers, the ones that many or most other XML-related specifications build on top of, the same way that HTTP builds on top of TCP/IP in the networking world. The most important core specification for XML is, of course, XML itself [XML]. The XML Recommendation defines the basic pieces that all XML-related specifications have to use, at least if they want to use the term XML. Fortunately, as this is the most basic level, it is also the level with the best software and even hardware support. Programmers can choose from a large selection of libraries for parsing and generating XML markup, users can choose from a smaller selection of XML editing and browsing software, and system designers can buy off-the-shelf hardware appliances for XML processing and networking. Ironically, then, although the XML Recommendation is the most important specification, programmers and users do not usually need to concern themselves with its details.

The XML Recommendation does not stand quite alone at the bottom of the core, however. Three other specifications are so closely tied in that it is difficult to separate them from XML itself: XML Namespaces, XML Infoset, and Canonical XML. Of the three, XML Namespaces [NAMESPACES] is the most important. Although the Namespaces Recommendation itself still generates hostility from some XML specialists, nearly all XML libraries and user tools have incorporated it, and the current versions of the most popular higher-level XML-based specifications, such as RSS, XSLT, and SOAP, all require it. Namespaces provides a mechanism built on top of XML for creating globally unique names, using URLs or URNs in the same role that package names play in Java or Perl or that namespaces play in C++. When you combine a URL, `http://example.org/ns/`, with an element name, such as `price`, you get a compound name that is guaranteed to be unique within the entire world. Not owning the `example.org` domain name, anyone else who wanted to use a `price` name in XML would have to use a different URL. Globally unique names make it possible to recognize information inside documents of different types and to create documents that mix different vocabularies—for

1.4 XML-Related Specifications

example, XSLT style sheets use namespaces to distinguish the XSLT markup information from template markup.

The XML Information Set [XML-INFOSET] Recommendation provides a formal data model for XML, specifying what the low-level XML markup syntax means. The Infoset has little practical use for the typical person working on an XML project, but it plays an important role for other XML specification writers, as it describes what kinds of information must be available from an XML document.

Finally, Canonical XML [CANONICAL-XML] creates a bridge between the syntax of the XML representation and the data model of the Infoset. Canonical XML is a way of normalizing an XML document so that two documents that share the same Infoset are guaranteed to have the same syntactic representation. Because it defines a standard representation for performing comparisons, Canonical XML is particularly important for security, generating hashes for digital signatures, and so on.

1.4.2 Embeddable Specifications

An *embeddable specification* is designed to sit between basic, low-level XML and a top-level document type. Embeddable specifications provide standard ways of encoding information that many different XML document types need; in other words, embeddable specifications are standard ways of using XML.

The XML Recommendation itself contains some features that are not part of the core syntax and could have been separated into embeddable specifications, such as the `xml:lang` and `xml:space` attributes. XML Namespaces, discussed in Section 1.4.1, is, technically, an embedded specification itself but is so widely used that it is no longer optional and needs to be treated as part of the core.

Most of the XML-related embeddable specifications have come from or through the W3C. The earliest embeddable specifications dealt with handling human-readable XML documents in browsers and included Mathematical Markup Language [MATHML], for marking up mathematical expressions, and Scalable Vector Graphics [SVG], for marking up vector graphics, such as line drawings and charts. Listing 1.1 is an example of a simple MathML equation embedded in an XML document fragment using presentation markup.[8]

Listing 1-1 Embedded MathML

```
<para>Energy varies relative to the square of the velocity:</para>

  <example>
<mth:math xmlns:mth="http://www.w3.org/1998/Math/MathML">
    <mth:mi>e</mth:mi>
```

---

[8] MathML has two markup sets: *presentation* markup, for rendering equations; and *content* markup, for processing or solving equations.

```
      <mth:mo>=</mth:mo>
      <mth:mfrac>
        <mth:mn>1</mth:mn>
        <mth:mn>2</mth:mn>
      </mth:mfrac>
      <mth:mi>m</mth:mi>
      <mth:msup>
        <mth:mi>v</mth:mi>
        <mth:mn>2</mth:mn>
      </mth:msup>
    </mth:math>
</example>
```

Without MathML available, the designers of this document type would have had to define their own complete mathematical markup language—a major undertaking—or offer limited or no mathematical support and require users to load equations as external graphics. MathML acts as a reusable component, like a software library, that document type designers can use to plug in new kinds of functionality.

Reusing the embeddable MathML specification brings several advantages.

- Specification designers save time because the mathematical markup is already defined and documented.
- Information authors save time because their skills and training are more easily transferable; once they know MathML, the authors can use it inside many different XML document types.
- Software engineers save time because they can use existing libraries and style sheets for working with MathML rather than designing mathematical support from scratch.

The key to all these savings is the XML Namespaces specification. Because MathML uses its own namespace (http://www.w3.org/1998/Math/MathML), designers can use it in any XML document type without fear of naming conflicts, and software can recognize it in any XML document, even though the software knows nothing about the top-level document type.

This ability of MathML or SVG to combine and embed vocabularies was one of the major reasons for the creation of the XML Namespaces specification: The most enthusiastic supporters imagine a world in which XML document type designers do their work mainly by assembling collections of embeddable specifications. MathML and SVG have had some success, both in XHTML Web pages and in other XML-related applications.

Other Web-related embeddable specifications from the W3C have had mixed results. *Associating Style Sheets with XML Documents* [XML-STYLESHEET], for linking a style sheet to an XML document, is generally supported, although because sites rarely use document types other than (X)HTML on the Web, people make relatively little use of it. (HTML has its own mechanisms for specifying style sheets.) The XML Linking Language [XLINK] and the XML Pointer

1.4 XML-Related Specifications

Language [XPOINTER] provide standard ways to encode links in and make references to XML documents, but those specifications never caught on. The Resource Description Framework [RDF] has a contorted XML syntax specifically so that people can embed RDF metadata in Web pages, but virtually no one has done so.[9] In general, these embedded specifications have had limited success not because of any inherent problems in them but simply because they were based on a failed vision. People imagined that XML would replace HTML on the Web, and that XML documents of any type would therefore support the basic Web operations, such as linking and style sheets. XML in the browser did not happen in any meaningful way, so there was no real problem for these specifications to solve.[10]

Newer W3C embedded specifications take a different tack, recognizing that XML's success has come on the server side rather than on the client side. The closest to the old, XML-in-the-browser specifications is XForms [XFORMS], which defines a sophisticated and generalized replacement for the simple forms support in HTML. Although it *could* be used in a browser embedded in XHTML, XForms can also be used to generate HTML forms on the server side or to drive specialized client software. Other W3C specifications cater more to business-to-business requirements, including XML Signature [XML-SIGNATURE] and XML Encryption [XML-ENCRYPTION].

As a final note, one popular embedded specification long predates XML: the CALS Table Model [CALS-TABLE].[11] Table models are complicated things to design and even more complicated to support with rendering software; as a result, many SGML and XML document types have used the CALS table model, usually through cut-and-paste. OASIS maintains the CALS table model but has recently met with competition from the simpler but better-known HTML table model.

1.4.3 Utility Specifications

Whereas embedded specifications describe components that people can use inside XML documents, *utility specifications* describe how people can work with XML. These specifications may or may not be XML based. The intended audience for most utility specifications is technologists, whether computer programmers, publishing specialists, or Web page designers; few utility specifications would interest an author using an XML editing system, for example.[12]

---

[9] RDF's focus inside the W3C has since shifted to standalone documents in a Semantic Web [SEMANTIC-WEB] rather than metadata embedded in HTML or XHTML pages. Outside of the W3C, RDF has had success as the base layer for some versions of RSS but remains controversial.

[10] People were imagining XML in the browser during the late 1990s, at the same time that people thought that Java applets would become pervasive on the client side. In the end, both Java and XML migrated to the server, where they have carried on a happy, existence ever since; the browser still belongs to HTML, CSS, and JavaScript.

[11] CALS (Continuous Acquisition and Life-Cycle Support) was a major U.S. Department of Defense initiative that kept many SGML specialists employed during the 1990s.

[12] One possible exception is the OASIS XML Entity Catalog [XML-CATALOG] specification, which is useful for setting up an authoring environment in which documents refer to local copies of schemas and other files.

The most basic level of utility specification is the application program interface (API) for XML software libraries. The best-known APIs for XML are the Document Object Model [DOM] and the Simple API for XML [SAX]. Both of these APIs have bindings for various programming languages, such as Java, Python, Perl, and C++. DOM is a tree-based, or random-access API, whereas SAX is a streaming, or serial, API. DOM implementations are easy to use, but DOM is slow and memory intensive, making it inappropriate for use in high-performance environments, such as servers. SAX implementations require more complicated programming but have low time and memory overheads. One of the first skills an XML programmer acquires is the ability to judge when to use a tree-based API and when to use a streaming API.

Standardized APIs bring a basic but important advantage to XML programming: They protect projects from locking into a single vendor or organization. For example, a project that starts using a DOM-based XML parser from Microsoft can easily switch to one from Apache, or vice versa, by changing only a couple of lines of code. Standard APIs also reduce the number of interfaces that an XML programmer needs to learn and make it easier to design books and training, as there is not a different interface for each parser. Using standard APIs, people can design higher-level software, such as an XSLT processor, that can work with any parser rather than having to design a separate version for each product.

Although SAX and DOM are important for programmers, the best-known XML utility specification is XSL Transformations [XSLT]. XSLT was designed as part one of a two-part specification for formatting XML documents—the second part is the formatting information itself—but a standardized transformation language turned out to be so popular that XSLT took on a life of its own. The same cautions that applied to the DOM apply to XSLT: XSLT implementations are relatively easy to use, but they are slow and memory intensive, so they generally do not make sense for high-performance environments, such as servers. XSLT is still a standard designed for technicians, but those technicians do not need to be programmers; in fact, people generally consider XSLT to be a separate skill, akin to Web design. XSLT also provides no standard way to access external information in databases or other locations, so it is not suitable for more complicated kinds of transformations—at least, not without proprietary extensions.

One special case of an XSL transformation is that from another XML format to HTML for display in a Web browser. The major browsers—Mozilla and Internet Explorer—both support using XSLT as a browser-side style sheet; the browser downloads an XML document and an XSLT style sheet, then applies the style sheet to create an HTML document for display. Because XML has had very limited success in Web browsers so far, this is not a very common use of XSLT; more typically, the transformation to HTML happens on the server side, but it is supported and can make for interesting demonstrations at conferences if nothing else.

XSLT has become so popular that people use it for applications beyond simple transformations, including rudimentary searching and querying of data stored in XML. The W3C has been working on a more elaborate standard, XQuery [XQUERY], to provide full query and reporting from XML documents, similar to the functionality that the SQL query language [SQL] provides for relational databases. At the time of writing, XQuery is not finished yet, although

1.4 XML-Related Specifications

some prototype implementations exist. It is not clear what impact XQuery will have on the large, existing XSLT developer community.[13]

Schemas, a type of utility specification, cause much concern and confusion; in fact, many nonspecialists believe that schemas are a required component of XML rather than simply one type of optional utility specification. The confusion probably comes from the fact that XML's predecessor, SGML, allowed only one type of schema, called a *document type definition* (DTD), required its use for all documents, and embedded it right in the document. To maintain compatibility with SGML, XML retained the DTD but made it optional. If present, a DTD must be inside the logical XML document but need not be present at all.

In fact, schemas have two main utility applications for XML, serving as

1. Templates for generating XML in authoring tools
2. A special kind of style sheet for processing XML

The second point needs a bit of explanation. Style sheet languages, such as XSL and cascading style sheets [CSS], are essentially filters that take an XML document as input and generate something else—HTML, PDF, another XML document—as output. A schema is a filter that takes an XML document as input and generates a Boolean value—valid/not valid—as output; a schema may also produce a transformed document containing default values filled in.

Because XML does not require an internal (DTD) schema, XML does not need to be limited to a single schema language. Some XML-related standards, such RDF (Resource Description Framework) [RDF], have developed their own specialized schema languages that are not applicable to other types of XML documents, and other proposals have come and gone without much impact. But two types of general-purpose XML schemas have drawn a lot of attention: the W3C's XML Schema specification [XML-SCHEMA] and RelaxNG [RELAXNG], pronounced either relax-N-G or relaxing, from OASIS, with an ISO blessing. XML Schema includes support for describing both structure and data typing: The specification is not popular with all developers,[14] but it attracts much attention in business circles and the Web Services world. RelaxNG is more popular among hard-core XML types, and the window dressing of an ISO blessing may help adoption in governments. RelaxNG does not have its own data typing system but can work with the one from XML Schema.[15]

---

[13] XQuery is designed for pulling information out of an XML document rather than iterating through it, whereas XSLT is designed for both approaches. Thanks to Ken Holman for suggesting, through private correspondence, a way to make the distinction so clearly.

[14] The W3C's XML Schema is so unpopular among some XML specialists, in fact, that many of them refuse to use the official name. They prefer such terms as *W3C Schema* or the namespace prefix used in the specification's examples: *XSD*.

[15] ISO has a project under way, DSDL (Document Schema Definition Langues) [DSDL], to create a framework for applying various types of schemas to the same document for more complete validation.

In addition to RelaxNG, OASIS has had some moderate success with its XML Entity Catalog specification [XML-CATALOG]. Back before XML, external files, such as DTDs, had identifiers that could not be resolved in any standard way, so developers and system designers used catalogs to map those identifiers to locally stored files. XML standardized on URIs—typically, URLs—for system identifiers, so that a DTD or any other resource could be loaded by any computer connected to the Internet. However, doing so did not entirely solve the problem: Computers are often not connected to the Internet, and even when they are, external resources may become unavailable, the delay retrieving a file over the Internet may be unacceptable, or for security reasons, an organization might not want to leave a footprint in someone else's server logs. As a result, some people still find catalogs useful, and the OASIS XML Catalogs specification provides a convenient, portable way to create and share them.

Other utility specifications happen to use XML but can be applied to any type of digital information. For example, the XML Signature Recommendation [XML-SIGNATURE] from the W3C defines an XML encoding for authenticating the signatory or content of any digital information, including an XML document; likewise, the W3C's XML Encryption Recommendation [XML-ENCRYPTION] defines an XML encoding for any kind of encrypted digital information. Neither of these specifications had gained significant implementation at the time of writing, however.

1.4.4 Application Specifications

The remaining XML-related specifications are not part of the core, are not designed primarily for embedding, and are not utility specifications for working with XML documents; instead, they are applications of XML to specific areas, such as accounting, news, technical documentation, or Web logs. The vast majority of XML-related specifications—many hundreds or possibly thousands of them—fall into this category. The good news is that you can ignore most of them and concentrate only on the ones that happen to do something that you need.

Of the many hundreds of XML application specifications, perhaps a couple of dozen, at most, have seen any serious implementation, and only a tiny handful of those could be called unqualified successes. Furthermore, many of the application specifications are tied to specific software, negating XML's advantage of sharing information. For example, Microsoft Excel, the KOffice spreadsheet, the Star Office and Open Office spreadsheet, and the Gnumeric spreadsheet all use XML-based formats for saving spreadsheets to disk and loading them back in; however, they all use *different* XML-based formats, so XML brings relatively little value.

The whole point of XML is sharing information independently of hardware, operating system, software, or even software type. Unlike a spreadsheet or a word processor file, an XML document may be processed in any number of ways by any number of applications. The ability to share, together with the amount and type of sharing going on, is the best gauge of an XML-based specification's success. One big company using a specification internally or one big software package using the specification counts for little; many different organizations using the specification to share information and process it in different and unexpected ways counts for a lot.

1.4 XML-Related Specifications

By that measure, the most successful XML application specifications at the time of writing are likely RSS and DocBook. DocBook, an XML format designed for technical documentation, has become the documentation format of choice in the open-source movement; most Linux distributions, for example, contain prepackaged tools for generating HTML, PostScript, PDF, and plaintext output from DocBook master files. RSS is the foundation of the Web log, or blog movement (see Section 5.3.5 for details). Like RelaxNG, DocBook is maintained by OASIS; RSS exists in separate, competing versions, with no single recognized maintainer.

Aside from these two special cases, XML has had little impact on how the world at large exchanges information, so the best-known XML-based application formats remain speculations on how people might someday do work rather than descriptions of how they work now. Despite the availability of XML-based XHTML (Extensible Hypertext Markup Language) [XHTML], for example, most Web designers still use basic, non-XML HTML. SVG and MathML have had some success, but this chapter groups them under the embedded specifications described in Section 1.4.2.

Nevertheless, some application specifications have succeed in small niches. The Text Encoding Initiative [TEI] maintains a set of markup specifications for textual analysis and research, and these specifications have been popular in academia in both SGML and XML. RDF, described in Section 1.4.2, can also serve as a standalone file format for metadata, and is the foundation of the W3C's Semantic Web project [SEMANTIC-WEB]. RDF's rival, XML Topic Maps [XTM], has a smaller but equally dedicated group of followers. XML Metadata Interchange [XMI] provides a common format for sharing Unified Modeling Language [UML] models in the programming world.[16]

Of course, many more XML specifications have gained a small amount of importance; for example, a governmental agency might require submissions in XML, or a new file-sharing application might happen to use an XML-based save format. Nonetheless, in early 2004, the lack of killer applications that enable widespread information sharing is remarkable. The fact that the formats are in XML brings little benefit to the users. With luck, this statement will no longer be true by the time you read this book, but it is a great, if rarely discussed, disappointment for the XML community. One area of great promise is XML networking, which includes Web Services, blogging, and information syndication (see Chapter 5).

The best source of up-to-the-minute information on XML application specifications is Robin Cover's XML Applications and Initiatives page [http://xml.coverpages.org/xmlApplications.html]. Go there first, if you are looking for XML application specifications in your field.

---

[16] At the time of writing, the version of XMI implemented by UML user tools does not provide a standard way of sharing *diagrams,* which is the part most people care about, so it is still not possible to save a UML diagram in one UML modeling tool using XMI and then load it into another. In this regard, XMI provides even less interoperability than the Rich Text Format [RTF] for word processors.

1.5 Special Topics

Aside from the overview of specifications and the groups that create them, two special standardization topics deserve attention:

1. The difference between *de facto* and *de jure* standards
2. Consistency and compatibility among XML-related specifications

1.5.1 *De Facto* versus *De Jure* Standards

Sometimes, standards develop not through a formal committee process but simply through widespread adoption; these are *de facto standards*, in contrast to the *de jure standards* of international bodies and industry consortia. De facto standards differ from ad hoc standards; ad hoc standards are still designed to be shared specifications, whereas de facto standards are often accidents.

For example, two proprietary Adobe specifications have become de facto standards across the information technology world: the PostScript language for printing and the PDF file format for read-only, fixed-format documents. Adobe has published both specifications and allows their use royalty-free, and good third-party implementations—open source and commercial—of both exist. As a result, there is no significant demand to replace either with a formal, de jure standard.

In the XML world, however, de facto standards have tended not to be important, despite the best efforts of some vendors to introduce them. Like the Internet, XML has a culture of following open, published specifications, and the community applies a fair bit of pressure to anyone who mistakes a proprietary vendor API or format for an open standard. In fact, one of the major reasons for the success of SAX and the DOM was that they free programmers from tying their code to a single parsing library; as a result, large companies were unable to lock in developers to their interfaces and had no foothold to force other proprietary practices on developers and users.

Still, de facto standards may emerge in XML. The best kind of de facto standard is one based on an open, published specification with no legal encumbrance: Anyone may implement it, and many different people and organizations do. Again, Adobe's PostScript is a good example of this kind of standard; there are PostScript implementations other than Adobe's, including open-source ones, and they are all interoperable. The worst kind of de facto standard is one that locks users to a single vendor, stifling innovation and stimulating a dangerous software monoculture. Some commercial word processor and spreadsheet formats are good examples of the bad kind of de facto standard; as more people exchange information using the proprietary formats, others are forced to buy software from the same vendor in order to participate.

De jure standards also have their disadvantages, however. As mentioned earlier, many, if not most, de jure XML specifications and standards are written *in advance* of real implementation. Instead of solving an existing industry problem, these specifications are R&D masquerading as standardization, and many turn out to be unnecessary, incompatible, or even unimplementable, but their blessing as official standards tends to choke out other proposals that might have a better

1.5 Special Topics

chance of success (see Section 1.2.1). On the other hand, a good de jure standard is one that finds common ground in the way people are already doing things and formalizes that common ground to make it easier for people to work together. One of the very few of these in XML is XML itself, capturing the common ground of various SGML subsets that existed before it; when they do appear, they have a high probability of success.

In the end, neither de jure standards, written in advance of real implementation, nor de facto standards, locking users into a specific vendor, are healthy for XML. The key to success, for either kind of standard, is a lot of implementers using a specification successfully to share information. When that key exists, a specification is a true standard and is probably worth using; when it does not, a specification is probably safe to ignore, no matter how big and important the standards body, organization, or vendor that backs it.

1.5.2 Consistency and Compatibility

XML provides a minimum amount of compatibility among XML-related specifications: Because all the specifications are related to XML in some way, implementers can take advantage of shared, reusable resources, such as the following:

- XML software, including parsing libraries, content-management systems and repositories, authoring and browsing tools, search and query tools, and publishing systems
- XML training and reference materials, including books, articles, Web sites, Web logs, slide shows, tutorials, and courses
- XML skills available from employees, contractors, vendors, and consultants
- XML publicity and goodwill in industry, government, and academia

These are all important advantages, but it is easy to overstate them. After all, XML is a very low-level markup format. The availability of an XML parsing library is an advantage, of course, but it solves only a very small part of the information-interchange problem; it is only one level above character-set compatibility and many levels below the type of logic that people need to exchange information usefully. For example, companies need to exchange business objects, not tags; technical writers need to exchange tutorials and user manuals, not tags.

To be genuinely useful, XML-related specifications have to provide the same advantages as XML itself but at a higher level. In other words, the specifications have to be *consistent*—doing the same kinds of things in the same way—and *compatible*—able to coexist in the same environment without conflict.

One well-known example of inconsistency, on a fairly low level, is XML Namespaces and document type definitions. XML inherited DTDs from its predecessor, SGML; however, whereas SGML was designed to work in isolated islands of information, XML was intended for sharing information globally across the Internet and other networks. Under those circumstances, naming collisions and confusion were a serious concern. Different organizations might use an XML element or attribute with the same name for something entirely different. The W3C considered various possibilities and eventually decided on a scheme whereby XML elements could declare namespaces, similar to Java or Perl package names, and bind them to prefixes. The problem was that this approach did not work comfortably with DTDs. Consider the following.

- If two elements or attributes use the same prefix mapped to different namespaces, an XML processor will consider them equivalent during DTD validation but not during namespace processing (see Listing 1-2).
- If two elements or attributes use different prefixes mapped to the same namespace, an XML processor will consider them equivalent during namespace processing but not during DTD validation (see Listing 1-3).

Listing 1-2   Equivalent by DTD Validation
```
<container>
  <a:name xmlns:a="http://www.example.org/ns#"/>
  <a:name xmlns:a="http://www.acme.org/namespace/"/>
</container>
```

Listing 1-3   Equivalent by Namespace Processing
```
<container>
  <a:name xmlns:a="http://www.example.org/ns#"/>
  <b:name xmlns:b="http://www.example.org/ns#"/>
</container>
```

This low-level problem is an irritant for hard-core XML aficionados, not a major impediment to XML adoption. There are simple ways to work around the problem, and DTDs are falling out of use in any case, to be replaced by new schema languages (see Section 1.4.3).

Incompatibilities become more obvious at higher levels. For example, the W3C has spent years designing an entire suite of specifications for working with XML documents, such as XSLT, XML Schema, XLink, and XQuery; because they work directly on syntax, all these assume that there is, more or less, a 1:1 match between XML syntax and the information model underlying the syntax. At the same time, the W3C has been basing its Semantic Web initiative on RDF, which allows a large number of syntactic variations for representing the same information. As a result, even though RDF and the Semantic Web are based on XML, most of the W3C's XML-related specifications do not work with RDF, unless restricted to a small syntactic subset: RDF ends up with its own schema language and will likely end up with its own query language and other support specifications as well. Thus, RDF will need its own separate set of software tools, separate training materials, separate publicity, and so on.

The incompatibilities and inconsistencies between DTDs and namespaces or between RDF and the major XML utility specifications draw most of the attention and criticism within the XML community, but the most costly problems exist at an even higher level: XML-based application

Table 1-1 Element Names for a Book Title

XML Document Type	Element Name
DocBook	`citetitle`
XHTML	`cite`
Text Encoding Initiative	`title`
Dublin Core	`dc:title`

specifications are unnecessarily inconsistent with one another, even on the minor details. For example, as Table 1.1 shows, major XML document types do not agree even on something as simple as how to tag a book title.

Does the inconsistency matter? After all, it is easy enough to change, say, `citetitle` to `cite`, using XSLT. But to look at the question differently, assume that you wanted to write an XML software tool to locate book titles in *any* XML document. Could you do it? Obviously, not without knowing the document type in advance; for example, `title` in an XHTML document does not refer to a book title, whereas `title` in a TEI document does. The more XML-based document types that you want to handle, the more special cases you need to build into your software. In the end, if you have to handle every XML-based format as a special case, XML's advantages become rather limited.

Other kinds of inconsistencies and incompatibilities exist as well. For example, XML document types have no standard way to refer to real-world objects using unique identifiers, so it is not easy to tell whether two XML document types are referring to the same thing, even where identifiers exist. For example, one XML document might put an ISO currency code in an attribute named `iso`, whereas another might put it in an element named `currency`. XML document types that model data also tend to use entirely different kinds of markup to model entities, relationships, and attributes, although RDF and XTM are trying to standardize data representation.

In the end, XML makes information sharing easier only if various XML specifications are in some way compatible. Simply choosing XML is not enough; in fact, it may raise costs without bringing any real benefits. Making XML-based specifications more consistent and compatible, possibly by using more standard element sets, such as the Dublin Core [DUBLIN-CORE], where appropriate, is the next big job for the XML community. PRISM and RSS 1.0 both build on top of common layers, such as RDF and the Dublin Core, making them more interoperable; whether these individual specifications fail or succeed, they provide good early models for how to build future XML-based specifications.

1.6 Final Words on Standards

When standards work, they work marvelously. The Internet is cheap, effective, and ubiquitous because everyone uses a core set of networking standards, allowing information to flow seamlessly from a computer through a local network, any number of backbones, and another local network to a different computer. North American rail transportation is cheap and effective because all the major railroads use a standard track gauge, allowing cars and coaches to move seamlessly from one rail line to another. Beer in pubs is cheap because all establishments use a standard system for measuring volume, allowing drinkers to move from establishment to establishment, comparing prices.

When standards don't work, however, they can impose high costs. A technology project might end up running far over budget simply so it can support a proposed standard that no one ends up using. Even the suggestion that a major organization is planning to develop a public specification can throw an entire software industry into fear, uncertainty, and doubt.

In fact, it is worth noting that standards are almost always suboptimal when implemented from scratch, because to be conformant, people have to spend time or money on some things that they would not otherwise have to do. For example, a company might want to use XML-based remote procedure calls (see Chapter 5) but might not require all SOAP's messaging and error-handling capabilities; implementing those extra features is wasted time and money.

When a standard is successful, however, the extra costs are diluted so far through economies of scale that they virtually disappear. Vendors and free-software authors can encapsulate the extra programming effort in shared libraries and tools, with the initial cost, in time and money, of supporting the standard benefiting hundreds or thousands of users. Likewise, the extra time required to learn standards and train staff may be offset by a faster implementation time and better interoperability using off-the-shelf components.

For a new specification, however, little or none of these benefits might exist, and the early implementer is left bearing all the extra present costs in the hope of uncertain future benefits. With few other organizations wanting to share information using the standard, few or no production-grade libraries and software tools to support it, little or no published training material, or few people already available with the appropriate skills, it becomes very difficult to make a case for supporting a new specification: The costs will almost certainly outweigh the benefits. In that case, a user is entirely justified in choosing to ignore a specification, no matter how heavily that specification has been blessed by ISO, the W3C, the WS-I, OASIS, or any other body. In fact, there is not even an early-adapter advantage; if the specification succeeds as a standard, competitors will be able to build better systems faster and more cheaply using off-the-shelf components. If the specification fails, competitors will not have wasted money on it. Except for researchers or vendors working on products for future release, supporting unproven specifications makes little business sense.

A more dangerous situation comes when a specification has good-quality support but only from a single vendor. Users can buy most or all of what they need off the shelf and wave the flag of standards compliance, but in fact, this is one of the most insidious forms of vendor lock-in: the project will end up beholden to the vendor just as much as if it were not following the specification but will be caught much less prepared. An open, published specification is no protection from vendor lock-in; only an open, published, *widely implemented* standard can help.

So sometimes, standards can bring huge benefits to users, but other times, users are better off going it alone. What can a user do to minimize the costs and risks in a situation like that?

1.6 Final Words on Standards

First, the user can take advantage of open, well-implemented standards as far as possible, so that at least parts of the system will be interoperable and vendor neutral. Next, the project team can modularize the project and isolate the parts that might become standardized in the future; for example, the designers might isolate a proprietary directory service behind a simple, generic interface, in the expectation that they will replace it with a standards-compliant directory service in the future. Sometimes, components can masquerade behind standardized interfaces: For example, programmers occasionally use SAX or DOM interfaces for non-XML information, so that XML tools, such as XSLT engines, can still work with it.

Deciding whether to use standards should be part of a cold-blooded cost/benefit analysis. Vendors that shun standards in the—usually vain—hope of locking in customers, and users who take up every new standard in the—usually vain—hope of benefiting from shared development costs and better interoperability are both equally misguided. In the end, you need to ask yourself four questions about any XML-related specification.

1. Is it well supported with off-the-shelf software and training materials?
2. Do people want to use it to share information with you, now?
3. Is it supported by many vendors or free-software authors?
4. Will you finish your project more quickly or more cheaply by supporting the standard, or will the project be measurably more valuable with the standards support?

If you answer three or four of the questions with yes, going with a specification is a very good idea. The more no answers you come up with, however, the more likely it is that you will be better off ignoring the standards and specifications for now. Standardization is a good thing—the basis, in fact, of much of the prosperity of the industrialized world—but it is not a substitute for good judgment.

CHAPTER 2

Planning an XML Project

So, you want to plan an XML project. Have you spent time thinking about standards and software for your project? What about people?

Some XML projects do not involve anyone but you. For example, if you have decided to tag a textual corpus for your academic research project or if you are the only tech writer at a small company and have decided to produce your documentation in XML, your only concerns about XML will be technical ones: where you can find good software, what specifications you should use, and so on. As soon as the project involves people other than yourself—whether it's an ad hoc group of four or five volunteers collaborating by e-mail on an open-source project or a team of hundreds of technologists working at a Fortune 50 company—you will quickly discover that, for XML, people are as much of a challenge as technology is.

XML is a *disruptive technology*; it requires people and machines to change the way they work. Other disruptive technologies, such as the World Wide Web, have brought great benefits to the world, but there are often losers as well as winners, such as the old proprietary network CompuServe, and these people will resist any change. Furthermore, the transition to a disruptive technology is expensive, involving throwing out a lot of old infrastructure and replacing it with something new.

This chapter starts by walking through the stages of a typical XML project—from planning to production—to show both the similarities and the differences between XML projects and other technological projects. The chapter then dives into the details, looking at common pitfalls and best practices, both for technology and for human beings, in XML project planning.

2.1 Components of an XML Project

XML is nothing more than a way of adding structure to information, so you can use XML for almost any purpose; in that sense, there is no such thing as a *typical* XML project. XML can show up in technical publishing, networked games, spreadsheets, air traffic control, news publishing, blogging, or just about anything you can imagine that involves passing information from one system to another.

Still, many XML projects involve performing similar operations on XML information, even if the final result is different. The operations described in this section and illustrated in Figure 2.1 are not low-level libraries and tools, such as parsers, as important as those are, but high-level stages in the life cycle of an XML document:

- Creation
- Storage
- Search
- Archiving
- Transformation
- Rendering
- Transport

To illustrate these stages, this section describes a hypothetical production system for a retail catalog. The designers chose XML because the company needs to publish the catalog in print for mailing to telephone customers and online for use by Web customers. (For more information on single-source publishing, see Section 3.1.1.)

For *creation,* the developers build a Web application with forms that authors can use to enter information directly into a database. In this system, the authors deal with only a tiny amount of XML. Photographers upload digital photographs of products, filling in metadata fields with basic information about each picture: date, product number, and so on. Writers write product information in various fields of a Web form, including product number, colors, and styles, and a short description, which allows a few simple types of in-line markup. When it is time to generate the complete XML master catalog, a script issues SQL database queries to collect information and then assembles it into an XML document, matching photos with descriptions and extracting current pricing and shipping information from other data tables.

The *storage* is the relational database, which holds the product photographs as binary large objects (BLOBs), and puts textual information directly into relational tables. The database also contains other product information, such as price, size, and weight, all keyed on the product bar code.

Figure 2.1 Components of an XML project

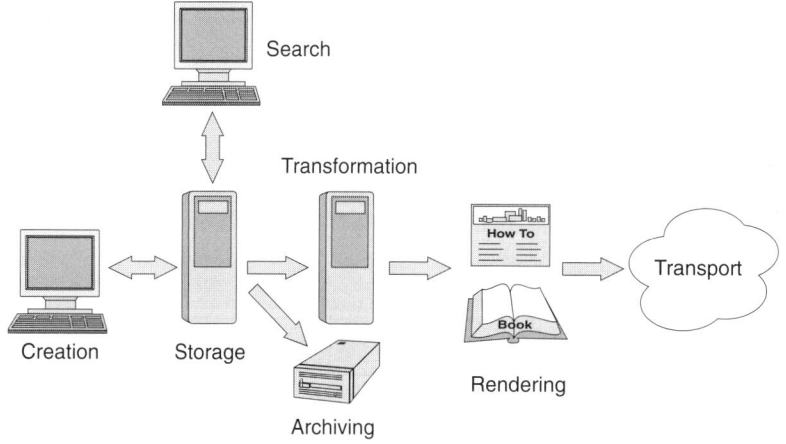

2.1 Components of an XML Project

Search takes place through the standard database query language [SQL]. For information already in database tables, a specialized XML search engine is not needed. A separate Web application translates user search criteria into SQL database queries, runs them against the database, and then formats the results as HTML pages with links into the catalog.

Because the catalog is updated and published relatively infrequently, XSLT is adequate for *rendering,* despite its performance problems in high-speed environments (see Section 8.3 for more information). A series of XSLT templates generates HTML and prints renditions from the XML master file exported from the database during the creating stage.

Transport takes place in various ways, depending on the catalog media. For the printed version, the transport is nothing more than regular mail; for the Web version, the transport is a Web server using HTTP. The catalog company also sends the raw XML version of the catalog to sales partners through a secure FTP server so that they can customize it and then generate their own formatted output, using their own XML systems.

As XML systems go, this one is fairly straightforward. Authors can use simple forms-based interfaces rather than unfamiliar XML editing tools, and searching and storage use standard relational database facilities. This kind of approach does not always work, however, particularly for less structured information, such as reports or news stories. The following subsections discuss the various approaches people can take for each stage.

2.1.1 Creation

Normally, an XML system starts with an XML document, which has to come from somewhere. Two common ways of creating the starting XML document are to

1. Have authors create it directly, using a text editor or a custom XML authoring tool
2. Have software assemble it automatically from other sources, such as database tables, non-XML data files, or even other XML documents (see Section 2.1.4).

The second approach will not always work, but where it does, as in the retail catalog example earlier, it will be significantly cheaper and easier than using XML authoring tools. Automatic software assembly generally works for data-oriented XML (see Chapter 4) but not for document-oriented XML (see Chapter 3). Direct XML authoring allows for richer information and works well with document-oriented XML, but it comes with higher ongoing costs for training, technical support, and staff time, as well as a higher probability of resistance from users.

Larger XML projects sometimes combine the two approaches. Authors write basic in-line content and possibly skeleton structures in XML; then automated processes flesh out the document with automatically generated boilerplate text, tables, figures, and other data. A project producing maintenance manuals for large machinery might follow this approach, using the database to hold part numbers, standard procedures, warnings and cautions, diagrams, and other reusable information. Changes to the database will automatically appear in the XML document without requiring human editing.

2.1.2 Storage and Archiving

Now that you have created an XML document, either by hand or through scripts, you might need somewhere to keep it. That is not always the case, though; in XML networking (see Chapter 5), your system might simply generate the XML, blast it out over the network, and then forget about it. Even if you need to keep the XML around, simply saving it to the hard drive or LAN, the same way you would with a spreadsheet or word-processing file, might be sufficient. You can get a little fancier by keeping the XML in a revision-control system, such as Concurrent Version System (CVS) or Microsoft's Visual SourceSafe, without having to buy or build any specialized XML software.

You cannot always get away with the easy solutions, however. You might need to allow several authors to work on different parts of the same XML document simultaneously, be able to maintain snapshots of hundreds of documents in a consistent state, or automate workflow through the authoring and editorial processes. For the first requirement, vendors sell custom XML databases that can manage each element in a document as if it were a separate file, but these databases have not had good results in the field. More typically, people will store XML documents in relational databases, either by decomposing them into data tables or by storing them as BLOBs or *character large objects* CLOBs.

The major database vendors, such as Oracle and IBM, provide special support for working with XML in their products. Normally, even large projects can avoid the need for simultaneous authoring by dividing documents into small files. For example, a system could store an XML manual as 500 separate files, one for each task, rather than as a single, large file—that way, it is easy for different authors to work on different tasks without conflict. Larger repositories will almost always require some search ability: see Section 2.1.3 and Chapter 6 for more information.

Archiving is a special case of storage. One of the major selling points of XML is future proofing: In 50 or 100 years, it may be difficult to read proprietary binary formats, but XML is designed to be easily accessible. Archiving may have special requirements, such as optical rather than magnetic media, and may also impose additional requirements on XML information, such as encryption, digital signatures, and metadata about when, how, why, and by whom each document was created. Archives typically also require an ability to search.

2.1.3 Search and Retrieval

Chapter 6 deals with the complex topic of XML searching. When an XML project contains dozens, hundreds, or even thousands of individual XML documents, authors and others working on the project will require some form of search and retrieval to find information. Following are several common approaches, from least to most complex, for searching XML documents:

- Batch searching
- Full-text indexing
- Database metadata
- Structural indexing

With batch searching, a program reads all the documents for every search, similar to the way the Unix `grep` command searches plaintext files. Batch searches can be relatively slow, taking anywhere from a few seconds to a few hours or more; however, because there is no preindexing, there are no built-in limitations about the kinds of searches people can make. Batch searching is most appropriate when searches are rare but possibly complex and delays are not a problem.

Full-text searching uses pregenerated indexes to speed up searching but simply treats XML documents like any other text documents, filtering out the markup and indexing the content and, possibly, attributing values. Although full-text searching is a blunt tool, it can be surprisingly effective, and many well-tested free and commercial indexing and retrieval tools are available off the shelf. Some full-text search engines allow labeled fields, so it is possible to add the name of the element containing text to the index, providing some simple structural search ability. Full-text indexing is most appropriate when content consists mainly of prose, such as novels, Web logs, or newspaper stories.

Database metadata is a useful approach for finding XML documents based on preselected criteria. When a user checks an XML document into the system, the system scans it once, extracting predetermined information, such as names, organizations, country codes, dates, headlines, and so on, and stores that information in regular relational database tables. The system is then able to find XML documents using normal SQL database queries. This approach is most appropriate for documents that consist mainly of highly structured information, such as lists, tables, or fields, or for documents that include explicit metadata, such as news stories.

Like full-text searching, structural searching uses indexes to speed up operations. However, instead of indexing only the text, the software also indexes the XML structure that goes with it. As a result, it is possible to formulate complex queries combining XML structure with text content. Both the XML Path Language [XPath] and the forthcoming XML Query Language [XQuery] can take advantage of structural search engines when they are available.

2.1.4 Transformation

Many XML systems include a *transformation pipeline*. A preliminary, raw XML document starts out at one end of the system and moves down the pipeline like a virtual assembly line, going through various stages of transformation until a finished XML document emerges from the other end. Transformations may involve rearranging or removing information that is already in the XML document, adding information from external sources, merging several smaller XML documents into one larger one—such as assembling chapters into a book—or splitting a large XML document into several smaller ones, such as breaking a book up into smaller Web pages.

Transformation components typically go through at least two iterations. First, developers prototype the transformations by using simple, template-based tools, such as XSLT processors; then, to improve efficiency and reduce memory requirements, developers rewrite the transformations in custom source code. In some cases, if speed is not essential and memory restrictions are not a problem, a system will continue to use XSLT right into production. One advantage of custom coding, however, is that it is easier to include information from non-XML sources, such as relational databases.

Typically, transformation tools require more custom coding than storage or searching, but they are not overly complex or expensive. See Section 8.3.4 for more information.

2.1.5 Rendering

Rendering is a specialized form of transformation (Section 2.1.4) intended for human consumption rather than machine use. Rendering is also a complex topic, and Chapter 3 examines it in more detail.

In practice, rendering components nearly always convert XML documents to HTML for online display and PDF or PostScript for printing. Normally, it is necessary to write separate code for rendering print and HTML, as the primitives are entirely different: HTML documents have tables, paragraphs, and links, whereas printed documents are usually formatted as a series of nested boxes on the page.

Online rendering has some special possibilities. The simplest, most portable, approach is to convert the XML to HTML in advance, but some Web sites store only the XML and generate HTML on the fly when requested; modern browsers can handle XML directly without a conversion step, a just-in-time rendering approach that allows the user to set preferences and customize the appearance or content of the rendered document. Both of the major browsers—Mozilla and Microsoft's Internet Explorer—support client-side XML rendering using XSLT or CSS, but very few sites take advantage of this capability.

2.1.6 Transport

The final major component is transport: Once the information is ready, it needs to get to the end user. Chapter 5 is devoted to XML networking and deals extensively with transport issues.

Very simple forms of transport include burning information onto a CD-ROM and mailing it, sending it as an e-mail attachment, or making it available through an FTP or HTTP server. More sophisticated projects may require scheduled, guaranteed delivery, publish-subscribe, and other features supported by advanced XML-related networking specifications.

For some projects, transport is the most important part. For example, financial information services, such as Bloomberg and Reuters, make their money from getting information to a customer as quickly as possible, and wire services add extensive metadata to their news stories to help customers process it automatically. The Web log movement is built almost entirely around the ability of RSS to make transport simple. Such specifications as NewsML [NEWSML], RSS [RSS], and Internet Content Exchange [ICE] deal with transport in great detail.

2.2 XML Project Pitfalls

The components listed in Section 2.1 deal with the technical side of an XML project; this section looks at pitfalls that come mainly from the human side, including unspoken expectations, unrealistic expectations, and resistance to change. A larger XML project in a government or corporate setting will often encounter threats from several groups of people and may face more risk from overenthusiastic supporters than from opponents.

2.2 XML Project Pitfalls

2.2.1 Unspoken Expectations

XML still gets a lot of media attention. Sometimes, managers approve XML projects simply so that their customers and shareholders will see that they are using the latest technologies. Nothing is wrong, in principle, with using XML as a marketing technique; the problem is that this goal is almost always unspoken. Nobody tells the project team that it is participating in a marketing exercise, and even if the team realizes that fact, it is still forced to act as if it were implementing a real project. In fact, the situation is worse, because often the team is the designated scapegoat, starting with a set of fictitious written goals that it has little hope of reaching, thereby setting the team up to take the blame for the project's technical failure. To make things even worse, management will often announce an excessively large XML project for maximum publicity but then spend as little as possible on development once the headlines have quieted down, starving the project of money and resources.

The best way to work around this problem is for management to be honest about the project's goals and requirements, in writing. If market visibility is one of the project's main goals, *write it down,* along the lines of "the major goal of this project is to raise BigCorp's visibility in the market by showing our commitment to new technologies like XML." Two years later, new managers and new team members will be able to measure their progress more fairly, and it may turn out that the project was a marketing success even though it was a technological flop.

2.2.2 Unrealistic Expectations

Difficult or impossible requirements are not always the result of devious maneuvering, however; sometimes, they come about honestly and sincerely not only from management but also from the developers. Managers and developers attend conferences and listen to zealots promoting the latest XML specifications, then rush out and make support for those specifications into requirements before evaluating their value and the level of available support, as discussed in Section 1.6. If the specifications chosen are not widely supported, the project's developers will not be able to use off-the-shelf software and will end up doing a lot of custom development to support a specification that brings little or no value to the organization. In many cases, no one has yet proved that the specifications even *can* be supported in a production environment.

This problem is especially common when a specification has endorsements from large companies and organizations. Those endorsements can give the impression that the companies are planning to use the specification or even to produce off-the-shelf software to support it, but that's rarely the case: Large companies wait for proven demand before making major investments in technologies. The name *IBM, Microsoft,* or *Oracle* on an XML-related specification simply means that the company authorized one or more of its employees to serve on the standards committee, not that it is about to release shrink-wrapped software to support the specification.

Starting out with unrealistic expectations can quickly leave developers and managers frustrated. The so-called standards mean more work rather than less, and there are no extra rewards for following them. The expected software and tool support never appears, and customers or suppliers that were talking about exchanging information using the new specification never get around to doing it. In the end, all the XML has to be converted back to an older, legacy information format anyway, and the XML ends up as an expensive and unnecessary extra step in the information pipeline.

The best way to work around this problem is to plan for the present, not for the future. How well is a specification supported *today*? How many partners, customers, or suppliers want to exchange XML-based information *today*? How many products and components are available off the shelf *today*? If the answer to each of these questions is close to zero, postponing support for the specification is probably the wisest choice.

2.2.3 Resistance to Change

Incremental technical innovations often have mild and benign social effects. For example, the change from rotary to touch-tone dialing did not initially have a major impact on people's lives, although eventually it did allow for automated telephone systems; likewise, the change from roof antennas to cable television simply built on what people were already doing—watching TV—but expanded their choice.

Disruptive technical innovations, on the other hand, have immediate and unavoidable social effects, both positive and negative, with clear winners and losers. Consider, for example, the effect of peer-to-peer file sharing on the music industry (losers) or the effect of cellular phone technology on real estate agents (winners). As happened with the music industry and peer-to-peer file sharing, the people who fear that they might be losers will fight long and hard against the change, believing that they are better off with the status quo.

XML typically falls into the disruptive group, so XML projects can face serious resistance. Although big companies—even the ones with the most to lose from open file formats—have embraced XML, XML still poses the same kind of apparent threat to individual users that file sharing poses to the music industry. The best place to start is the separation of content and formatting, one of the central assumptions of XML.

It is common in the XML world to be dismissive about WYSIWYG word processors, such as OpenOffice Writer or Microsoft Word, but authors using such WYSIWYG systems have an enormous amount of control over their work. Although they may be required to use a specific template and to follow a standard style guide, they can still add formatting directly and see more or less what the published version of their work will look like. They can add page breaks, rearrange paragraphs, add tabs and indentation, and fiddle in many other ways until their text not only reads well but looks good. Taking away control over formatting and presentation wipes out much of what gives document authors pride in their work.

It is not simply a matter of control, however, but of prestige. To balance the authors' freedom in a writing team using word processors or desktop publishing software, there is often a set of complex rules, both written and unwritten, enforced by editors and senior writers. Many of these rules are related to formatting and software; mastering these rules, especially the unwritten ones, gives the senior people a position of power over the junior ones. Switching to XML immediately weakens or eliminates that power: XML-driven editing software can enforce many structural rules that used to have to be enforced by editors or peers, and formatting rules become mostly irrelevant. The new XML-based system may be just as complex, but the senior people no longer have an advantage: They have to learn it from scratch, just like the junior people do, and probably will not be able to learn it as quickly.

A third, related problem is simple overwork and frustration, even from people who are not otherwise opposed to the project. An XML-based system often requires people to learn a software product that may be buggy and incomplete. At the same time, unless the group using the XML project is brand new, such as a start-up or a recently created division of a company or organization, the users likely have to keep up with their regular work during the transition. Structured markup requires a new way of thinking, and a new way of thinking takes time to sink in; if, as is typical, users are not given any extra time—or even if they suspect that they won't be—they will be enormously hostile to any new system, XML or otherwise.

Even the people who will not be using the system directly will likely be skeptical, as they are with any big technical change; they'll be concerned about—or jealous of—the resources being devoted to the XML project and will be eager to jump on the first weakness that turns up.

So, to summarize, following are four major reasons that people will be secretly or openly hostile to a new XML project in any company or organization.

1. Authors do not want to give up control over the physical appearance of their work.
2. Senior people do not want to lose their advantage of experience with the current system over the coworkers.
3. Users do not want to devote the time to learn a new system, risking falling behind in their existing work.
4. All members of the company or organization may be skeptical that the project's benefits will justify the cost.

How can an XML project deal with these obstacles? The best place to start is an admission that, sometimes, the naysayers are right. An XML project may fail or underperform, especially if it involves desktop authoring tools. Employees may initially find their work less pleasant once they've lost some control over it. Senior people are at real danger of being left behind by any technological change. Employees will find that their managers expect them to learn and to adopt complicated new technologies without any temporary decrease in productivity. All together, like most other workplace innovations, a big change like XML can make for a bad situation and, eventually, a poisoned working environment.

2.3 How XML Projects Can Succeed

The previous section ended on a sour note, but your XML project does not have to end the same way. To sweeten it up, you need to work hard in two areas:

1. The *social* side of XML, helping the users who will be most affected by a project
2. The *technical* side of XML, planning from the start to avoid bloat and maintenance problems and to minimize the risks from working with new, unproven specifications and techniques

2.3.1 Winning Friends and Influencing Users

As mentioned earlier, XML is a big troublemaker.

- It takes away authors' control over the layout and appearance of their documents.
- It disrupts the pecking order by reducing or eliminating the value of senior people's experience.
- It increases the workload for users, especially during the initial transition to XML.
- It generates hostility from rivals promoting other technologies or approaches.

The key to dealing with these problems is to try to minimize their impact by giving users back some control, working to protect the authority of senior people, managing users' workload during the transition to XML, and finding ways to placate rivals and involve them in the XML project. Obviously, these factors go far beyond the power and authority usually granted to a technological project team and will require the cooperation and understanding of management. It is best to raise the issues early, however, before a project is in trouble; otherwise, management may, rightly, see the issues simply as excuses for the project team's failures.

2.3.1.1 Keeping Users in Control   When users switch to XML, they lose the ability to fine-tune the appearance of their documents. XML specialists will try to explain that the users are not so much giving up control over their work as trading one kind of control for another; they have less control over how their text *looks* but more control over what it *means*. Previously, for example, users might have used—or abused—bold italics and indentation to mark a warning; now, they can tag the whole thing with a `warning` element. If another writer or editor works on the text later, there's no ambiguity about what the original author intended.

Still, the loss of formatting control can be stressful for authors. People do need to be able to see the results of their work quickly and frequently, and an XML system that takes human factors into account should budget some time and money accordingly. Many writers like to use paper printouts for proofreading, for example, and many want to be able to show drafts to people who do not use XML editing software. XML projects that involve human authors usually end up giving them a way to preview and print out their work frequently, with formatting attached: Building the preview/print support early, debugging it thoroughly, and showing it to the authors the first time they try the system can help restore their sense of control over what they are doing. They do not have to take it on blind faith that their documents will look nice some day, far in the future.

2.3.1.2 Preserving the Pecking Order   The pecking-order problem is a lot trickier to deal with. For example, an organization may be introducing XML precisely to avoid depending so much on senior people; in that case, shaking up the office power structure is one of the project's goals rather than merely an unintentional side effect, and the project team can do nothing other than dig deep trenches and wait for the bombardment to begin. The people with the most to lose from the old system are often in the best position to thwart the new one because of the influence they hold.

2.3 How XML Projects Can Succeed

If the company does not want to destroy the current pecking order, the best approach is to bring some of the senior people onto the XML design team itself somehow, especially for designing document types. Involving these people in the project is tricky, but it has two significant advantages.

1. Because they are involved in the design, the people have a personal stake it the new system and are less likely to attack it.
2. Because they learn the new system before anyone else and also know about the process that led to its design, the senior people retain their knowledge advantage over their junior coworkers.

Putting the senior people on the design team can also backfire. If they are still in an obstructionist mood, they can easily slow down or destroy the project. Even if they are cooperative, they may introduce many new, unnecessary, and expensive requirements in an attempt to display their knowledge and experience. Realistically, the team implementing an XML project usually lacks any authority to transfer or fire employees, so placating them is normally the only option.

2.3.1.3 *Managing User Workload*

The workload problem is probably the most difficult one to solve, as it usually originates in the company or organization's work culture. XML simply exacerbates the problem, as XML authoring systems require such a different way of thinking and thus a lot of training and practice. The best solution is to explain the problem to management in advance and to try to convince them to reduce the users' workload during the transition period. Some companies may be willing to do so, but others, especially those that try to make employees work extra hours during evenings and weekends, are not likely to cooperate.

At that point, the XML team has to start looking for solutions that are within its power. One promising approach is to bring in XML very slowly to spread out the burden on the users. The XML team can start by introducing XML into noncritical areas, where bugs or lack of familiarity will not slow employees down in their main work and make them cancel vacations or miss weekends with their families. The users can learn the ideas of XML and the specific software gradually, and the XML team can slowly expand the system without leaving the users too far behind. This approach also helps the XML team, as the members can learn more about how the users work with XML and what the real requirements are. In fact, if users become familiar with XML through simple systems—say, through virtual timesheets or expense reports—and they become convinced that XML *can* make their work easier, they will end up as XML advocates themselves.

2.3.1.4 *Placating Rivals*

The problem of jealousy between departments, divisions, committees, projects, or other administrative units is the most difficult one to deal with in any major technological project. Because XML is a new and still unproven technology, however, it is especially vulnerable to attacks. As it did with hostile users, the XML team can try to win over rivals by involving them in the XML project design; in doing so, however, the team runs the risk that those people will try to sabotage the project from the inside by smothering it with requirements or simply stalling at every stage.

A safer solution is to start XML projects very small. Rivals are not likely to consider a small project as a threat, and by the time the project grows, it will be well established and more capable of surviving attacks. Starting small may seem counterintuitive for XML—after all, it represents a disruptive technology, a bold new way of doing things, and all that—but it provides a good opportunity for people to learn XML and for the project to grow.

2.3.2 Successful XML Technology

This chapter has spent a lot of time on the people affected by—or scheming against—an XML project. Obviously, however, getting the human factors under control is not the only requirement for a successful project. Once you've won everyone over, you still have to deliver a system that works. Building working systems on time is surprisingly difficult in all areas of computer technology but is especially tricky with newer, experimental technologies, such as XML. This section looks at two areas that matter a lot for building good, robust XML systems:

1. Forward-compatibility and extensibility
2. A markup budget

2.3.2.1 Forward Compatibility and Extensibility Consumer desktop software is almost always *backward compatible* but very rarely *forward compatible*. If you buy the latest version of a word processor, for example, you should be able to load files created with any earlier version (*backward compatibility*); however, if you save a file with the latest version of the word processor—even if you do not use any of the new features—people running the older versions may not be able to read your file (*forward compatibility*). Obviously, it is in the vendor's interest not to be forward compatible: As soon as a certain proportion of users upgrade, the rest are forced to upgrade as well so that they can still share files. The fact that consumers rarely complain about this forced upgrade march is a measure of how low their expectations of desktop software have fallen.

There are, of course, some legitimate justifications for the forward incompatibility that is prevalent in the software industry, both in shrink-wrapped software and in custom projects. What *should* an older application do when it finds a feature that it does not support? Should it silently skip the feature? Should it display a warning? Should it try to fall back to something simpler? Should it simply give up completely? Most applications have traditionally chosen the last option, but over the past decade, HTML and the Web have shown us all that there is an alternative.

From early on, HTML included a simple rule for Web browsers: If the browser sees any markup it does not recognize, it should ignore the tags and attributes but render the content (text). The following is an HTML paragraph with the non-HTML `special` element included in its content:

```
<p>This is a regular HTML paragraph with
<special>specially marked content</special>.</p>
```

2.3 How XML Projects Can Succeed

When it renders this paragraph, an HTML browser will ignore the start and end tags of the unrecognized `special` element but will render the text inside it, as follows:

```
<p>This is a regular HTML paragraph with
specially marked content.</p>
```

Because of this approach, Web browsers do not fail completely when they run into something they do not recognize but rather fail gradually and, usually, gracefully: In this case, an older browser will fail to apply any special formatting for the `special` element but will render the content. Sometimes, this approach does produce awkward results. For example, the content of HTML tables looked strange in early browsers that did not include table support, Web sites that use frames have to explicitly include alternative text for older browsers, and Web developers have to surround scripting code in comments so that older browsers will not render the code on screen.[1] Nevertheless, the approach has worked fairly well.

The point of forward compatibility is not to allow people to use keep using ten-year-old browsers—although some undoubtedly do—but rather to make it possible for information formats to evolve without too much resistance from the installed software base. Much of what gives HTML its expressive power—from pictures to tables to forms to applets and scripts—was not present in the initial HTML specification. Forward compatibility made it possible to experiment with various ways of adding these features without disrupting current users. If everyone *had* been forced to upgrade their browsers before every major advance, such as tables, forms, or scripts, the Web would have evolved considerably more slowly, if at all, and would not be nearly as popular and useful as it is today.

Like HTML, XML is all about sharing information, and sharing information is most valuable if many people or organizations are participating. However, the more users there are, the less likely that they will all be willing or able to upgrade their software at the same time; that means that the more popular an XML-based format becomes, the more difficult it will be to change it. Forward compatibility offers an escape from this trap, allowing the introduction of new features without forcing users to upgrade immediately; they can wait until they decide that supporting the new feature is worthwhile and then upgrade on their own schedules, if at all.

In certain cases, on the other hand, forward compatibility is not a good thing. For example, an XML-based format may go through a significant change to add security features, or it may change the meaning of some markup; in those cases, it is better for a client application to fail than to produce inaccurate, incomplete, or insecure information. Likewise, if lives depend on the XML—say, for medical operations or weapons systems—incomplete information may be worse than none at all.

Whether forward compatibility is desirable or not, it is essential for every XML-based specification to state clearly how client software should behave when it finds unrecognized markup,

---

[1] This problem is largely the Web developers' fault. A better solution is to place the scripting code in a separate file, to avoid mixing the view and controller layers.

and this statement should be drawn up as early in the planning stage as possible, as it will affect every other part of the project's design. The forward-compatibility and extensibility statement can be as simple as a short list.

- If a client application encounters an element that is not part of this specification, the application shall ignore the element and its attributes and process the element's content as if it appeared in the same location as the unrecognized element.
- If a client application encounters an attribute that is not part of this specification, the application shall ignore the attribute and its value.

It is often worthwhile to make finer distinctions. For example, an unrecognized element in front matter or metadata might be treated differently from an unrecognized element in the main body, and an unrecognized element inside a paragraph might be treated differently from an unrecognized element between paragraphs. Namespaces can also come into play; for extensibility, a specification might allow unrecognized elements and attributes in *other* namespaces but not in the specification's primary namespace. The XML document as a whole might include a `version` attribute, and the compatibility and extensibility rules will depend on the version number.

The important point is to allow some room for extensibility and future changes, if possible, and to specify precisely what the rules are for processing unrecognized markup. If a specification or a project does not go to the trouble of defining rules for compatibility and extensibility, different implementers will choose different approaches, and serious interoperability problems may follow. A good forward-compatibility and extensibility policy will make for a robust and sustainable project.

2.3.2.2 Markup Budget The previous section showed how to make it easy to introduce new markup in future versions of an XML-based format. In many ways, markup is a good thing: It adds meaning and structure to a document, making it possible for computers to do more with them automatically. However, it is important to note that, although markup is undoubtedly good, it is *not* cheap; each individual element or attribute in an XML-based specification triggers a cascade of costs of both time and money. Containing these costs—budgeting markup—is an important step in managing any XML-based project.

Consider, for example, the costs of only a single XML element in a documentation project.

- A DTD or a schema designer has to declare the element and include it in the appropriate content models.
- A technical writer has to learn about the element and document its usage, possibly in several contexts.
- A style sheet writer has to add style support for the element in the authoring tool.
- Software engineers writing transformations for publishing and archiving have to support the element in their code.

- Layout designers have to support the element in the specifications they design for the publishing engine.
- Users have to be trained to use the element properly.

And, unfortunately, that's not the end of the costs. For a living project, the preceding costs are ongoing: Every time the writer has to revise the documentation, for example, or every time someone has to update the schema, an extra complexity cost for each element or attribute is added. Increased size also brings increased risk: Each extra element or attribute is one more place that bugs or security flaws can creep into a system.

Obviously, an XML project has to pay the costs for some markup, or it would not be an XML project. However, people designing technology projects have an unfortunate tendency to design defensively. Instead of building what they need right away, they build everything that anyone thinks they might need for many years to come, and, of course, most of those guesses end up being wrong, resulting in huge wastes of time and money. The result is systems that are unnecessarily complex and therefore end up either failing or coming in late and over budget.

Section 2.3.2.1 discusses how it is possible to design a change-tolerant XML system by defining forward compatibility and extensibility behavior explicitly from the start. If future changes are not expensive, why build in too much markup now? For example, it might be that authors do not currently require the ability to tag part numbers but that they might want that in 5 years when or if the company implements a new inventory system. Should version 1 of the document type include part numbers as an option? If it does so, it will trigger all the time and money costs for something that authors may never end up using. On the other hand, if the new inventory system is imminent, authors might want to be able to tag part numbers now so that they will not have to go back and edit all their documents later. In that case, you can make a good argument for including the element in the markup budget.

Over all, a successful XML project should run on a tight markup budget. Limiting the project to the smallest possible schema or DTD will bring benefits throughout the project's life cycle, from planning to full deployment.

2.4 Final Words on Planning

XML is both disruptive and new. An unproven technology with enemies can make a shaky foundation for any major project, so starting small and growing incrementally is almost always a good choice, from both the technical and human perspectives. A small project can allow users to ease into XML, allow developers to learn from less expensive mistakes, and allow both to avoid the wrath of jealous rivals.

That said, XML can bring enormous benefits to projects. Breaking away from proprietary data formats allows an organization to own its own information rather than effectively lease it from a software vendor. The Web changed the world by making it easy for people to share information, and XML may make it easy for computers to share information the same way. Part Two of this book shows how projects can use XML in various areas and includes a frank discussion of the advantages and disadvantages of XML in each one.

PART TWO

XML Implementation

Part One focused on the higher-level strategic questions. The chapters in Part Two focus on the midlevel details of making an XML project work.

Originally, people divided XML projects into two groups: *XML documents* and *XML data*. Recently—with the rise of Web Services—a third group, *XML networking,* has emerged. Many XML specialists hate these distinctions, arguing that they gloss over everything that different kinds of XML projects have in common. Nevertheless, these distinctions provide useful starting points for understanding the various ways that people use XML; this book keeps to the best-known classifications.

Chapter 3 introduces the most traditional of the three XML project types: using XML for publishing documents, such as manuals, books, Web sites, and so on, intended for human readers. XML publishing is difficult and expensive, but in some specialized areas, it can provide a significant return on the time and money invested.

Chapter 4 examines the use of XML for communicating with machines rather than with people. XML is a popular export and interchange format for machine-readable data, and XML data publishing, although not easy, does not have most of the serious pitfalls of XML document publishing.

Chapter 5 takes a look at the newest area of XML work, where XML starts to blur the line between the network protocol and the network payload. XML is already wildly successful for syndicating Web logs, or blogs, and many large corporations are betting that Web Services based on XML will be the next great technology wave. Nevertheless, outside of blogging, XML networking is still a new, unproven concept.

CHAPTER 3

XML Documents

Generic markup was originally designed for *documents,* such as technical manuals, books, and articles. XML is a direct descendant of the the Standard Generalized Markup Language [SGML], which was released in 1986; SGML, in its turn, was a descendant of the Generalized Markup Language (GML), developed by Charles Goldfarb, Ed Mosher, and Ray Lorie at IBM in the early 1970s, initially for tagging documents in the legal department.[1] This kind of in-line markup traces its way back further to formatting codes for typesetting machines and on to editorial marks on paper copy.

Over time, document markup has become increasingly generic: Codes for type styles, such as "italics," have given way to more general codes, such as "title," that say what text represents rather than how it should be formatted. This pattern occurred not only with XML but also with other document languages, such as TeX and TROFF, which implemented high-level macro packages, such as LaTeX and MS, to hide low-level formatting codes. For example, a LaTeX document often contains no low-level formatting code at all, as in Listing 3-1.

Listing 3-1   LaTeX Markup
```
\documentclass{article}
\title{Sample document}
\author{David Megginson}

\begin{document}
\maketitle

This is a simple LaTeX document.

\end{document}
```

That example is not, functionally, much different from a similar document in XML, as in Listing 3-2.

---

[1] Many people believe that GML stands not for Generalized Markup Language but for Goldfarb, Mosher, and Lorie.

Listing 3-2 XML Markup
```
<article>
  <title>Sample document</title>
  <author>David Megginson</author>

  <para>This is a simple XML document.</para>
</article>
```

Behind the scenes, however, the LaTeX example hides the formatting code inside macro definitions, whereas the XML example has no direct link to formatting at all. Even so, the ideas behind XML and SGML are familiar to people in computer technology, math, and science, who have been working with formats like LaTeX for many years. That fact that HTML was inspired by, but not initially based on, SGML lexical conventions also smoothed the introduction of XML into the documentation world.

It is XML's document origin that explains specialized syntactic features, such as mixed content and CDATA sections, that seem to make computer processing of XML more difficult than it should be, especially in terms of whitespace handling. Although these features cause technical problems, they exist to allow XML to work with human-readable, publishable information, such as books and articles. For machine-readable data (see Chapter 4), simple lists and tables are usually sufficient, as in Listing 3-3.

Listing 3-3 Sample XML Data, Without Mixed Content
```
<parts>
  <part>
    <number>16687</number>
    <name>locknut</name>
  </part>
  <part number="16687">
    <number>35581</number>
    <name>washer</name>
  </part>
</parts>
```

This example has a clear distinction between markup and content: Every element contains either text or other XML elements but never both. Documented-oriented XML, on the other hand, tends to be messier, as in Listing 3-4.

Listing 3-4 Sample XML Document with Mixed Content
```
<para>The film <title>Gone with the Wind</title> appeared in
<date>1939</date>, looking back to the U.S. Civil War while much of
the rest of the world was already preparing for <event>World War
II</event>.</para>
```

3.1 Advantages of XML for Documents

This second example has no clear distinction: The content of the `para` element consists of both text and other elements mixed together. The presence of this kind of mixed content is a strong indication that an XML file is intended as a document rather than as a data collection.

These days, XML-encoded documentation is about as common as SGML or LaTeX documentation was before it—people use XML mainly in large, complex technical documentation systems or small, private research projects—but documents are no longer the main use for generic markup. Interest in using XML to exchange data and to set up distributed computing (Chapter 5, XML networking) now far exceeds any interest in XML for documentation. Many of the initial XML document-oriented specifications (XLink [XLINK], XPointer [XPOINTER], and XSL-FO [XSL-FO]) now either languish with few users or have been coopted for use with data or networking (XSLT [XSLT], XPath [XPath]), whereas data- or networking-oriented specifications keep on appearing. The world appears to be satisfied with the Hypertext Markup Language [HTML] for online documentation and Microsoft Word for print and is not eager to embrace XML with all its extra complexity.

Obviously, because of that extra complexity, XML is not a general-purpose solution for all documentation projects, but in some situations, using XML for documents makes a lot of sense, particularly when you need to publish and republish large amounts of technical information in multiple formats, combine human-written material with information from databases, or customize publications for individual recipients. This chapter examines both the advantages and the disadvantages of XML documents and introduces some of the special issues involved with XML publishing.

3.1 Advantages of XML for Documents

Enterprise-grade XML documentation and publishing systems are expensive custom jobs, so they are most useful when XML can bring significant savings in labor later on. The classic case for XML documents is *single-source publishing,* whereby a single master XML document can generate output in many different formats. But XML can save time and money in other ways: For example, an XML publishing system can create *hybrid documents,* combining information from human authors with information extracted from a database. XML also simplifies *custom publishing,* whereby a document needs to be published in different versions for different users. XML supports information *reusability,* using the same fragment, such as a chapter or a task, in several documents. And finally—and perhaps most important—XML preserves more of the author's knowledge and intent in a document than other document formats can, exposing that information to enable smarter processing, searching, and archiving.

3.1.1 Single-Source Publishing

XML's biggest promise for documentation is *single-source publishing*. From a single master XML document, someone can generate outputs in many different formats and media. One of the most common examples is publishing to both print and the Web; a simple script can split a long document into a series of linked pages for Web publication but still produce a nicely formatted

Figure 3-1 Single-source publishing

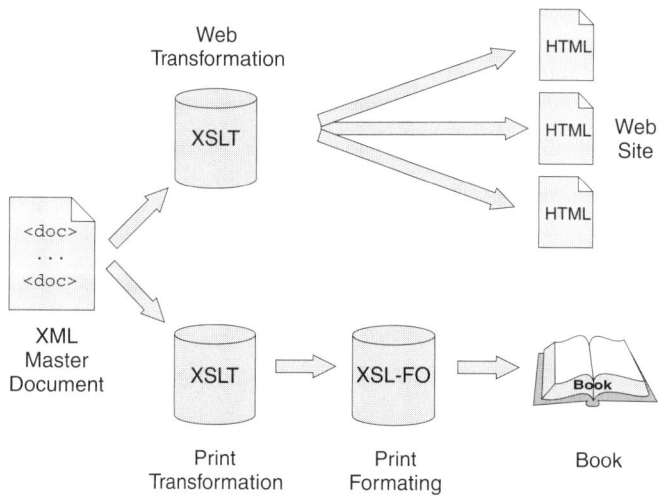

book for print, as illustrated in Figure 3-1. This book, in fact, is written entirely in XML but can be converted to high-quality HTML or any number of other formats—plain text, PostScript, PDF, RTF, Braille, and so on—automatically.

Single-source publishing works because XML markup specifies what text represents rather than how it should appear; in other words, XML specifies *meaning* rather than *formatting*. For example, an element named `book-title` might generate italic text on a printed page, blue text on a Web page, and a different voice pitch in an automated voice reader. An element named `chapter` might generate a page break and a new number for a printed book and a new Web page online. The key to all this is the use of XML together with external style sheets or transformation templates: A style sheet provides a set of rules about how to convert the generic XML markup to specific typefaces, sounds, colors, or other formats. The same style sheet can be used to convert hundreds or thousands of XML documents following the same markup language to the same output format, so any initial cost of developing the style sheet can pay itself back many times.

Single-source publishing is a well-proven technique, dating back over a decade and a half to SGML and other, more limited single-source formats, such as TeXInfo and TROFF. Single-source publishing systems are used frequently in government, big industry, and the free-software community; in fact, much of the technical documentation for the open-source Linux operating system and software commonly used with it comes from XML or SGML master documents written in the DocBook [DOCBOOK] format, and standard Linux distributions have the tools preinstalled for generating output from a single source. Although DocBook is in many ways an awkward, cumbersome document type, the availability of easy-to-use tools ensures its continuing success, an important lesson for anyone promoting a new specification.

3.1 Advantages of XML for Documents

3.1.2 Hybrid Data Publishing

A second area in which XML document publishing is a good fit is hybrid publishing, or combining human-authored text with live information from a database. For example, a catalog needs to have the latest prices: A person could edit and proofread the catalog every time a price changes, but that would be labor intensive and error prone. Instead, the original author can simply insert a database reference in the XML markup, as in Listing 3-5.

Listing 3-5   Catalog Entry before Transformation
```
<item>
  <source>Henrickson</source>
  <name>Acoustic Guitar</name>
  <description>This guitar includes a mahogany fret board, gold-plated tuning pegs, and a solid top.</description>
  <price dbref="g3905778/price"/>
<item>
```

Note that the author does not have to know the price at authoring time. When the XML document goes through its transformation to print or Web pages, the transformation engine automatically looks up the `g3905778` reference and generates new XML before formatting, as in Listing 3-6.

Listing 3-6   Catalog entry after transformation
```
<item>
  <source>Henrickson</source>
  <name>Acoustic Guitar</name>
  <description>This guitar includes a mahogany fret board, gold-plated
    tuning pegs, and a solid top.</description>
  <price>
    <status>sale</status>
    <expiry-date>2005-01-01</expiry-date>
    <currency>USD</currency>
    <amount>1999.00</amount>
  </price>
<item>
```

According to the generated XML, this is a sale price. If the company ran the XML through the transformation engine again the next week, a different price might come out of the database if the sale were over, as in Listing 3-7.

Listing 3-7   Catalog Entry after Another Transformation
```
<item>
  <source>Henrickson</source>
  <name>Acoustic Guitar</name>
```

```
    <description>This guitar includes a mahogany fret board, gold-plated
       tuning pegs, and a solid top.</description>
    <price>
       <status>regular</status>
       <expiry-date>2005-01-08</expiry-date>
       <currency>USD</currency>
       <amount>2499.00</amount>
    </price>
<item>
```

Note that no human intervention was involved: The price will change automatically every time the XML document goes through the transformation engine. The transformation might be a weekly batch job, and the catalog will stay up to date even if the author is away on vacation.

3.1.3 Custom Publishing

Custom publishing is similar to single-source publishing except that both the content and the format can change. Consider a simple source document like this:

```
<para>BigCo purchased a 45 percent share of ACME Widgets for <money
currency="GBP">48M</money>.</para>
```

A reader in the United Kingdom would be happy to see the following text:

> BigCo purchased a 45 percent share of ACME Widgets for £45M.

A reader in the United States, on the other hand, would likely prefer to see the value in local currency:

> BigCo purchased a 45 percent share of ACME Widgets for $72M (£45M).

An XML-based publishing system can handle this kind of conversion easily and automatically. Not only can such a system save money by minimizing the need to pay editors to localize documents, but it can also save time by allowing the document to be published more quickly.

More typically, custom publishing appears in heavily regulated environments. An airliner from Airbus, Boeing, or Bombardier, for example, comes with dozens of manuals, some of which are tens or hundreds of thousands of pages long. The manufacturer must customize these manuals for each customer to cover only the engines and other systems installed in that customer's aircraft and must republish some of the manuals with updated information every few months. Managing such a task by hand requires a small army of employees just to sort the paper and bind the manuals; a customized XML-based document publishing system, although expensive to set up, can provide indisputable time and money savings.

3.1.4 Reuse

XML documents can include other files, so an XML publishing system can easily assemble smaller documents and fragments into larger ones: For example, each news story, chapter, or task can be a separate XML file. In fact, producing a document from XML source is very similar to compiling and linking a computer program from C or C++ source. Just as computer programs can link in libraries and other reusable code, XML documents can include reusable fragments; for example, several maintenance manuals might include the procedure in Listing 3-8.

Listing 3-8 Reusable Fragment
```
<procedure>
<title>Extracting a Phillips screw with a worn head</title>

<step>Ensure that your screwdriver head is the correct size
and does not show visible wear.</step>

<step>Apply a small amount of gripping compound to the head of
the screwdriver, apply strong downwards pressure, and attempt
to turn the screw.</step>

<step>If the screwdriver head still cannot grip the screw,
use a small grinding tool to cut a large slot across the
screw head, then attempt to turn the screw with a screwdriver
fitted with a slotted head.</step>

<step>If the screw still will not turn, drill it out using an
electric drill and a drill bit designed for metal work.</step>
</procedure>
```

Because the manuals include the procedure by reference rather than by cut-and-paste, any change to the procedure's content will automatically appear in all the manuals the next time they are formatted, just as a change to a computer library will appear in all programs that use it the next time they are linked.

In addition to sharing the same information among multiple documents, XML makes it possible to use the same information more than once inside a single document. For example, a standard warning about handling acids might need to appear a dozen times. Using a single XML source for the warning ensures that it will always be consistent and that changes to it will propagate automatically.

See Section 3.4.2 for more information on reusing XML fragments in publishing, including a discussion of the difficulties involved.

3.1.5 Knowledge Preservation

Documents capture people's knowledge. Whether a document contains a fictional story, technical procedures, or business transactions, its text serves as a persistent record of information that the writer knows and wants to record. Typically, however, a writer records knowledge not merely through words themselves but through punctuation and formatting as well. Consider the following unformatted text:

```
THEDOORSSONGTHEENDINTHEOPENINGCREDITSOFAPOCALYPSENOWCREAT
ESASTRONGCONTRASTBETWEENTHESLOWALMOSTHYPNOTICMUSICANDTHEV
IOLENTWARSCENESONTHESCREENMARTINSHEENSCHARACTERBEGINSTHEM
OVIEINHISOWNSCENEOFQUIETSELFDESTRUCTIONINAHOTELROOMMIRROR
INGBOTHTHEQUIETMUSICANDVIOLENTIMAGESOFTHEOPENING
```

Two thousand years ago, written documents were sometimes very similar to this: With a little work, it is possible to read the passage, but much of what the author knew is lost in the unadorned text. Now consider the same passage with modern formatting, capitalization, and punctuation added:

The Doors song "The End" in the opening credits of *Apocalypse Now* creates a strong contrast between the slow, almost hypnotic music and the violent war scenes on the screen. Martin Sheen's character opens the movie in his own scene of quiet self-destruction in a hotel room, mirroring both the quiet music and the violent images of the opening.

The formatting, whitespace, punctuation, and capitalization provide a lot of additional information.

- Spaces show where words start and end, and capitalization and periods show where sentences start and end.
- The second word is capitalized to indicate that Doors is a proper noun: the name of a musical group, in this case.
- The phrase "The End" is capitalized and in quotation marks to show that it is a song title.
- The phrase *Apocalypse Now* is in italics to show that it is a movie title.
- The comma between "slow" and "hypnotic" shows that the two adjectives stand in apposition: They both describe the same thing.
- The words Martin Sheen are capitalized to show that they are proper nouns—a person's name, in this case.
- An apostrophe appears between "Sheen" and the following "s" to show that this is a possessive form modifying the word "character" that follows.
- The comma before the word "mirroring" shows that the remainder of the sentence stands in apposition to the first part, providing a description of it.

Obviously, markup existed long before XML; people use complex markup every time they write, usually without giving it any conscious thought. However, our traditional markup is ambiguous: Is a word in quotation marks because it is a song title, a definition, or a direct quotation? Is a phrase italicized for emphasis or because it is a book or movie title? Is a word capitalized because it is a proper noun or because it begins a sentence? Does a comma indicate apposition, or does it simply separate items in a sequence? Does an apostrophe indicate the possessive or a contraction? People rarely have problems with these ambiguities, because we understand the meaning of the text well enough to resolve them.

Computers, on the other hand, have very limited abilities to make sense of natural-language text and so do a poor job interpreting the ambiguous markup of punctuation, whitespace, and formatting that humans prefer. In fact, even humans can have a difficult time interpreting formatting and punctuation if they do not share the writer's background. For example, someone who had never heard of the musical group The Doors or the film *Apocalypse Now* might have some difficulty understanding even the formatted passage.

XML markup provides a way for the writer to make this extra information unambiguous by using tags and attributes to annotate the text explicitly. Linguists and philologists will sometimes do away with capitalization, punctuation, and significant whitespace altogether and annotate a text using XML exclusively. More typically, however, XML documents still use punctuation and interword whitespace for basic grammatical markup, with XML serving only to replace typefaces and other layout, as in the following:

```
<p>The <band>Doors</band> song <song>The End</song> in the opening
credits of <film>Apocalypse Now</film> creates a strong contrast
between the slow, almost hypnotic music and the violent war scenes
on the screen. <actor>Martin Sheen's</actor> character opens the
movie in his own scene of quiet self-destruction in a hotel room,
mirroring both the quiet music and the violent images of the
opening.</p>
```

This example is still fairly easy for a person to read, but it also captures more of the author's knowledge: *The Doors* is a band, *The End* is a song, *Apocalypse Now* is a film, and *Martin Sheen* is an actor. As described in Chapter 6, this kind of markup can make search engines much smarter. It is also useful for generating lists and indexes, but most important, it will make it possible for computers or even human users in different cultures or time periods to make sense of the text.

3.2 Disadvantages of XML for Documents

XML-based documentation systems can be surprisingly difficult and expensive to set up. A researcher or free-software author can sit at home and write and format a manual, article, or book using easily accessible free software, but attempts to introduce XML document writing into a larger, enterprise work environment often end in frustration. The biggest problem with XML documents is the people who have to write them: An individual writing XML at home has a positive attitude toward XML and understands how to use it; at a workplace, it is necessary first to win people over and then to educate them. After that, there's the problem of software: XML desktop applications are not as easy to buy or install as regular office software, and both initial purchase and customization can be expensive.

Other problems with XML documents have to do with the technical limitations of XML publishing systems. Although these systems do a good job with basic technical material, they are not yet up to the creative layout necessary for glossy magazines, advertising, or other special uses.

3.2.1 People and Software

Section 2.3.1 discussed human factors relating to XML in detail, but it is worth a quick reminder that XML-based publishing systems need XML content going in one end to get formatted publications out the other. In some cases, the XML can come straight out of a database; for example, a company might keep a database of collectable dolls and generate a simple XML catalog directly from those database tables, with no human intervention. In a situation like that, authors deal only with filling in normal database forms, so they never have to worry about markup. Most of the time, however, that approach is not adequate for documents, so an XML documentation project can either

1. Train and convince authors to create their documents in XML
2. Allow authors to create documents in different formats, such as plaintext or a word-processing format, and then add the XML markup later

The first approach does not seem as though it should be that difficult. Based on the number of functions available and the amount that people have to learn to get started, XML authoring tools are no more complicated than word processors or spreadsheets and are much simpler than most drawing or paint programs. In fact, many academic researchers and open-source software programmers create hundreds or thousands of pages of XML with minimal training and primitive tools, such as plaintext editors.

The problem comes down to familiarity. In the early 1990s, during the initial growth of the SGML community, there was hope that the structure-oriented SGML editor would eventually replace the format-oriented word processor in the business world, just as the word processor had replaced the typewriter and the typewriter had replaced the pen. Things did not turn out that way, of course: The word processor had a head start of more than a decade, and by the early 1990s, it had reached a critical mass; people had used it for years, had become familiar with it, and had then gone out and taught others. Even if a structured SGML editor brought some new advantages, they were not strong enough to justify starting the learning process all over again. Word processors do enough of what people need that people will stick with them even if better alternatives come along.

This kind of sudden change followed by a long period of conservatism is not new. For example, English spelling varied enormously over the Middle Ages, both from place to place and from decade to decade, reflecting, partly, differences in local pronunciation. Then, in 1476, William Caxton brought the printing press to England, and English spelling froze. More than 500 years later, English spelling still represents, more or less, the pronunciation of London and the

3.2 Disadvantages of XML for Documents

East Midlands in the fifteenth century and has very little to do with how English speakers talk anywhere in the world.[2] Structured editing, whether SGML or XML, arrived too late to catch the big wave of the personal computer revolution, and people still create electronic documents essentially the same way they did in 1982.

Given that observation, getting authors to write XML directly is always going to be difficult; unlike word processing or spreadsheet design, structured XML editing is not a skill that most job applicants bring with them, especially if they are already required to be subject-matter experts in another field, such as finance, engineering, or law. Both new and existing employees will need training to use XML tools properly, and existing employees will likely resist any big change in their work environment.

Aside from winning over and training the employees, a company will have to purchase, deploy, customize, and support the XML authoring software. Without the economies of scale that make other types of computer programs relatively inexpensive, large-scale XML authoring can cost a lot in software licenses alone. Some organizations try to limit their costs by restricting XML to a smaller number of people: Authors create their documents in plaintext or a traditional word processor; then human editors or computer programmers add the tags. This approach is tempting because it can avoid most of the costs of training all authors in XML and supplying software for them, but it has some serious drawbacks.

- After the tagging has been added, the original authors can no longer go back and make further revisions without learning XML.
- The authors typically know more about what they are writing than anyone else. Having them add XML tagging is a way of encoding that knowledge into the document. Allowing someone else to do the tagging is a matter of replacing authors' knowledge with someone else's guesses.
- Trying to add XML markup automatically nearly always fails, even if the authors provide clues, such as special styles. Computer programs know even less than human editors, after all.

In the nearly two decades since SGML first appeared, later to be replaced by XML, no one has yet found a universally effective solution to the problems of people and desktop software. Getting a large group of people to use XML in an office environment is difficult and expensive, so the anticipated benefits will have to be high to justify the costs.

3.2.2 Layout Control

The second disadvantage of XML publishing is the loss of fine layout control. Most of XML's advantages come only when formatting and publishing can be automated. When an author adds or removes information, the system automatically repaginates and reformats the document, saving time and money.

---

[2] To illustrate how arbitrary English spelling now seems, George Bernard Shaw famously suggested the spelling "ghoti" for *fish*, with "gh" as in *cough*, "o" as in *women*, and "ti" as in *station*.

XML document formatting systems do a reasonably good job with the kind of layout required for journal articles, technical books, and most other kinds of publications in which the content is the most important part. However, visual layout is at least as important as content in many other kinds of documents:

- Glossy magazines
- Marketing and advertising material
- Illustrated children's books
- Newspapers

All these types of documents require a careful balance of content and other concerns, such as visual appeal or advertising space, and that balance comes only from human intervention. For a further discussion of XML's formatting limitations and how to work around them—sometimes—see Section 3.4.

3.3 Formatting and Production

Once the higher-level issues are resolved and the authoring system is installed, it is time to turn to the nitty-gritty details of formatting. In many cases, there will be no problems at all; XML, together with transformation and formatting software, does a good job of handling the typical, routine tasks of formatting, particularly if the XML master document contains a single text flow continuing over several pages, such as a technical manual.

Unfortunately, things are sometimes not so simple. This section examines some of the physical aspects of printed documentation that can cause problems for XML publishing. Sometimes, these problems will not surface until late in a project, when there is not enough time or money left to fix them properly; learning to anticipate them can make a big difference to an XML publishing project's chance of success.

3.3.1 Change Markup

Technical publications often include various kinds of change information to make it easy for users to find differences between versions, and encoding this kind of information in XML markup probably represents the single biggest difficultly in XML publishing. The final change information in a printed text can take many forms:

1. Vertical bars in the margin beside changed text
2. Separate textual descriptions of changes made and the reasons for them
3. Different font combinations to show text removed and added
4. Differently formatted section headings to show sections that contain changes

Even finding the differences between two versions of the same XML document in the first place can be a problem, although more open-source and commercial software is becoming available. Some XML differencing algorithms scale badly with large documents, so it is worth load

3.3 Formatting and Production

testing your intended differencing software early in any project. Assuming that you do have some mechanism—even manual identification by the author—in place for locating changes in an XML document, this section examines some of the problems with inserting the change markup into XML documents for publication.

3.3.1.1 Markup Issues Change markup in XML documents causes publishing difficulties on several levels. Most basically, changes do not tend to fit neatly into XML markup trees. Consider the following:

```
<p>[...] There are 203 authorized service depots in Southeast
Asia.</p>

<p>The authorized service depots all provide [...]</p>
```

A change in the company's technical-support structure could cause the content to change, as follows:

```
<p>[...] There are 55 service partners in the Asia-Pacific
region.</p>

<p>The service partners all provide [...]</p>
```

What kind of markup should a system add to this document to show where the changes are? The change begins in one paragraph and ends in the next one, but XML does not allow an element to start and end inside different parent elements, so it is not possible to tag the entire changed sequence as a normal XML element.

The first option is to put empty tags at the start and end of the changed text:

```
<p>[...] There are <change-start/>55 service partners in
the Asia-Pacific region.</p>

<p>The service partners<change-end/> all provide [...]</p>
```

A variation on the same theme is the use of processing instructions, to avoid contaminating the main element tree:

```
<p>[...] There are <?change-start?>55 service partners in
the Asia-Pacific region.</p>

<p>The service partners<?change-end?> all provide [...]</p>
```

Unfortunately, XML publishing tools normally apply formatting based on element boundaries, and many of those tools are not capable of recognizing a span from one empty element to another. Custom-written Perl or Python scripts or very clever and complicated XSLT templates can handle this kind of markup in many cases, but developing them will use up a disproportionately large amount of time on any project.

A second option is to split up the change so that it falls into element boundaries:

```
<p>[...] There are <change>55 service partners in
the Asia-Pacific region</change>.</p>

<p><change>The service partners</change> all provide [...]</p>
```

This approach is much more practical for working with formatting tools, as they can apply normal formatting based on element context, but can cause awkward problems when additional information is attached to the change markup. Consider the following:

```
<p>[...] There are <change desc="Change to new service system.">55
service partners in the Asia-Pacific region</change>.</p>

<p><change desc="Change to new service system.">The service
partners</change> all provide [...]</p>
```

If the publishing system is also generating a list of changes or is adding marginal notes or footnotes describing the changes, the change will show up twice. If authors add change markup by hand, splitting a long change—say, over several paragraphs or steps—will be tedious and could lead to errors.

A third option is to use a single change element placed higher up in the document tree:

```
<change desc="Change to new service system">

<p>[...] There are 55 service partners in the Asia-Pacific
region.</p>

<p>The service partners all provide [...]</p>
</change>
```

This approach has the advantage of avoiding duplicate change elements, but it can end up tagging far more text than has changed. An even coarser variation on this approach is to mark changes only on the element level, using attributes:

```
<p changed="y" desc="Change to new service system">[...] There are
55 service partners in the Asia-Pacific region.</p>

<p changed="y" desc="Change to new service system">The service
partners all provide [...]</p>
</change>
```

3.3 Formatting and Production

This approach can be useful for specialized applications, such as legal texts, with individually numbered paragraphs or subparagraphs. In the general case, however, it has the disadvantages of both including too much *and* duplicating change information.

The last solution is both the most elegant and the most brittle: Track changes outside of the document by using, for example, XPointer expressions to describe the start and end of each change:

```
<change type="update">
  <description>Change to new service system</description>
  <span>
    <start>//step[@id="foo"]/p[2]/text()/point()[position()=247]
    </start>
    <end>//step[@id="foo"]/p[3]/text()/point()[position()=20]
    </end>
  </span>
</change>
```

Although this approach allows tracking the change precisely, without duplication, it also requires an enormous amount of coordination between the out-of-line index and the authoring system; if they are not kept perfectly synchronized, the whole thing will fall apart.

So far, this section has not mentioned the problem of marking changes in attribute values. Because attribute values cannot contain tags or processing instructions, marking changed attributes is always awkward; therefore, tracking changes externally might be the best option in this case. XML projects sometimes ensure that all information that needs to be marked as change appears within elements.

3.3.1.2 Custom Publishing Issues Although the tagging issues for change markup can be tricky, the more serious problems come with custom publishing. The change information in the final published document has to represent changes visible to the reader, not necessarily changes visible to the author.

In custom publishing, documents are typically assembled from text objects that have rules governing when they should or should not appear. For example, a warning may apply only to aircraft that use a certain engine or to reactors that use a certain cooling process. If the rule for the text object changes, it may suddenly appear in one customer's document or disappear from another's. Consider this warning:

```
<warning applicability="0050-0200">Using the wrong grade of
lubricant can cause engine failure.</warning>
```

The warning is applicable for serial numbers 0050–0200 of a product; a custom publishing system will include it in publications for customers owning products with those serial numbers and omit it for all other customers. Now, an author makes a couple of small changes to the warning:

```
<warning applicability="0100-0250">Using the wrong grade of
lubricant can cause valve damage.</warning>
```

The customer with product serial number 0150 should see essentially the same warning, with the phrase `engine failure` changed to `valve damage`:

```
<warning>Using the wrong grade of lubricant can cause <change>valve
damage</change>.</warning>
```

The customer with product serial number 225 previously did not see the warning at all, so the whole thing requires change markup:

```
<change><warning>Using the wrong grade of lubricant can cause valve
damage.</warning></change>
```

The customer with product serial number 0075 previously had the warning, but the change in effective serial numbers means that it will no longer appear in that version of the manual, so the change in this case is a deletion:

```
<change><warning>[Deleted]</warning></change>
```

Any descriptions of the changes also need to make sense from the reader's perspective. Many projects do not need to report changes with this level of accuracy, but when they do, it can end up being a major project in itself.

3.3.2 Looseleaf Publishing

Another challenging problem for any automated formatting system is page-based updates, otherwise known as *looseleaf publishing*. Some kinds of technical documents, such as maintenance manuals and regulatory documents, need to be updated frequently. A standard practice in the paper-based publishing world is to distribute the entire document once, in a binder, and then to send new or updated pages at regular intervals, perhaps every month or a few times a year, with instructions on where to add, remove, or replace pages in the current manual. The instructions, called *change pages*, might look like this:

- *Remove* pages 1-3 to 1-5, 1-7, 1-18, 1-26 to 1-44
- *Add* pages 1-3 to 1-5, 1-7, 1-18, 1-26 to 1-48

To ensure that the publications do not fall out of sync, the publishers will periodically issue a *list of effective pages* (LEP) showing what pages should be in the binder. Normally, page

3.3 Formatting and Production

numbering starts fresh in each section or chapter, so that a page inserted in one part of the publication will not force renumbering of all pages.

The advantage of any automated publishing system is its ability to free authors from worrying about formatting details, such as pagination, but in this case, pagination matters quite a bit. For page-based updates, a publishing system has to be able to manage the following tasks:

- Preserve page numbers from the last revision, whenever possible
- Preserve page breaks from the last revision, whenever possible
- Identify and print changed pages, with instructions for adding, removing, or replacing, as necessary

This process is not easy to automate, as a lot of judgment is involved: How much whitespace should the system allow at the bottom of a page before changing a page break, for example? Another problem is that formatting information, such as page breaks and numbering, has to be preserved somehow and kept in sync with the XML markup. One option is to design a system that will insert the information back into the XML document after each formatting run:

```
<para>Airspace above FL180 is Class A, and is restricted to
aircraft flying IFR.</para>

<pagebreak n="F.12"/>

<para>Some class E airspace may require a mode C
transponder.</para>
```

As an alternative, a system could store pagination information externally as a set of pointers into the XML document. In that case, however, the authoring system will need to be able to update the pointers as authors make changes to the XML document, so a fairly elaborate technical infrastructure will be required.

Unfortunately, this problem has no simple, technically elegant solution. It blurs the boundary between content and presentation, a boundary that is usually very important for XML work. The best anyone can do is identify the requirement early and, once again, allow a lot of time and money for meeting it. In time, page-based updates will disappear as publishers distribute more and more information electronically; it is generally easier to redistribute an entire electronic document rather than only changed pages. Also, if sections are small, it is sometimes easier to redistribute an entire changed section rather than individual pages. (XML publishing systems will manage that task much more easily.) Note that documents that use page-based updates generally also require change markup, described in Section 3.3.1.

3.3.3 Multiple Text Flows

A text flow is a single sequence of text meant to be read from start to end. In a simple publication, all the text flows occur in sequence: for example, an introduction, followed by several chapters, followed by several appendixes. Multiple text flows in sequence are not much more difficult to work with than a single text flow.

Some types of publications, however, take advantage of both dimensions of the page to present text flows in parallel. One obvious example is a newspaper: Several stories can appear together on the same page, and some stories can continue on other pages, wherever space is available around paid advertisements.

Automating the layout of a newspaper from an XML master document would be a difficult task. Fitting stories together on a newspaper page is a bit like a jigsaw puzzle, except that it involves answering hundreds of subjective questions as well: Editors have to decide what stories are important, and marketable, enough to appear on the front page and, in a broadsheet, above the fold. A certain amount of variety in the story selection is needed: Unless something important had occurred, a newspaper editor would not want too many stories about the same person or event to appear together at the front, even if they would otherwise be the highest-priority stories. During an election, the newspaper editor may want to be careful not to appear to be biased by giving one candidate a disproportionately large amount of front-page coverage. (Or, on the other hand, the editor may indeed want to favor one candidate that way.)

Off the front page, the paper is, of course, divided into sections, and related stories tend to be grouped together. Advertising pays a big part of the newspaper's expenses, so ad placement is critical, and the editor also has to watch for conflicts; for example, the lawn-care company ad must not appear too close to the story on the danger of pesticides. Visual appearance is also important; some stories have pictures attached, and the stories must be arranged so that the pictures are spread out evenly among the pages. Without a lot of care, the newspaper could end up with five pictures on one page and solid text on the next.

Can all of this decision making and design be automated, with or without XML? Fortunately for the job security of newspaper editors, it does not appear so. At best, an XML-based publishing system can chip around the edges by adding metadata to each story, including its priority and subject codes, so that the computer system can help the editor find and organize the stories more easily.

The newspaper is an extreme example, but the same problems arise in other, more routine kinds of publications. Footnotes, for example, are a separate kind of text flow, but one that many automated formatting systems, such as TeX, handle fairly well. Tables and illustrations are a little more difficult, as they need to be placed close to the text that references them without creating too many widow and orphan lines on the page, and sidebars make the problem a little more difficult yet. Although automated systems are not yet ready to handle newspaper or glossy magazine layout at all, they can handle footnotes, sidebars, tables, and illustrations, but many publishers find the result a little sloppy, and they still employ human layout artists working with interactive programs, such as Adobe FrameMaker, rather than fully automated publishing systems.

So right now, automated formatting systems can handle some kinds of multiple text flows well enough for technical publications but not well enough for, say, glossy magazines or advertising material; those still require the services of human layout designers. In those cases, XML is most useful for the content of individual text flows—marking paragraphs, special text, and so on—rather than for the document as a whole.

In the future, this problem will solve itself as more and more publishing moves online. Most attempts to do newspaper- or magazine-style layout online look horrible and are awkward to use on current computers. Instead, a typical magazine or newspaper Web site consists of a list of headlines and, possibly, summaries, with links to individual stories on their own pages. Computers will still probably not be smart enough to lay out advertising material or glossy magazines on their own, but they will be able to handle the bulk of information moving out to the world.

3.4 Special Topics

This section takes a higher-level look at four special topics for XML document production: *client-side XML, reuse*—introduced in Section 3.1.4—*documentation idioms,* and *content management*.

3.4.1 Client-Side XML

Single-source publishing allows people to write documents in XML and then convert them to multiple formats, such as PDF or PostScript for print and HTML for the Web. However, the World Wide Web Consortium [W3C] did not design XML simply to be a source for other formats; many people intended XML itself to be a delivery format for the Web, replacing HTML. Beyond XML is a family of W3C specifications, such as XML Linking Language [XLINK], XML Pointer Language [XPOINTER], cascading style sheets [CSS], and XSL Transformations [XSLT], all designed to help browsers display XML documents directly.

In many ways, this work has succeeded. Both Microsoft's Internet Explorer and the variants of Mozilla contain extensive XML support: They can display a raw XML document without a style sheet, or they can use style sheets to make an XML document in a browser window indistinguishable from HTML for the casual user. Behind the scenes, however, client-side scripts can perform sophisticated tricks based on the XML source, providing a richer browsing experience for users. Although the XML support in the two browsers has incompatibilities, and some specifications, such as XLink, are barely supported, if at all, there is also a surprising amount of compatibility, especially in comparison with the bitter browser wars of the late 1990s.

Both the standards and the software are in place for delivering XML directly to users without going through a middle format, such as HTML or PDF, and most users not only have the software installed on their system but use it daily for viewing HTML pages. Nevertheless, XML on the Web is almost nonexistent, as HTML is good enough for almost everything that anyone wants to do on the Web, and the extra benefits of delivering XML directly do not make up for the costs of new training, new authoring tools, and incompatibility with the minority of users who still have old, pre-XML browsers installed.

Although client-side XML has failed to take off the way that HTML did in the mid-1990s, the tool availability is still a benefit for XML documentation projects. Instead of purchasing and installing special XML viewers, authors can preview formatted versions of XML documents directly in their familiar Web browsers. On intranets and other areas where browser versions are more uniform, client-side XML viewing is a useful ability, even if it has failed to become a social phenomenon on the Web.

3.4.2 Reuse

Documentation always fits awkwardly into technology projects. Technical writers complain about programmers who make changes at the last minute, forcing the writers to redo most of the documentation; programmers, in turn, complain about writers who seem unable to write most of their documentation until just before a release deadline.

In fact, programmers have long created and used systems to help them write and maintain documentation aimed at other programmers. In the 1980s, Donald Knuth promoted *literate programming,* whereby the source code for a program, such as TeX, was embedded inside its own documentation and extracted automatically for compilation; anyone editing the documentation would edit the code at the same time, and vice versa, ensuring that the documentation and the code remained synchronized. In the mid-1990s, as the Java programming language increased in popularity, the opposite approach became common: Programmers embedded documentation in the source code as specially formatted comments and extracted it automatically for publication. (Earlier programming languages, such as Emacs LISP, had already used this approach on a smaller scale.) The JavaDoc system proved extremely effective for generating programmer's API documentation and has been much imitated for other programming languages.

JavaDoc and literate programming work for programmer's documentation because the documentation nearly always follows the structure of the source code. When the programmer deletes a class or a method, the documentation disappears with it; when adding or modifying a class, the programmer simply needs to modify the documentation that is right there on the screen with it.

Unfortunately, things are not so easy for most technical writers. Normally, their documentation is designed for users rather than for programmers, so it is based on tasks or concepts rather than source-code structure. As a result, there is no natural connection between the changes a programmer makes to the source and the changes a technical writer has to make to the documentation. A single user task, such as creating a new account, might touch code from dozens of source code modules managed by different programmers; a single source code module might affect dozens of different task descriptions. Even a trivially small change to the source code can have an exponential impact on the documentation.

Consider a simple code module that displays a dialog box containing a message and two buttons labeled `Accept` and `Cancel`. The quality-assurance specialist sends a note to the programmer, saying that, for consistency, the first button should be labelled `OK` rather than `Accept`; the programmer takes 5 minutes to change one line of code, test, and commit, and the documentation specialist then announces that it will take 2 weeks to revise the tutorial and manual. What happened?

First, dozens of different parts of the code might invoke that dialog box, and each may be used by dozens of different tasks. Suppose that a manual has text like the following:

Select `crop` from the `File` drop-down menu.
A confirmation dialog will appear. Select `Accept` to continue.

For each instance, the writer will have to change `Accept` to `OK`, and then the writer—or editor or quality-assurance specialist—will have to recheck all the documentation against the software.

3.4 Special Topics

Even worse, the manual may contain screenshots of the dialog in different contexts, all of which will have to be recaptured and recropped. If a small change like this can cause so much trouble, it is not difficult to understand how a more fundamental change could throw technical documentation into chaos.

This kind of problem was common in computer programming as well until the structured programming movement, beginning in the 1970s, and the object-oriented programming movement, beginning in the 1980s, helped programmers get better at writing reusable code. Programmers have learned to encapsulate reusable code in a single place, such as a function or an object or even a library, rather than duplicating the same code over and over again in their programs; database designers do the same thing when they normalize their database. In fact, document writers have been able to do this for centuries before computers existed, simply by embedding a reference in a text, such as "(see Job 8:8–10)."

Modern technical documents could use the same include-by-reference approach as modern computer programs, in which case their documents might look like this:

To create a new document, take the following steps:

(See p.145)
(See p.251)
(See p.18)
(See p.44)
(See p.182)

It would be easy to write documents this way, especially with word processors that can track references and automatically fill in page numbers, but it would not be easy to *read* such a document. Following cross-references and keeping track of previous locations are a lot more difficult for humans than for a computer, and people reading documentation like this will quickly get frustrated or simply lost. Documents—at least in the final form that readers see—are necessarily highly redundant, or what a database specialist would call *denormalized*: They *have to* repeat information.

This is where another of XML's big promises comes in. XML, like its predecessor, SGML, is designed to allow writers to reuse text the same way that programmers reuse code: A single change in the XML source document can automatically propagate itself throughout the output formatted document at the other end of the XML publishing system.

XML has several mechanisms for allowing reusable text, among which the simplest is the internal text entity. In the internal DTD subset, an author includes a declaration like the following:

```
<!ENTITY accept-button-name "Accept">
```

Then, in the main text, the author enters a reference to that entity:

```
<step>A confirmation dialog will appear. Select
&accept-button-name; to continue.</step>
```

Although this approach is dead simple for a single author creating XML in a text editor, it can cause problems in a large, multiuser environment, in which regular authors should not be able to modify the DTD, where the entity declarations appear. In those cases, system designers come up with more elaborate methods for reusable text. For example, in a maintenance manual, the following caution might appear many times:

Caution: Use calibrated torque wrench. Overtorquing may cause the bolt to shear.

In a big project, an author might create this caution once, possibly as an independent XML document like the following:

```
<caution>Use calibrated torque wrench. Overtorquing may
cause the bolt to shear.</caution>
```

An author who needs to include this caution will include it by *reference,* often through a custom-designed dialog box added to the editing system, as follows:

```
<caution-inclusion ident="cautions/overtorque001"/>
```

The same technique should work for shared steps in tasks, boilerplate legal text, and anything else that gets repeated throughout a document.

This approach looks like the ideal bridge across the discontinuity between the way coders code and the way writers write, but experience in field use has been disappointing. First, in technical writing, repeated text tends to be similar but not identical: A part name in the middle of a caution or the transition text at the beginning of a paragraph will change, depending on its context. Even when the text does not change, managing and locating small, reused chunks of text is mind-numbing work. Most authors would probably prefer to simply to retype when necessary, rather than spend several minutes each time searching through a repository of reusable steps to see whether one is appropriate. Even if authors were willing to use such a system, the savings would not be as great as forecasted. For example, if the same step were used in 200 places and the step were changed, authors or editors would still have to check all 200 places in the text to make sure that the change was appropriate in context, and checking the 200 places will usually take as long as retyping them.

It may be that new tools and new ways of running projects make reusable information more common in the future; for now, however, XML is not a universal solution to the documentation discontinuity.

3.4.3 Idioms

Although reusable text is a bit of a chimera, single-source publishing is a real benefit that can come from an XML publishing system. However, single-source publishing also has its limitations, and it is important to understand them before starting on a major XML publishing project.

3.4 Special Topics

Single-source publishing is an exciting idea that also happens to be easy to explain to non-specialists. You create a single XML source document, then use scripts or templates to transform it automatically into different publication media, such as print, Braille, an automated voice telephone system, or the Web.

Much of the time, people want to publish from XML source documents only to print and the Web. For publishing to print, the typical data formats are TeX, PDF, RTF, PostScript, and MIF; for publishing to the Web, the typical data formats are HTML and XHTML but sometimes also PDF or Flash. XML specialists learn quickly that they need to write separate transformation style sheets for print and the Web, even if the core content is identical. The obvious problem is that they are transforming to different primitives: HTML deals with abstractions, such as paragraphs and lists, whereas print formats tend to deal with concrete layout elements, such as blocks, fonts, and spacing. This difference is not simply a design problem that could be fixed. Print formats are fundamentally page-based, whereas HTML is fundamentally screen-based. Each has pros and cons.

Page-based formats allow a designer to take advantage of all the available space, by including multiple texts and graphics in different parts of a single page, with fine control over the placement and size of each item. However, page-based formats are also brittle: A document needs to be optimized for a specific size and aspect and will not move easily across different display devices. (Try viewing a U.S. letter- or A4-sized PDF document on a handheld computer.)

Screen-based formats are inherently more flexible and, when properly used, will work for many different display sizes. However, that flexibility comes at the cost of surrendering control over the finer points of layout. (Try placing sidebars and graphics precisely in HTML.)

The real problem, then, is that a Web page is not simply a print document online but rather a fundamentally different kind of thing. That is why Web pages need their own style sheets. That's not such a big problem, however: Writing two, or even ten, style sheets accounts for very little overhead when you will be using them hundreds or thousands of times to transform XML for publication.

Single-source publishing works well for both print and the Web, as long as you are publishing the right kind of thing. A technical manual for a software program, or a novel, can easily pass from a single XML source document through a couple of different style sheets to print and Web versions, all without human intervention. You do end up, usually, with Web pages that scroll a lot (say, one page for each chapter). That will not be a problem if the user has decided to read a book or manual online, but it is not what you normally expect to find in a Web page. Web pages are typically short, dynamic, and interactive, not long and static.

There is no reason that a person cannot design an XML document type that takes dynamic content into account, so that the HTML rendition can contain animations, applets, forms, and so on, but doing so requires that you place new constraints on your XML document type in advance: You cannot publish just *any* document and have it look good both online and in print. This is not a medium problem but an *idiom* problem. You can print a Web page on paper or put a novel online, but neither fits naturally there, because Web pages and novels are fundamentally different kinds of things. Many other idioms cause trouble for single-source publishing. Consider, for example, slides, online help, and Unix man pages: Each of these follows a fundamentally different set of constraints and carries a different set of reader expectations, and it gets more and more difficult to generate all of them from a single XML source document. In the end, XML cannot deliver on all its promises for single-source publishing; it can allow you to publish to multiple *formats* from a single master document, but publishing to multiple *idioms* is much more difficult.

Is universal single-source publishing a hopeless case, then? Not quite. It turns out that, although all these idioms have drastically different top-level structures, they share much in common at the lower levels. Many of them, for example, have paragraphs of text with special-purpose phrases contained in them, and many use lists and tables. For the lower-level content, XML truly can deliver on at least some of the promise of single-source publishing: the same table might appear on a slide, a man page, a Web page, and in a printed book, all in significantly different contexts, appropriate to each idiom.

Furthermore, people are often willing to accept deficiencies for the sake of saving money or having easier access to information. For example, a state legislature might accept simple, unimaginative, automatically generated Web pages for its online legislation in exchange for a cost savings of $100,000 a year. The Web site for a popular magazine, on the other hand, will not likely be willing to make the same trade. Designing and implementing an XML-based publishing system is largely a matter of managing expectations. Raising false hopes about single-source publishing will lead to disappointment and hostility later on, but if both the implementers and the users understand and agree to the tradeoffs in advance, XML publishing can work *and* save money.

3.4.4 Content Management

This chapter has already emphasized that the biggest real benefits for XML publishing come with large, highly structured technical publications, such as regulatory documents, dictionaries, legislation, or maintenance manuals for complex equipment, such as aircraft or weapons systems. Such documents typically have many authors and a formal and often complex editorial review process. These living documents are under continual revision for their entire lives. With a dictionary, for example, lexicographers write individual entries, which will then pass through several stages of editing and approval before being added to the dictionary proper. As corrections and new slips—usage examples—come in, lexicographers will revise an entry and start the entire review process again. At some major projects, the lifespan of the documents is longer than that of the authors: For the *Oxford English Dictionary,* for example, this process has continued nonstop for almost a century and a half. There's never any concept of a *finished book;* each edition is only a snapshot of a never-ending work in process. Exactly the same process applies to the aircraft maintenance manual for a large airliner, for example, except that the snapshots are published every few months rather than every few decades.

Obviously, this kind of publishing was possible before computers, much less XML, but it was labor- and paper-file-intensive: precisely the kinds of operations that can benefit from some kind of content-management system. Many computer programmers are already familiar with source-code-management systems, such as CVS or Visual SourceSafe. Content-management systems for documentation are very similar: They allow authors to check objects, such as documents

3.4 Special Topics

or pictures, into or out of a central repository, which tracks revisions and often also allows searching, indexing, and even final document assembly. A documentation content-management system may also have a workflow component attached to it, so that it can both track the status of each object through the editorial process and manage the process by sending files to the people who need to approve them.

None of these features is unique to XML, but they are especially likely to be required in a large, multiauthor XML documentation project. Some systems go further: Instead of managing each XML document as a single object, the same as a picture or word-processing file, they allow users to check out *part* of an XML document—say, the third `task` in the second `chapter`—while other users work on other parts of the same XML document. Typically, the system parses the XML document and converts it into a series of entries in a specialized database, then reconstructs it as XML when needed.

For a large project with multiple authors, a content-management system is often a requirement: The only question is whether to use a traditional system or a special XML-aware one. It is best to approach this problem backward and start with the non-XML solution. Assume that a company is creating a large amount of technical documentation in XML, using a team of authors and editors. At any time, authors will have lists of items assigned to them for writing or revision, and editors will have lists of items assigned to them for editing and approval. The technical documentation itself consists mostly of independent tasks. Listing 3-9 shows a fragment of a simplified DTD.

Listing 3-9   Top Level of a DTD
```
<!ELEMENT doc (intro, chapter+)>
<!ELEMENT chapter (title, chapterintro, task+)>
<!ELEMENT task (title, taskintro, partlist, toollist, step+)>
```

Most of the authoring items moving through the workflow chain are tasks with their associated graphics; the editors will assign tasks to individual authors, who will then pass the tasks back up to the editors for approval. When a task requires revision, the cycle repeats itself.

Would an XML-aware CMS bring much benefit to a project like this? No. Authors do not need to check out a single step or title or an entire chapter, only tasks. The CMS can handle each task as a separate XML document without needing to know anything about the task's internal markup structure.

To require an XML-aware content-management system, there would have to be no standard unit for authoring, editing, or workflow; the author would need to be able to check out and lock anything from a single list item to the entire document. The author of this book has not yet seen such a requirement in the real world. Every big multiauthor project has standard units of work, whether they are tasks, dictionary entries, or newspaper articles.

Content-management systems also typically offer searching, indexing, and packaging. A full-text search is sometimes sufficient, but because XML markup can provide much more detailed content, a good case can sometimes be made for making the search XML-aware. For more on this point, see Chapter 6.

3.5 Final Words on Documents

Using abstract markup to produce human-readable documentation is a long tradition, dating back to SGML, TROFF macro packages, TeX macro packages, and even earlier, to phototypesetting languages and editors' scribbles on paper copy. Computer programmers, academic researchers, technical writers in the military or aerospace manufacturers, and others have used packages like these for decades: For these people, XML is an easy adjustment, and much of the XML documentation extant, such as that in the Linux Documentation Project, comes from them.

On the other hand, XML documentation has failed to break out into the wider world, where authors have spent two decades using visual editing tools similar to Microsoft Word and Adobe FrameMaker. Writing a document in XML is a lot like writing a document in LaTeX but has almost nothing in common with creating a document using a graphical word processor. These people are not likely to switch to XML easily or even willingly: Attempts by XML software vendors to sell editing tools that look like word processors have failed to win many people over.

When a lot of simple manual work is involved in document production, such as customizing manuals for customers or reformatting documents for the Web, or when there are strong requirements for intelligent searching and archiving, an XML documentation system can make a lot of sense: The ongoing savings can offset the high initial cost of building the system. The most obvious users for XML documentation should be technical book publishers, but they have shown little interest in XML. There does not appear to be a pressing business demand for single-source publishing in the book industry, at least not until electronic books become more common. Also, as discussed in Section 3.4.3, there is often a difference between online and print publishing that is more fundamental than differences in formatting or pagination, and these differences can easily make automated single-source publishing impractical or even impossible.

Before XML's arrival, SGML-based documentation systems made some progress in highly regulated, multiauthor environments, such as case law, aircraft and weapons system documentation, and legislation, but authors in these areas have often used complicated proprietary documentation systems in the past rather than the usual word processors. XML has continued SGML's progress into these areas and is gradually replacing the legacy SGML systems as well. This, most likely, is the near-term future of XML documentation: It will continue to make headway in areas in which people are already accustomed to creating documents without word processors, growing its niche but failing to gain widespread acceptance among organizations and individuals who find the combination of word processing and HTML presentation adequate for their needs.

CHAPTER 4

XML Data

XML document files (see Chapter 3) are designed for people; XML data files are designed for machines. There is always some amount of mixing, of course, but in most XML projects, one of the two is clearly dominant.[1] A project for publishing electronics user manuals from XML source files is clearly an XML document project, even though it may deal with a large amount of tabular data; a project for exchanging raw meteorological observations among various weather services is clearly an XML data project, even though it may contain segments of prose written by humans and intended ultimately for human readers.

The majority of business-to-business (B2B) work involves XML data, as the whole point of XML-based B2B is automated processing. If a human has to read an invoice and extract information from it, XML is of no benefit. Sometimes, XML data can be a business in itself, as is the case with vendors that collect and sell information on books, music, or the stock market. XML data, then, is the style of XML that deals with *automation*: The goal of all XML data-oriented initiatives is to allow computers to talk to each other directly, sharing information, negotiating contracts, managing inventory, and performing many other similar exchanges.

The difference between XML documents and XML data is visible not only in their purposes but also in their markup styles.

- XML document files tend to be loosely structured, with large amounts of natural-language text and mixed content—elements mixed in with text on the same level—while
- XML data files tend to be highly and repetitively structured, with fielded information, strict use of identifiers and cross-references, and little or no mixed content.

XML document files use markup for some basic, generic structure, but they rely on natural language, which people are good at understanding, for most of their context. XML data files use natural language for leaf values in their fields but rely on markup and cross-references, which computers are good at understanding, for most of their context.

Data is a natural fit for XML, not only because XML markup is well suited to representing many kinds of structure but also because XML fills an empty niche. Although XML's designers paid a lot of attention to documents—to the point that an XML file is typically called an *XML document* even if it contains only data tables—and many people promoted XML initially as a replacement for

---

[1] Recently, however, XML networking has also joined the fray; see Chapter 5.

the Hypertext Markup Language [HTML] on the Web, there was little popular demand for XML documents. The HTML-based Web is good enough for most users, and single-source publishing (see Section 3.1.1) remains a niche technology. On the other hand, the data world had no equivalent of HTML, no robust way to publish and share information in a portable way; current formats, such as delimited text, were severely limited. So although the world turned to the Web in the 1990s and started sharing documents, data stayed locked up, shared only with difficulty.

XML has not yet made it as easy to share data as HTML has made it to share documents, but it has improved the situation. Unlike XML documents, XML data does not generally require complex software interfaces: Only rarely is it necessary to build user applications for authoring or viewing. Instead, scripts sitting on the edges of databases typically create and consume XML data. Such specifications as the Resource Description Framework [RDF] and XML Topic Maps [XTM] propose higher-level, data-oriented layers on top of XML to make data sharing easier, and database vendors, such as Oracle and IBM, continue to add to and improve native XML support in their own products.

4.1 The Advantages of XML Data

In many of the other chapters in this book, the lists of the advantages and disadvantages of XML are close to even; for sharing data, however, XML is a much more obvious choice. Of course, there are disadvantages that will rule out XML for certain projects, but in most cases, XML's advantages far outweigh the disadvantages, because there really is no general, portable alternative to XML for exchanging data with complex structure.

Behind the scenes, many companies are already using XML for internal data sharing, but despite its value, XML data itself is no longer a hot topic. Although the vendors continue to add support for XML in databases and other applications, the spotlight has moved on to XML networking (Chapter 5) and, especially, Web Services. However, even XML networking is still, at heart, using XML for data: Nearly all the networking specifications are simply combinations of XML data with a network transport layer, such as HyperText Transfer Protocol [HTTP].

XML brings clear and persuasive advantages for data exchange in five areas:

1. Platform and storage independence
2. Self-documentation
3. Reusability
4. Verification
5. Archiving and auditing

4.1.1 Platform and Storage Independence

In the past, save files for PC-based databases, such as FoxPro, sometimes became a de facto interchange format, just as Microsoft Excel spreadsheet files are a de facto standard for exchanging simple tabular data. Spreadsheets and other data applications also support some more portable formats, such as comma-delimited text or the sequels to the old Data Interchange Format

4.1 The Advantages of XML Data

(DIF). None of the portable alternatives, however, is particularly good at exchanging complex structured data.

XML can model arbitrarily complex data structures and is not tied to a specific vendor or product. With XML and Unicode, there are no byte-order, line-end, or character-encoding problems moving from machine to machine or even from country to country or culture to culture. All major and many minor programming and scripting languages have good support for XML, as do most databases.

XML's independence, however, goes far beyond simply avoiding platform incompatibilities. As discussed in Section 4.3, XML can represent data in its *logical* format rather than its physical storage format. Whereas a relational database might divide information into a series of separate, cross-linked tables, using attributes for order, XML can pull everything into a single, ordered, logical document.

XML's abstraction encourages loosely coupled data interchange. It does not matter whether the data provider and the data consumer arrange their databases differently, with different tables linked in different ways, because that physical level is not fossilized in XML as it would be in a series of comma-delimited table dumps. This fact, perhaps, matters more than all the other portability issues.

4.1.2 Self-Documentation

For humans, although not for computers, XML documents are at least partly self-describing, as discussed at length in Section 7.1.2. It might seem inconsistent, at first, to suggest that human readability is an advantage, when this chapter has been emphasizing that XML data is intended for machines. However, in practice, people still have to implement the programs or scripts to work with XML. Because XML documents normally have human-readable names for elements and attributes, developers will find it easier to produce, process, transform, and, most important, debug XML input and output. Human-readable names also make it possible to automate the creation of forms and other human interfaces for data entry.

4.1.3 Reusability

This advantage is related to storage independence (see Section 4.1.1). Well-designed XML data is almost always loosely coupled; it does not slavishly follow the structure of a spreadsheet, a set of database tables, or any other source but rather reorders the information into an abstract, logical presentation. Therefore, XML data is not limited to a single purpose. Data exported from a database can be read into another database, of course, but can also be edited, displayed, analyzed for statistical patterns, transformed, searched and queried, or even published to a Web page or print. The original data provider does not have to be able to anticipate all the uses people might have for XML data. Once the information is in XML format, XML tools and utilities will simply be able to work with it any way the recipient desires.

4.1.4 Verification

Developers often spend a lot of their time developing and testing code for data validation. With XML data, it is possible to do basic structural validation and, in some cases, data-type validation (see Section 4.5.3), using schema languages with off-the-shelf software tools and libraries. Writing an XML schema or DTD is a specialized skill, but it can sometimes be much easier and more robust than writing custom code to perform the same structural checks.

XML data allows verification in other ways as well. Because XML is plaintext, people can easily examine it for problems that automated tests might have missed, the same way that people can examine text-based Internet protocols, such as HTTP, SMTP, or Post Office Protocol v. 3 (POP3), manually for verification and debugging. And, like any text file, XML is relatively simple to sign digitally.

4.1.5 Archiving and Auditing

XML data consists of files, not bits on the wire—like a networking protocol—or application-specific binary data—like a spreadsheet file. Because XML is not tied to an application that may no longer exist in a few years, XML data will still be useful in an archive 50 or 100 years from now; because it can be saved to disk, every transaction can be archived and audited, something that is difficult with protocols.

These points are especially important for companies or other organizations that face complex legal and reporting requirements. A saved XML transaction, like a saved e-mail, provides an ongoing record of what was happening in a company at a specific time. In case of a security breach, people can go back and review not only logs but also past transactions to track down the problem.

4.2 The Disadvantages of XML Data

Besides XML's advantages for data interchange, there are nonetheless some disadvantages. The first thing new users notice is that you cannot simply load arbitrary XML into an application or database the way that you can load a spreadsheet. That level of interoperability requires higher-level specifications, and those have been slow to gain acceptance. Without those specifications, XML processing still, unfortunately, requires a lot of custom coding and a not insignificant amount of processing time.

4.2.1 Interoperability

XML alone is not sufficient for sharing data: higher-level specifications are required to define what information should appear in the XML and how it should be structured. It is difficult to write a general-purpose, off-the-shelf tool to import XML into a database, but people can provide off-the-shelf tools to import NewsML [NEWSML], Extensible Business Reporting Language [XBRL], or many other such formats.

Higher-level XML data formats, however, are difficult and expensive to create, and there are too many of them. These problems might seem to contradict each other. In fact, people propose many higher-level XML formats but implement few of them, as discussed in Section 1.4.4: The proliferation of proposals causes confusion without providing solutions that people can build around.

Because there are rarely middle layers between low-level XML and high-level data formats, most XML data specifications are stovepipes, built from low-level XML on up. Although most of them share common concepts, such as identifiers, references, entities, attributes, and relationships, they all implement them differently, destroying the chance to use shared code—and shared user knowledge—to lower costs. As a result, there are few useful off-the-shelf components for dealing with data and no significant economies of scale or network effects.

XML networking specifications (see Chapter 5) are helping this problem somewhat by providing general-purpose data formats for the networking payloads. These data formats may not be optimal for exporting large amounts of information from databases or publishing data on the Web, but they will at least provide a starting point.

4.2.2 Abstraction

Abstraction can also be a problem. If one organization exports its data to XML, a second organization probably will be unable to read that data into its system immediately but will have to write transformation and import scripts to change the XML to a format that its system can use. That is the major problem with XML for data sharing: Its abstraction gives it many advantages, but it also means more work. You cannot simply save or load any arbitrary XML data the way that you can save or load a spreadsheet file.

4.2.3 Resources

XML has a reputation, partly deserved and partly undeserved, as a resource hog. XML is plaintext, and XML data is usually in an abstract, logical format, so reading XML into an application often requires two steps: parsing the XML from plaintext and transforming the parsed XML so that the application, such as a database, can use it.

Parsing and transformation take time, as does generating XML for output. Chapter 8 discusses how to avoid some of the worst inefficiencies in XML processing, but in an extremely high-speed environment, the time and processor use of XML might still be unacceptable.

4.3 Common Data Styles

What does XML data look like? Three popular ways of modeling machine-readable information are

1. The tabular style, familiar from spreadsheets
2. The graph style, familiar from relational databases and the World Wide Web
3. The hierarchical style, familiar from computer file systems

XML can use any of the three styles, but it is optimized for the hierarchical (or tree) style. Database specialists are particularly fond of the graph style, as it simplifies database import and export and is most suited for fully normalized data. Developers of desktop applications often prefer the tabular style, especially for initialization files, as it is easy to set up; some use simple lists, which are equivalent to a single-column table. This section looks at the strengths and weaknesses of all three styles.

4.3.1 The Tabular Style

At their best, tables are a space-efficient way of representing structured information for machines or for humans. A column in a table represents a labeled field—one piece of information about a thing—whereas each row represents all the fields for the same thing, as in Table 4-1.

The arrival of the consumer spreadsheet with VisiCalc in 1979 gave end users their first chance to work with structured information directly, and its tabular format proved easy to understand and work with. Twenty-five years later, the spreadsheet is still at the center of many business applications; in fact, much business software is nothing more than customizations built on top of Microsoft's Excel spreadsheet.

The tabular style is especially effective when every data object has roughly the same kinds and quantities of information. But this style becomes awkward quickly when different objects have different kinds of information or when information can repeat itself. In Table 4-1, it could be that the more senior employees have more than one specialization; for example, Janet Mulville might also have 5 years of experience with C++ programming and 3 years of experience with application server design. How would that fit into this table? The initial solution is to start repeating the Specialization and Years columns, as in Table 4-2.

Because the structure is a table, Ahmed Said and Julie Fujikawa have blank fields for additional specializations hat they do not have. If a new employee arrives with five specializations, the

Table 4-1 Simple Data Table

Employee	ID	Title	Unit	Specialization	Years
Janet Mulville	e000234	Senior Consultant	Database	Data modeling	9
Ahmed Said	e000345	Project Manager	Systems	System integration	11
Julie Fujikawa	e009122	Intern	Systems	System integration	1

Table 4-2 Messy Data Table

Employee	ID	Title	Unit	Spec-1	Years-1	Spec-2	Years-2	Spec-3	Years-3
Janet Mulville	e000234	Senior Consultant	Database	Data modeling	9	C++	6	Appl. servers	3
Ahmed Said	e000345	Project Manager	Systems	System integration	11				
Julie Fujikawa	e009122	Intern	Systems	System integration	1				

4.3 Common Data Styles

table will add columns for *all* the rows, so again, all other users will have more unnecessary blank fields. When Julie is temporarily assigned to the Database unit for 50 percent of her time, an additional Unit column will be needed as well, and so on, until it becomes extremely difficult for a person or a machine to make much sense of the information.

XML has techniques to make tabular information a little more readable and efficient, however. As a starting point, consider Listing 4-1, which is a direct rendition into XML of the information in Table 4-2.

Listing 4-1   Raw Table in XML

```xml
<table>
<title>Employee Information</title>
<tgroup cols="10">

<thead>

<row>
<entry>Employee</entry>
<entry>ID</entry>
<entry>Title</entry>
<entry>Unit</entry>
<entry>Spec-1</entry>
<entry>Years-1</entry>
<entry>Spec-2</entry>
<entry>Years-2</entry>
<entry>Spec-3</entry>
<entry>Years-3</entry>
</row>

</thead>

<tbody>

<row>
<entry>Janet Mulville</entry>
<entry>e000234</entry>
<entry>Senior Consultant</entry>
<entry>Database</entry>
<entry>Data modeling</entry>
<entry>9</entry>
<entry>C++</entry>
<entry>6</entry>
<entry>Appl. servers</entry>
<entry>3</entry>
</row>
```

```
<row>
<entry>Ahmed Said</entry>
<entry>e000345</entry>
<entry>Project Manager</entry>
<entry>Systems</entry>
<entry>System integration</entry>
<entry>11</entry>
<entry></entry>
<entry></entry>
<entry></entry>
<entry></entry>
</row>

<row>
<entry>Julie Fujikawa</entry>
<entry>e009122</entry>
<entry>Intern</entry>
<entry>Systems</entry>
<entry>System integration</entry>
<entry>1</entry>
<entry></entry>
<entry></entry>
<entry></entry>
<entry></entry>
</row>

</tbody>
</tgroup>
</table>
```

XML can improve on that representation in several ways while still staying in the spirit of the tabular approach. First, because XML already labels every element, a header row labeling the columns is not needed; instead, the column labels can appear as element names. Then, once each entry is labeled, the blank ones need not be included.[2] The result is the much more readable and space-efficient XML table in Listing 4-2, although it is still far from ideal XML markup.

Listing 4-2   Readable Table in XML

```
<employees>

  <employee>
    <name>Janet Mulville</name>
```

---

[2] In fact, the blank entries in Listing 4-1 could have been left out anyway, as they are all trailing; however, any nonblank entries at the ends of the rows would have had to be included.

4.3 Common Data Styles

```
    <id>e000234</id>
    <title>Senior Consultant</title>
    <unit>Database</unit>
    <spec-1>Data modeling</spec-1>
    <years-1>9</years-1>
    <spec-2>C++</spec-2>
    <years-2>6</years-2>
    <spec-3>Appl. servers</spec-3>
    <years-3>3</years-3>
</employee>

<employee>
    <name>Ahmed Said</name>
    <id>e000345</id>
    <title>Project Manager</title>
    <unit>Systems</unit>
    <spec-1>System integration</spec-1>
    <years-1>11</years-1>
</employee>

<employee>
    <name>Julie Fujikawa</name>
    <id>e009122</id>
    <title>Intern</title>
    <unit>Systems</unit>
    <spec-1>System integration</spec-1>
    <years-1>1</years-1>
</employee>

</employees>
```

This XML is more flexible than a spreadsheet table because adding a new field for one row does not affect the rest of the table. Still, it is fully denormalized: The specialty name "System integration" appears in more than one place, creating potential maintenance problems, and repetition, such as Janet's multiple specialties, is handled awkwardly.

4.3.2 The Graph Style

Relational databases are collections of indexed tables that can be connected to each other by using common *keys,* or identifiers, so they can model complex information more efficiently than a spreadsheet can. Relational databases take any information that can be repeated or shared and move it into a separate table. For example, the employee names and job titles could appear in a single table, as in Table 4-3. To assign skills to the employees, the relational approach adds a separate table linking skills to employees (Table 4-4), repeating only the unique employee

Table 4-3 Employee Names and Titles (Relational)

EmployeeID	Name	Title
e000234	Janet Mulville	Senior Consultant
e000345	Ahmed Said	Project Manager
e009122	Julie Fujikawa	Intern

identifier to connect the two tables. The skills are in a separate table, so it is possible to add as many or as few skills as necessary for each employee.

Table 4-5 takes a similar approach for another kind of repeatable information: the units to which employees are assigned. In this case, employee ID e009122 has two rows, as that employee is assigned to both the Systems and Database units. Again, for employees who are *not* assigned to additional units, no extra, blank rows or columns need to be added.

It would be possible, of course, to decompose the information further. For example, an employee might hold more than one job title, and it would be better to make a separate table holding the names of units and skills, each with a unique identifier of its own, so that the system can attach information to those as well. Once a designer has broken up the information as far as it will go in this way, the information is said to be fully *normalized*.

Table 4-4 Employee Skills (Relational)

EmployeeID	Skill	Years
e000234	Data modeling	9
e000234	C++	6
e000234	Application servers	3
e000345	System integration	11
e009122	System integration	1

Table 4-5 Employee Units (Relational)

Employee ID	Unit
e000234	Database
e000345	Systems
e009122	Systems
e009122	Database

4.3 Common Data Styles

This is the worldview of both the entity-relationship information model and the World Wide Web: There is a series of uniquely identified objects—*entities* or Web pages—each of which can have information attached directly—*attributes* or text content—and connections to other objects—*relationships* or Web links. When you draw a diagram of a collection of entities or a collection of Web pages, you end up with a graph: The lines connecting objects move in many different directions.

Just as it can represent a single, denormalized table, XML markup can represent a complex set of normalized entities and their relationships, as illustrated in Listing 4-3.

Listing 4-3 Fully Normalized XML

```
<rdf:RDF
   xmlns:rdf="http://www.w3.org/1999/02/22-rdf-syntax-ns#"
   xmlns="http://www.acme.com/namespaces/hr/">

  <employee rdf:ID="e000234">
    <name>Janet Mulville</name>
    <jobtitleref rdf:resource="#t000188"/>
    <unitref rdf:resource="#u000100"/>
    <experienceref rdf:resource="#ex123456"/>
    <experienceref rdf:resource="#ex123457"/>
    <experienceref rdf:resource="#ex123458"/>
  </employee>

  <experience rdf:ID="ex123456">
    <skillref rdf:resource="#sk008"/>
    <years>9</years>
  </experience>

  <experience rdf:ID="ex123457">
    <skillref rdf:resource="#sk010"/>
    <years>6</years>
  </experience>

  <experience rdf:ID="ex123458">
    <skillref rdf:resource="#sk012"/>
    <years>3</years>
  </experience>

  <employee rdf:ID="e000345">
    <name>Ahmed Said</name>
    <jobtitleref rdf:resource="#t000050"/>
    <unitref rdf:resource="#u000200"/>
    <experienceref rdf:resource="#ex123458"/>
  </employee>
```

```xml
<experience rdf:ID="ex123458">
  <skillref rdf:resource="#sk014"/>
  <years>11</years>
</experience>

<employee rdf:ID="e009122">
  <name>Julie Fujikawa</name>
  <jobtitleref rdf:resource="#t000263"/>
  <unitref rdf:resource="#u000200"/>
  <experienceref rdf:resource="#ex123459"/>
</employee>

<experience rdf:ID="ex123459">
  <skillref rdf:resource="#sk014"/>
  <years>1</years>
</experience>

<jobtitle rdf:ID="t000050">
  <name>Project Manager</name>
</jobtitle>

<jobtitle rdf:ID="t000188">
  <name>Senior Consultant</name>
</jobtitle>

<jobtitle rdf:ID="t000263">
  <name>Intern</name>
</jobtitle>

<unit rdf:ID="u000100">
  <name>Database</name>
</unit>

<unit rdf:ID="u000200">
  <name>Systems</name>
</unit>

<skill rdf:ID="sk008">
  <name>Data modeling</name>
</skill>

<skill rdf:ID="sk010">
  <name>C++</name>
</skill>
```

4.3 Common Data Styles

```
<skill rdf:ID="sk012">
  <name>Application servers</name>
</skill>

<skill rdf:ID="sk014">
  <name>System integration</name>
</skill>

</employees>
```

Listing 4-3 uses the *Resource Description Framework* (RDF),[3] a standardized XML model and syntax for representing normalized data. Each top-level element represents an entity with a unique identifier, supplied by the `rdf:ID` attribute, and empty elements represent relationships to other entities, specified by the `rdf:resource` attribute).

Normalized information like this is very easy to maintain and extend, as each piece of information is its own entity. For example, if the company wants to rename the skill "System integration" to "Enterprise deployment", it needs to make the change in only one place. It also is a simple matter to change the model and add new kinds of information without having to edit every entity individually.

On the other hand, it is difficult to deny that the XML markup in Listing 4-3 is verbose and is extremely difficult for a person to read because of all the cross-referencing. Computers are very good at following references, however, so why should human readability be a concern?

Anything that is difficult for humans to read makes systems difficult to debug and maintain. The success of the Internet was the victory of text-based, human-readable networking protocols over nonreadable binary protocols; the success of the Web was the victory of text-based, human-readable document formats over nonreadable binary document formats; the success of XML is the victory of text-based, human-readable data formats over nonreadable binary data formats. The trend is impossible to miss: Information that is easy for *people* to understand and debug leads to robust, widely deployed systems. Any step away from human readability abandons XML's biggest advantage.

That argument will likely leave old-school networking engineers and system designers unconvinced. A better argument is that any XML document that is difficult for people to understand is likely inefficient for computers to process. For example, the references in an XML document like the one in Listing 4-3 require the computer to jump back and forth; in other words, such references require *random access*. In XML processing, however, random access is expensive, as it requires storing the parse tree for an entire document in memory. Furthermore, in real life, some of the objects might appear in different XML documents, requiring network access to retrieve them. All told, processing a large, fully normalized XML document could be orders of

---

[3] See http://www.w3.org/RDF/.

magnitude slower than processing a denormalized one. Ironically, many database designers have discovered the same problem with their own technology: A normalized database is easy to maintain but slow to access. As a result, large organizations sometimes maintain two separate copies of a database: a normalized one for authoring and a denormalized one for efficient data publishing.

4.3.3 The Hierarchical Style

The third, hierarchical (or tree) approach models information in a series of nested levels, similar to folders and subfolders in a file system. Moving toward the leaves reveals more detail, whereas moving toward the root provides a higher-level of abstraction. This syntax fits more comfortably with XML syntax than either the tabular or the graph approach. Listing 4-4 is a recasting of the information from Listing 4-3 into a typical XML hierarchical style.

Listing 4-4   Hierarchical XML

```xml
<employees>

  <employee>
    <name>Janet Mulville</name>
    <jobtitle>Senior Consultant</jobtitle>
    <unit>Database</unit>
    <experience>
      <skill>Data modeling</skill>
      <years>9</years>
    </experience>
    <experience>
      <skill>C++</skill>
      <years>6</years>
    </experience>
    <experience>
      <skill>Application servers</skill>
      <years>3</years>
    </experience>
  </employee>

  <employee>
    <name>Ahmed Said</name>
    <jobtitle>Project Manager</jobtitle>
    <unit>Systems</unit>
    <experience>
      <skill>System integration</skill>
      <years>11</years>
    </experience>
  </employee>
```

4.3 Common Data Styles

```
  <employee>
    <name>Julie Fujikawa</name>
    <jobtitle>Intern</jobtitle>
    <unit>Systems</unit>
    <experience>
      <skill>System integration</skill>
      <years>1</years>
    </experience>
  </employee>

</employees>
```

Listing 4-4 is much simpler for a human to read than Listing 4-3, but avoids some of the more serious problems in Listing 4-2 by allowing related information to be grouped in sub-elements instead of using numbered names, such as `spec-1`, `years-1`, `years-2`, and so on. As a result, most XML-based data specifications use markup very similar to what appears in Listing 4-4.

However, some problems remain. Because the information is not fully normalized, it is sometimes repeated; for example the skill name "System integration" and the unit name "Database" both appear twice in this short example and would likely be repeated many more times for a company with many employees. Why does normalization matter? After all, XML markup like this is not the database itself but a report generated from a database; it is unlikely that any sane company would choose to use an XML file as its primary storage for a large database. As long as the database from which the XML is generated is properly normalized, what difference does it make whether the XML itself is?

The answer is that, unlike a generated HTML page, generated XML often needs to be read back into a database again. If the information in the XML is not normalized, the second database cannot easily be normalized either. That is a significant difference between *information publishing* and *information exchange*.

Fortunately, compromises are possible. The most important part of normalization is not avoiding repetition but being able to identify reused information. You know that two people have the same job title because their job titles point to the same row in a database table, not because the strings describing the job titles happen to match. All that is required to get that advantage in XML is to attach unique identifiers and references to certain elements, as in Listing 4-5.

Listing 4-5 Hierarchical XML with Identifiers

```
<employees>

  <employee code="e000234">
    <name>Janet Mulville</name>
    <jobtitle>Senior Consultant</jobtitle>
    <unit code="t000188">Database</unit>
```

```xml
      <experience>
        <skill code="sk008">Data modeling</skill>
        <years>9</years>
      </experience>
      <experience>
        <skill code="sk010">C++</skill>
        <years>6</years>
      </experience>
      <experience>
        <skill code="sk012">Application servers</skill>
        <years>3</years>
      </experience>
    </employee>

    <employee id="e000345">
      <name>Ahmed Said</name>
      <jobtitle code="t000050">Project Manager</jobtitle>
      <unit code="u000200">Systems</unit>
      <experience>
        <skill code="sk014">System integration</skill>
        <years>11</years>
      </experience>
    </employee>

    <employee id="e009122">
      <name>Julie Fujikawa</name>
      <jobtitle code="t000263">Intern</jobtitle>
      <unit code="u000200">Systems</unit>
      <experience>
        <skill code="sk014">System integration</skill>
        <years>1</years>
      </experience>
    </employee>

</employees>
```

This subtle change—adding the code attribute to employees, job titles, administrative units, and skills—makes it as easy for a computer to reimport this information into a normalized database as it is to import the information in Listing 4-3, while still leaving the XML document easy for humans to read, understand, and debug.

4.4 Markup Issues

This section examines two markup issues that come up frequently when using XML for data: whitespace handling and non-XML content. Whitespace handling is a seemingly trivial problem that often trips up people approaching XML from the data side; to them, XML whitespace handling seems nonintuitive because it is also designed for the more complex requirements of documents. How to handle non-XML content, such as photos in an XML document—whether to include the whole thing in a text encoding or simply to point to it externally—is an ongoing debate in the XML community, and this section considers both sides.

4.4.1 Whitespace Handling

Much confusion exists about XML whitespace rules. For example, data specialists often complain about the way XML parsers handle whitespace in an XML document like the one in Listing 4-6.

Listing 4-6 Data-Oriented XML

```
<drm>
  <publisher>ACME Publishing Limited</publisher>
  <subscriber>ACE News</subscriber>
  <start-date>2004-01-01</start-date>
  <end-date>2004-12-31</end-date>
  <region>North America</region>
  <rights>
    <right>archiving</right>
    <right>publication</right>
  </rights>
</drm>
```

A data specialist would prefer an XML parser to report the information roughly as shown in Listing 4-7, but is stuck dealing with something more like Listing 4-8 instead.

Listing 4-7 Whitespace: What the Data Specialist Wants

```
startElement("drm")
startElement("publisher")
characters("ACME Publishing Limited")
endElement("publisher")
startElement("subscriber")
characters("ACE News")
endElement("subscriber")
// etc.
```

Listing 4-8 Whitespace: What the Data Specialist Gets

```
startElement("drm")
characters("\n ")
startElement("publisher")
characters("ACME Publishing Limited")
endElement("publisher")
characters("\n ")
startElement("subscriber")
characters("ACE News")
endElement("subscriber")
"characters("\n ")
// etc.
```

All the extra whitespace in Listing 4-8 is available for the document world, in which any whitespace might matter, and text and elements might be mixed together in any order, as shown in Listing 4-9.

Listing 4-9 Document XML

```
<p>However, XML is <em>not</em> a programming language; it is also
<em>not</em> a single format, like a word processor save format.</p>
```

So, as long as data-oriented XML applications, such as the Resource Description Framework [RDF], XML Topic Maps [XTM], or data binding (see Section 4.5.4) work directly at the XML level rather than at higher levels of abstraction, they will be forced to deal with whitespace because the XML parser is forced to report it.

XML does, however, have some features to reduce the workload.

- A validating XML processor will flag whitespace that is not part of text content according to a DTD or schema, making it easier to ignore.
- XML documents may use the `xml:space` attribute to indicate whether an application should preserve all whitespace.

For example, the `default` value for `xml:space` in Listing 4-10 indicates that the application does not have to preserve whitespace exactly. It can normalize whitespace—say, combining two spaces into one and removing newlines—or discard it, as appropriate.

Listing 4-10 The `xml:space` Attribute

```
<drm xml:space="default">
  <publisher>ACME Publishing Limited</publisher>
  <subscriber>ACE News</subscriber>
  <start-date>2004-01-01</start-date>
  <end-date>2004-12-31</end-date>
  <region>North America</region>
```

4.4 Markup Issues

```
<rights>
  <right>archiving</right>
  <right>publication</right>
</rights>
</drm>
```

An even stronger hint can come from a validating parser using a DTD like the one in Listing 4-11.

Listing 4-11 DTD Specifying Ignorable Whitespace
```
<!ELEMENT drm (publisher, subscriber, start-date,
               end-date, region, rights)>
<!ELEMENT rights (right+)>
<!ELEMENT publisher (#PCDATA)>
<!ELEMENT subscriber (#PCDATA)>
<!— etc. —>
```

Elements that contain `#PCDATA` in their content models have *mixed content,* whereas elements that do not, have *element content*. An XML parser is required to report all whitespace, but a validating parser must also flag the whitespace between elements in element content so that the application can distinguish it and ignore it, if appropriate, without a lot of special-case coding. In Listing 4-11, the `drm` and `rights` elements do not have `#PCDATA` in their content models, so a validating parser will flag any whitespace that appears immediately inside those elements as ignorable; the `publisher` and `subscriber` elements do contain `#PCDATA`, so any whitespace inside them is potentially significant, and a validating parser will not flag it.

Ideally, the data world will eventually agree on common higher-level standards on top of raw XML, so that people can concentrate on application and business logic rather than worry about details of whitespace. Until then, however, whitespace continues to be a trap for the unwary new XML developer.

4.4.2 Non-XML Content

Sometimes, XML documents need to include information that is not XML. When the information is naturally text based, it is usually possible to include it directly, escaping any non-XML characters, as in Listing 4-12.

Listing 4-12 Including Non-XML Text
```
if (x &lt; 3 &amp;&amp; y &gt; 4) {
do_process(x, y);
}
```

In some cases, the textual content will contain control characters that are not allowed in XML, but this approach normally works well both for non-XML textual content and for XML textual content being quoted literally.[4] For some cases, such as vector graphics [SVG] or mathematical equations [MATHML], reasonably well-supported XML formats are available, distinguished by their own namespaces, and you can also embed these directly in your documents, as illustrated in Listing 4-13.

Listing 4-13   Including an XML Vector Graphic
```
<para>The following diagram is an ellipse.</para>

<svg:svg width="2in" height="4in" version="1.1">
  <svg:ellipse cx="1in" cy="2in" rx="1in" ry=".5in" />
</svg:svg>
```

Most often, however, using XML markup for the structure of nontextual data is impractical or impossible—if, say, the binary information is signed or encrypted. In those cases, including binary information in an XML document can be done either externally, using a link—usually, a URL—or internally, using a binary-to-text encoding, such as base64.

Listing 4-14 shows an XML document linking to an external resource. This approach is very common for XML documents and is the only way to include pictures and other similar resources in HTML Web pages.

Listing 4-14   Referencing Binary Data Externally
```
<para>The following photograph shows Lisbon in 1943:</para>

<image type="image/png" url="lisbon.png"/>
```

Listing 4-15 shows an XML document including a binary file internally in base64 encoding. (An entire encoded photo would require many pages of this book, so the listing shows only the first few lines.)

Listing 4-15   Including Binary Data Internally
```
<para>The following photograph shows Lisbon in 1943:</para>

<image type="image/png" encoding="base64">
/9j/4AAQSkZJRgABAAEAWgBaAAD//gAfTEVBRCBUZWNobm9sb2dpZXMgSW5jLiBWMS4w
MQD/2wCEAAICAgICAgICAgICAgICAgICAgICAgICAgICAgMDAgIDAgIC
AwQDAwMDBAQEAgMEBAQEBAMEBAMBAgICAgICAgICAgMCAgIDAwMDAwMDAwMDAwMD
AwMDAwMDAwMDAwMDAwMDAwMDAwMDAwMDAwMDA//EAaIAAAEFAQEBAQEBAAAA
AAAAAABAgMEBQYHCAkKCwEAAwEBAQEBAQEBAQAAAAAAAAECAwQFBgcICQoLEAACAQMD
```

---
[4] Another option for non-XML textual content is the CDATA section, but it has some special restrictions that make it tricky for inexperienced users; escaping special characters using entities is a safer choice. I will admit that I did use CDATA sections for the examples in this book because I am typing them by hand rather than in an XML editing tool, and I know what to avoid.

4.5 Special Topics

```
AgQDBQUEBAAAAX0BAgMABBEFEiExQQYTUWEHInEUMoGRoQgjQrHBFVLR8CQzYnKCCQoW
FxgZGiUmJygpKjQ1Njc4OTpDREVGR0hJS1NUVVZXWF1aY2R1ZmdoaWpzdHV2d3h5eoOE
hYaHiImKkpOU1ZaXmJmaoqOkpaanqKmqsrO0tba3uLm6wsPExcbHyMnK0tPU1dbX2Nna
4eLj5OXm5+jp6vHy8/T19vf4+foRAAIBAgQEAwQHBQQEAAECdwABAgMRBAUhMQYSQVEH
[...]
</image>
```

Linking to a binary object externally has some important advantages.

- The object can be located anywhere on the Internet.
- The object can be changed without modifying the XML file.
- An HTTP server can deliver different versions of the object, based on user requirements.
- The XML document remains small and easy to edit and parse.

Including a binary object internally has a different set of advantages.

- There is no need to manage multiple objects.
- It is possible to keep matching versions together, so that an older version of the document does not accidentally pick up a newer version of the non-XML object.
- It is easy to ship and archive the information.

On balance, the external approach is probably better, simply because many XML tools—especially DOM libraries and XSLT engines—are not particularly memory efficient. There is little point running all the binary data through an XML parser and in-memory data structures every time the document needs to be processed, especially if the embedded binary data changes a 1 kilobyte document to, say, a 50 megabyte document. On the other hand, publish/subscribe systems, such as newswires, may want to keep all related information together in a single file, so embedding objects might sometimes make sense.

The XLink specification [XLINK] provides one method for referencing external objects, but XLink is rarely used, so a project will do just as well coming up with its own mechanism. There is no generally accepted specification for including binary data internally, although almost everyone agrees on using base64 encoding, which is XML safe. The NewsML specification [NEWSML] contains markup that supports both approaches.

4.5 Special Topics

This section introduces some special, higher-level topics associated with using XML for data:

- Identification
- Transactions
- Data typing
- Data binding

As suggested in Section 4.3.3, the most important feature for managing loosely coupled data in XML is not normalization but *identification*. If the objects described by an XML data file have unique and persistent identifiers, computers can recognize when two different sets of XML data are describing the same thing. That will be the basis of any kind of XML data web that might appear in the future.

Transactions are a complex but inevitable topic when discussing data management. Using XML data, especially with XML networking (Chapter 5), does not solve the transaction problem, but it does simplify it a fair bit. XML allows all related information for a transaction to be packaged into a single document, making error detection and recovery simpler.

Data typing is a vexing problem in XML. People coming to XML from a database background have long demanded data typing, and typing is the most popular part of the W3C XML Schema Recommendation [XML-SCHEMA]. On the other hand, the XML community has not gained enough experience with data typing yet, and it is not yet clear whether basic XML's original, loosely coupled *everything-is-a-string* philosophy will turn out to be a liability or an asset.

This section does not treat data binding, another controversial topic, in detail. Data binding attempts to hide XML by generating automatic interfaces of various kinds. Removing the complexity of worrying about XML—or the need to have custom I/O libraries to handle it—seems like an advantage, but the lack of transparency of data binding is also a significant risk, making debugging and performance tuning much more difficult.

4.5.1 Identification

If XML data starts to appear online on the Web rather than simply going directly from producer to consumer via HTTP or other point-to-point transport, Web practice will ensure that each XML data file is *addressable,* using a uniform resource locator [URL]. Like a Web page or a picture, each XML data file will have a unique URL, such as `http://www.example.org/financials/2003/balancesheet.xml`, that allows any computer connected to the Internet to locate and retrieve the file.

Addressability alone is not enough for online data, however: Data collections—whether in a corporate database behind a firewall or spread across the Web—often need to support identification. The distinction between addressability and identification is important.

- An address states how something can be located.
- An identifier states what something is.

For example, a person should have only one social security or insurance number—identifier—but may have many phone numbers, e-mail addresses, and street addresses. On the other hand, a phone number *is* a unique identifier for a phone line, physical or virtual, and an e-mail address is a unique identifier for an e-mail account. In fact, people work with many unique identifiers:

- Phone numbers
- E-mail addresses

4.5 Special Topics

- Bank account numbers
- Credit card numbers
- Government social insurance numbers
- Customer account numbers
- Postal codes

These identifiers all help machines work automatically, without worrying about street names, personal names, and all the other imprecise ways that people refer to things. You may be one of 10,000 John Smiths at your bank, but as long as you are the *only* John Smith with bank account #1033756, the bank's computer can easily determine which account to debit or credit when you do a transaction. Twenty phone lines may belong to Jane Does living in Topeka, but as long as each line has a different phone number, the phone company's computers can easily route your call to the correct line. A snack food company might distribute its products to hundreds of customers called Corner Grocery, but as long as each Corner Grocery has a different account number, the company's computer can easily issue the correct invoices to its customers.

Unlike computers, people care little about identifiers. We typically memorize a few phone numbers, but most of the time, we have to look them up. We know our own social security identification numbers, but we do not know those of our friends. Many people do not know their credit card numbers by heart. In fact, people are bad at working with arbitrary identifiers, such as long numbers, because we cannot remember them, but we are very good at working with the kind of incomplete or ambiguous information that stumps computers. We can remember that an invoice goes to the Corner Grocery near the park with the burned-out oak tree, that John Smith with the steel-rimmed glasses takes our travel expense reports, and that the Jane Doe who looks under 30 is probably the one who should get the high school shot put scholarship check.

The current Web contains mostly documents and other objects designed for people to use, so it has little need for unique identifiers for the things it describes. We can almost always tell from context whether two different Web sites are discussing the same topic, person, or product, even if they use different names, such as Elizabeth Windsor and Queen Elizabeth.

Computers, however, are not that smart. If they are going to work with online XML data themselves—say, to compare prices or perform calculations—they need identifiers, just like the *primary keys* that relational database systems use. If two data pages contain information on the same book, they will both need to include a unique identifier for that book so that a computer can collate the information; if two data pages discuss the same person or country or event, they will both need to include a unique identifier for that person, country, or event. The news industry has long been using special codes for these purposes when sending out wire stories, and some of these are now making their way into public specifications, such as NewsML [NEWSML], but those are not a general solution for all the things people might want to create data for. Without a central authority handing out identifiers, how will it be possible to provide the equivalent of primary keys for XML data spread out over the Internet?

4.5.1.1 Existing Identification Schemes
Although there is no generally accepted global identification scheme, specific domains have local schemes. For example, the ISO [ISO] publishes several collections of widely used codes for various areas:

- Countries and regions [ISO-3166]
- Language [ISO-639]
- Currencies [ISO-4217]
- Units of measure [ISO-1000]

Local agencies in more than 150 countries and territories assign a unique International Standard Book Number (ISBN) to every new book published, whereas the Uniform Code Council assigns a unique universal product code (UPC) to all kinds of retail products. There are, of course, many similar examples.

All these identification schemes share two important characteristics.

1. They are global.
2. There is, at least ideally, a one-to-one relationship between the identifiers and the things they refer to.

A *global* identifier refers to the same thing everywhere: For example, the same ISBN does not refer to different books in Mexico and India. Obviously, a global scope is essential for any identification scheme used for online XML data. It should not be necessary to check whether the XML data file is on a server in France, for example, before using the identifier.

Many popular identification schemes are not global. Stock ticker symbols are unique only to a single exchange, and although companies try to avoid confusion, it is not uncommon to find the same symbol referring to a different company on a different exchange. The lack of global scope already creates serious ambiguities for online trading, so Web sites often require users to specify the exchange or provide a list of alternatives to choose from. Another well-known example of an identifier with local scope is the postal code. Postal codes, such as U.S. zip codes, uniquely identify a small geographical area, such as a block of a street, but each country has a different coding system, and the same code could potentially be used for a different area in a different country. Many countries also assign unique identification numbers to each of their citizens, such as the Canadian Social Insurance Number; again, those numbers are specific to each country.

It is critical that an identifier refer to only a single thing; it is less clear how important it is for a single thing to have no more than one identifier. For example, many online businesses use e-mail addresses as user identifiers. Like ISBNs or ISO country codes, e-mail addresses have global scope, and ideally, every e-mail address should belong to only one person, group, or organization. On the other hand, one person may have many e-mail addresses, so online businesses have trouble determining when a person has opened more than one account. The relationship between e-mail addresses and people is many-to-one, which is difficult but still workable. On the other hand, identifiers that have a one-to-many relationship, such as personal names, are virtually useless for identification: There are simply too many John Smiths in the world.

4.5 Special Topics

4.5.1.2 Future Possibilities The types of identifiers presented in Section 4.5.1.1 share another important characteristic: No matter whether they have global or local scope or are one-to-one or many-to-one, they are all domain specific. No two products in the world should have the same UPC, for example, but there is no guarantee that a UPC will not be identical to some country's social security number or a phone number. An ISO country code is unique only compared to other ISO country codes but may be the same as codes used for other purposes. The same applies to any kind of global identification scheme, from an International Civil Aviation Organization (ICAO) airport identifier, such as KLAX, to the medium access control (MAC) address of your Ethernet card.

If there is some day a single, global XML database across the Web, identifiers need to be unique across the entire database. For example, consider the identifier KEST: Is it the ICAO code for Estherville Municipal Airport in Iowa or the stock symbol for Kestrel Energy Inc. on the OTC Bulletin Board market? How will a computer know?

To deal with this first problem, one promising idea is using uniform resource identifiers [URI] as identifiers as well as addresses. The XML community has already taken up this idea by using URIs to make element and attribute names globally unique [NAMESPACES], so it is not an enormous jump to use a URL or URN for data identification. For example, someone could use the URL `http://www.example.org/icao#` as the root for ICAO code identifiers and the URL `http://www.example.org/companies/otcbb#` as the root for OTC Bulletin Board market ticker symbols, as in Listing 4-16. When they are made into URIs, such as URLs, the identifiers are entirely distinct.

Listing 4-16 URIs as Global Identifiers
```
<charter-flight>
  <date>2004-04-01</date>
  <customer ref="http://www.example.org/companies/otcbb#KEST"/>
  <destination ref="http://www.example.org/icao#KEST"/>
</charter-flight>
```

This system works because it takes advantage of central authorities that already exist—the Internet Assigned Numbers Authority (IANA) and the International Corporation for Assigned Names and Numbers (ICANN)—which coordinate the assignment of IP addresses and domain names. Because each domain name can have only one owner at any particular time, that owner can create URL-based identifiers without any fear of conflict. Basing identifiers on domain names provides the best of both worlds: The identifiers are guaranteed to be globally unique, but the creation of identifiers is infinitely partitionable. Millions of domain owners can create their own identifiers without waiting for approval from any central authority, and they can further delegate the task internally, based on subdomains.

For example, consider an organization that owns the domain `example.org`. The organization wishes to publish XML data online about open-source software, the people who create the software, and the organizations that use it and wants that data to be able to integrate with other XML data on the Web; as a result, every object described needs to have a globally unique identifier, or primary key. Because it owns the domain, the organization can simply begin each identifier with `http://example.org/` and know that the identifier will be guaranteed not to conflict with any identifier created by any other organization.

This particular organization might be divided into three groups for managing data: one to manage data about software, one to manage data about people, and one to manage data about organizations. These groups work fairly autonomously and do not want to be slowed down by a lot of central bureaucracy. As a result, the organization decides to assign a separate path to each of them for creating identifiers:

- The software data group has `http://example.org/objects/software/`.
- The people data group has `http://example.org/objects/people/`.
- The organizations data group has `http://example.org/objects/organizations/`.

Now each of the groups can go ahead and create its own identifiers without fear of conflict and without the need for further coordination. The people group, for example, might choose to use the identifier `http://example.org/objects/people/00001` for Linus Torvalds, whereas the organizations group might choose to use the identifier `http://example.org/objects/organizations/00001` for the Free Software Foundation.

This kind of system can work very well: so well, in fact, that the W3C used it as the basis of its XML Namespaces [NAMESPACES] specification for creating globally unique element and attribute names. However, this system does have its weaknesses. At any given moment, a domain name has only a single owner, but owners can change over time. Next year, perhaps, a different group might own the `example.org` domain and would have no obligation to maintain the previous owner's identifiers. As a result, it could publish online XML data that used the identifier `http://example.org/objects/organizations/00001` for something entirely different, such as the United Nations. The W3C tries to mitigate this problem for its own namespace identifiers by building a date into every one, on the assumption that a future domain owner would be extremely unlikely to create an identifier such as `http://www.w3.org/1999/XSL/Transform`. Still, it is no guarantee.

Other organizations have decided to avoid URLs and use the other kind of URI, the uniform resource name (URN). Unlike URLs, which are based on domain names, or IP addresses, which can change hands, URNs are not private property. For NewsML, the International Press Telecommunications Council created a URN scheme for identifying news stories uniquely and persistently, using identifiers such as `urn:newsml:reuters.com:20000206:IIMFFH05643_2000-02-06_17-54-01_L06156584:1U`. This particular scheme still uses a domain name as a component, but as the format of the URN scheme is strictly regulated, the combination of the domain name with a date *does* guarantee that no future domain owner can use the same identifier. In the future, URN schemes could exist for standard identifiers, such as the UPCs, ISBNs, and ISO date, country, and currency codes mentioned earlier, so that people could freely use such identifiers as `urn:isbn:0136422993` or `urn:iso:639:fr-CH` in their online XML data without ambiguity.

It is possible, then, to work around the problem of changing domain-name ownership without too much trouble, either informally, as the W3C did by embedding dates in URLs, or formally, as the IPTC did with its NewsML URN scheme. Although it is relatively simple to keep an identifier from referring to more than one object, however, it is quite difficult to ensure that an object does not have more than one identifier.

For example, assume that there is no universally accepted standard for identifying listed stocks. One organization might come up with an identification scheme based on *its* domain name, including the exchange and exchange ticker symbol in the path, such as `http://example.org/objects/stocks/nyse/gm`, whereas another might come up with `http://foo.com/companies/gm.nyse` as an identifier. Each organization managed to create a unique identifier; unfortunately, however, there is no easy way to to tell that the identifiers point to the same thing.

If people ever create a global online database using XML data on the Web, this problem will be the most difficult one they have to solve. Even databases isolated inside organizations have the problem of duplicate identifiers, such as several social security numbers for the same person due to data entry errors or fraud; out in the wild, the problem will only be worse.

4.5.2 Transactions

The idea of a *transaction* is very important in the database world. Essentially, a transaction is a collection of information or instructions that must stay together. For example, if I transfer $100 from my checking account to my savings account, I'm passing two instructions to my bank.

1. Withdraw $100 from my checking account.
2. Deposit $100 into my savings account.

What would happen if one of these instructions failed? If I do not have $100 in my checking account, the withdrawal step will fail; in that case, the deposit must fail as well, or else I will end up with an extra $100 of the bank's money. Likewise, if the deposit fails—perhaps the account has gone dormant—the withdrawal must fail as well, or else the bank will end up with $100 of my money.

Even if both transactions are valid, something else might go wrong. For example, the network might go down after the withdrawal instruction has been transmitted to the bank's database but before the deposit instruction has gone out, or the data for one of the two might get scrambled. Obviously, database specialists have spent a long time thinking about how to deal with this kind of problem. What they came up with was the ACID (*atomicity, consistency, isolation, durability*) test.

- *Atomicity.* Transactions are all or nothing; if any part fails, the whole thing must fail.
- *Consistency.* The information in the database must make sense; if two withdrawals have the same tracking number, something has obviously gone wrong.
- *Isolation.* Transactions occurring at the same time must be fully independent; for example, if I am checking my bank balance at the same time as I am transferring the money, I must not

see the transfer half finished, that is, the money removed from my checking account but not yet placed in my savings account.
- *Durability.* Once a transaction is finished, its effects must be permanent. For example, it must be possible to retrieve the transaction from a log or other backup after a power failure.

Obviously, these rules have a lot to do with physical storage and networking protocols, neither of which applies directly to XML. However, XML has the potential to make implementing ACID much easier by providing atomicity for free. An XML document can encode all the information for a transaction in a single place instead of using separate network exchanges for each step of a transaction. Consider the normal sequence for passing a transaction like the bank transfer mentioned earlier.

1. Connect with the database.
2. Receive acknowledgment.
3. Signal the beginning of a transaction.
4. Receive acknowledgment.
5. Order a withdrawal of $100 from the checking account.
6. Receive acknowledgment.
7. Order a deposit of $100 into the savings account.
8. Receive acknowledgment.
9. Signal the end of the transaction.
10. Receive confirmation.

An extended, back-and-forth dialogue like this has a lot of opportunity for something to go wrong, such as a dropped network connection. Furthermore, to ensure durability, the server has to reconstruct the entire transaction as it arrives.

In an XML-based transactional system, the transaction could all be put into a single XML document, as shown in Listing 4-17.

Listing 4-17 XML Transaction
```
<transaction>
  <customer-no>12345</customer-no>
  <debit>
    <account>54321</account>
    <amount>100.00</amount>
  </debit>
  <credit>
    <account>98765</account>
    <amount>100.00</amount>
  </credit>
</transaction>
```

4.5 Special Topics

With all the transaction information together in a single, physical atomic unit—the XML document—communication with the database server becomes much simpler.

1. Send the XML transaction to the database server.
2. Receive confirmation.

If the entire XML document arrives intact, the server knows that it has all the required information; if not, it can report a failure right away. Logging for the server is simple, as the entire transaction is already in a form that can be saved and easily restored. Finally, after the commit, the server can simply return a message to the client that everything was successful. Even more important, the transactions are human readable, so debugging is easier. If a client is generating bad transaction information, a tester can simply open the transactions in an XML editor and see what they look like. For more on the use of XML data in network transactions, see Chapter 5, XML networking.

Database software still needs to implement complex technical tasks, such as two-phase commits, to support ACID properly. But XML and its natural atomicity can make transaction management a lot easier for servers and clients.

4.5.3 Data Typing

In the simplest kind of data model, every piece of information is a string, and it is up to the software processing that information to make conversions as needed. Consider, for example, the text 2004-06-01 in a data table. How should software process this information? One application might preserve its exact form, assuming that it is an opaque string, such as a serial number; a second might assume that it is a formula and reduce it to the number 1997 (2004 minus 6 minus 1); a third might assume that it is a date and normalize it to June 1, 2004.

Aside from the possibility of confusion, treating all data as strings is simply inefficient, both for storage and for processing time. For example, a binary-encoded date (year/month/day) will fit comfortably into two octets, whereas even a very efficient Y2K-compliant string-encoded date, such as 20040601, requires at least eight octets. Every time it reads or writes the data field, a program has to run a conversion filter, slowing down operations.

To work around this problem, both spreadsheets and databases borrowed the idea of *data typing* from programming languages.[5] When each field has a known type, such as integer, applications can process it more consistently and store it more efficiently.

XML arrived long after spreadsheets and relational databases had proved the benefits of data typing, so data specialists are usually surprised and dismayed to find that basic XML information is almost completely untyped. A minimal amount of data typing is applied to attribute values—

---

[5] Nearly all programming languages have data typing; some have *weak typing,* whereby a variable may be assigned data of any type, and some have *strong typing,* whereby a variable may be assigned to data of only a specific type. In both cases, however, the data itself is typed. In one famous counterexample, the programming language Tcl abandoned data typing and made everything a string. Tcl never achieved the popularity of Perl or Python, but it is unclear whether the cost of continual data conversion to and from strings was the primary reason for its failure.

and then, only if there is a DTD—and none at all to content. Consider Listing 4-18, which has many types of data all represented as strings.

Listing 4-18 Untyped XML Data
```
<account>
  <name>Imram Henderson</name>
  <active-status>true</active-status>
  <branch-no>0562</branch-no>
  <account-no>9943758</account-no>
  <type>value checking</type>
  <start-date>1998-01-18</start-date>
  <current-date>2004-03-19</current-date>
  <current-balance>$392.88</current-balance>
</account>
```

To a human reader,[6] it is obvious that the first field, `name`, should be processed as an opaque string: It would take about the same amount of storage space typed or untyped. The next field, `active-status`, may be a Boolean value (`true` or `false`), so a database or a spreadsheet could store it as a single bit, whereas this XML document requires from 4 to 16 octets (32 to 128 bits) for the same information, depending on character encoding.

The next two fields, `branch-no` and `account-no`, are trickier. Are these numbers or opaque strings? This matters, especially for the first one. If it is stored as an integer, the initial 0 will be lost, but that might be significant if the branch number is opaque. Because it is not always safe to assume that something consisting only of digits is a number, neither a human being nor a software application can know for certain how to handle `0562` or `9943758` without additional information.

The fifth field is more complicated than it might at first appear. The content, `value checking`, is obviously not a number, date, or other specialized data type. However, from the context, a human reader can assume that it is probably an *enumerated value;* that is, a value chosen from a fixed list. In this case, the bank might have five or ten kinds of accounts, such as investment savings, no-fee checking, and so on, and the content of the `type` field will always be one of these. In a programming language, a coder would most likely represent these options with integers rather than with strings. A single octet would be sufficient to represent up to 256 account types, which would be more than adequate for any bank. Comparing account types would require only a simple integer operation rather than a more expensive string comparison. With the XML data, however, these optimizations cannot be made, and the account type requires from 14 to 56 octets of storage, depending on the character encoding.

The next two fields, `start-date` and `current-date`, both contain string representations of dates and need to be parsed. The last field, `current-balance`, is slightly more

---

[6] But not necessarily to a computer: Things that are obvious to people are typically completely opaque to computers.

4.5 Special Topics

complicated: It contains both a currency sign—$—and a real number, although many applications might prefer to handle currency as a fixed-precision integer rather than a real number to avoid precision problems. Typically, an application will need to parse and remove the currency sign, then parse the remainder of the field as a number.

So XML shares the two inefficiencies of untyped data—waste of storage space and waste of processing power—both of which are inseparable parts of XML, which is, after all, a text format. People can mitigate the first problem, to a certain extent, through the use of compression technologies.[7] The second problem is simply a cost of XML processing, and because XML does not support embedded binary data, there is not likely to be any way to avoid it. However, it is important to remember that XML is designed for interchange, not for storage. In other words, XML is a way to get information from one system to another, not necessarily a way to provide long-term storage and access for multigigabyte databases. In that regard, the transparency of plaintext is likely to outweigh any space and time inefficiencies.

As shown in Listing 4-19, if transparency is the goal, however, a different kind of problem arises: The data types of the information in the XML document are *not* transparent. Should XML software treat every field as a string, or should it try to guess what is a string and what is a number or a date? Because of these concerns, the World Wide Web Consortium has included support for data typing in its *XML Schema* language, a higher-level specification that can be used together with XML.

Listing 4-19 XML Schema with Data Types

```xml
<xsd:schema xmlns:xsd="http://www.w3.org/2001/XMLSchema">

  <xsd:element name="account" type="AccountType"/>

  <xsd:complexType name="AccountType">
    <xsd:sequence>
      <xsd:element name="name" type="xsd:string"/>
      <xsd:element name="active-status" type="xsd:boolean"/>
      <xsd:element name="branch-no" type="xsd:string"/>
      <xsd:element name="account-no" type="xsd:decimal"/>
      <xsd:element name="type" type="AccountType"/>
      <xsd:element name="start-date" type="xsd:date"/>
      <xsd:element name="current-date" type="xsd:date"/>
      <xsd:element name="current-balance" type="xsd:string"/>
    </xsd:sequence>
  </xsd:complexType>
```

---

[7] In fact, *compressed* XML is often more space efficient than a customized binary format, because binary formats often have much unused space in their primarily fixed-width fields and contain many null octets. Try some of your own experiments and see.

```
  <xsd:simpleType name="AccountType">
    <xsd:restriction base="xsd:string">
      <xsd:enumeration value="value savings"/>
      <xsd:enumeration value="value chequing"/>
      <xsd:enumeration value="investment savings"/>
      <xsd:enumeration value="fixed-fee chequing"/>
      <xsd:enumeration value="fixed-fee savings"/>
    </xsd:restriction>
  </xsd:simpleType>

</xsd:schema>
```

This short schema provides a lot of information that an application can use to optimize its processing and storage of the XML document. It is clear now, for example, that the `active-status` field is a Boolean and can be stored in a single bit; `start-date` and `end-date` can be parsed and stored as dates; `account-no` can be treated as a number, whereas `branch-no` cannot; and `type` can contain only a short list of enumerated values, which can be stored internally as integer indices. The schema does not attempt to deal with the currency sign in the `current-balance` field but could use a `restriction` to force it to match a certain pattern, even if that would not help the application much.

Note that all this information is available to the application *even if the designer did not build in any information about this XML document type*. The data typing in the schema alone allows all these optimizations, and an application could perform similar optimizations for storing and processing a different document type, as long as it came with its own schema.

However, using a schema to get data-typing information also has drawbacks.

- The cost of XML processing is much higher, as the processor has to parse and compile the schema and apply it to the XML document, as well as parse the document.
- An external schema introduces security risks, as tampering with a schema could, obviously, change the interpretation and processing of an XML document.
- An external schema either introduces management complexities—the schema has to be kept with the document—or network-latency problems—the software has to go to an outside Web site and retrieve the schema whenever it needs it.

Some of these problems have workarounds, but they also are complex. In the end, using schemas for data typing is not a lightweight approach, especially as most XML applications *do* have built-in knowledge of the document types they are dealing with. The person who writes a banking application will know which fields contain dates and will design the source code appropriately. In that case, all the machinery of data typing and schemas offers no advantage. However, for designing generic XML tools, which have no advanced knowledge of specific XML document types—and in particular, for designing XML authoring tools—schemas and data typing can bring benefits.

4.5.4 Data Binding

For programmers, one popular way of exchanging information is through *data binding*. Instead of writing code or using libraries to parse XML documents and pull information out of them, programmers use a special support framework that makes XML documents look like objects or data structures in their normal programming language, so that XML processing is almost invisible. Alternatively, XML information is tied directly to relational database tables, so that programmers can work with the XML documents directly, without worrying about the underlying database implementation.

For example, consider the XML inventory information in Listing 4-20. A Java programmer would be very comfortable working with interfaces like the ones in Listing 4-21 to manipulate this information, but how do we get from the XML to Java data structures and back again?

Listing 4-20   XML Inventory Information
```xml
<inventory>

  <product>
    <name>Diet Pepsi (355ml can)</name>
    <sku>069000014257</sku>
    <price>0.75</price>
    <quantity>25</quantity>
  </product>

  <product>
    <name>Baked Lays (180g bag)</name>
    <sku>060410044001</sku>
    <price>1.49</price>
    <quantity>10</quantity>
  </product>

</inventory>
```

Listing 4-21   Simple Java Inventory Interfaces
```java
public interface Inventory
{
  public int getProductCount ();
  public Item getProduct (int index);
}

public interface Product
{
  public String getName ();
  public String getSKU ();
```

```
  public float getPrice ();
  public int getQuantity ();
}
```

The programmer could design the software to parse the document by using an XML parsing library, then use an interface, such as SAX or DOM, to extract the inventory information, but doing so requires a high level of XML expertise and makes for verbose and difficult-to-maintain code: The XML logic ends up scattered all over the source code base, and a small change to the XML format can trigger serious code changes. Data binding sounds like a much better option, as the programmer can simply run a utility that reads an XML schema or DTD and generates the XML parsing code and Java definitions automatically.

Unfortunately, the solution is not as promising as it might sound. For direct mapping to programming interfaces, different kinds of XML markup work better for different programming languages, so either the XML markup becomes somewhat unportable, or the binding interface becomes much more complex. Furthermore, data binding in programming languages often requires the use of a tree-based interface, such as DOM, which can be inefficient for memory and processing time. The worst problem, though, is the same one that comes up with other kinds of code-generation tools, such as Unix yacc: Because the resulting code is not transparent—it's not easy to see how it works—it is very difficult to debug.

In some cases, data binding can be beneficial, but in general, a better approach is to write custom import/export libraries for reading and writing XML-based information. With a library, XML becomes almost entirely invisible to the application, as in Listing 4-22. All the XML-related code is isolated in a single place and can be easily updated as required, and as persistent access is not required, there is no need to store an in-memory XML parse tree while working with the inventory information.

Listing 4-22 Reading XML with a Custom Library

```
try {
  Inventory inventory = InventoryInput.read("inventory.xml");
  // work with the inventory
  InventoryInput.write("inventory.xml");
} catch (IOException ex) {
  // handle an exception from reading or writing
}
```

Data binding is too complex a topic to treat in detail here. For more information, see Ronald Bourret's Web site on XML data binding resources: http://www.rpbourret.com/xml/XMLDataBinding.htm.

4.6 Final Words on XML Data

XML data is already widespread. Many applications, from spreadsheets to word processors to flight simulators, have XML-based save formats. The problem is that those applications are not designed for data interchange: Each one is intended and optimized for a single purpose, and people rarely share them among other systems and applications. As a result, although applications can produce XML data, they are nearly all stovepipes, reinventing XML data from basic XML markup on up, sharing little in common besides basic XML tools, such as parsers.

The best hope for the future of XML data lies in middle-level specifications, such as the Resource Description Framework [RDF] and XML Topic Maps [XTM], which capture a lot of the basic infrastructure for data, including identifiers and references, entities, classes, and attributes. At the time of writing, neither specification has captured a great deal of interest.

Fortunately, even with some custom coding required, XML is a useful and convenient way to move data around, making complex information transparent and platform independent. With time, perhaps better infrastructure will emerge.

CHAPTER 5

XML Networking

Traditionally, the two main fields for SGML and then XML have been *documents* (Chapter 3) and *data* (Chapter 4). Document-oriented projects are concerned with such issues as structured editing, repositories, and publishing engines, whereas data-oriented projects focus on such issues as forms, database interfaces, data typing, and normalization.

Recently, however, things have changed. When XML appeared in the late 1990s, the HyperText Transfer Protocol [HTTP] had already become ubiquitous on the Internet. As the preferred network transfer protocol for the Web, HTTP had support from nearly all operating system, application, and hardware vendors. It did not take long for people to put XML and HTTP together and realize that the two could generate new kinds of network protocols, generally referred to as *XML networking*. What started as a few experiments and open projects took only a few years to become the third major field of XML work: In fact, XML networking now attracts more interest from vendors, investors, and the press than data and documents put together.[1]

Although it has grabbed the imagination of people outside the XML, Web, and distributed-computing communities, XML networking has met some resistance from within. Parts of the older XML community are skeptical about mixing format—XML—and protocol—HTTP—arguing that XML's power comes from the fact that it is purely declarative, with a clean separation from any procedural information. Web specialists complain that XML networking is not always RESTful (see Section 5.3), moving away from the basic design principles that made the HTML and HTTP Web a success. Distributed-computing specialists worry about performance, security, and transactional integrity, especially with a lightweight, text-based protocol built on top of stateless HTTP.

Others are more enthusiastic. At the time of writing, networking and telecommunication companies are excited about new products and new markets, and the titans of the software industry, Microsoft and IBM, both have strategies that involve extensive use of XML networking.[2] The technology press gives much space to XML networking, especially Web Services. Many developers with no previous XML exposure are starting to use XML in their applications only because of XML networking.

---

[1] To be fair, though, one would have to acknowledge that most kinds of XML networking are an outgrowth of XML data, with a networking component added.

[2] Their use of XML differs slightly: Microsoft leans more toward Web Services, whereas IBM leans more toward grid computing.

One possible source of confusion is figuring out exactly what *XML networking* means. When vendors and investors use the term, they may be talking about either or both of the following: networking technologies that carry XML as their payload or networking technologies that use XML as part of their protocol.

This chapter considers XML networking from both perspectives: moving XML content over networks, using any protocol, and using XML to move content across networks, with any kind of payload. First, however, this chapter examines the advantages and disadvantages of XML as a network technology.

5.1 Advantages of XML Networking

XML and HTTP are a great combination: XML brings full internationalization, transparency, and extensibility; HTTP brings compatibility with the Web infrastructure and a high level of hardware and software support. Combining XML and HTTP makes it possible to have stateless, lightweight, decentralized, and distributed computing, the same way that HTML and HTTP made it possible to build a stateless, lightweight, decentralized, and distributed document base.

5.1.1 Internationalization

Many of the basic Internet protocols date back to the days when the Internet and its predecessor were a phenomenon primarily of the English-speaking parts of North America. International support for non-English characters and different writing directions is often either unavailable or tacked on.

XML, on the other hand, was designed from the ground up for full internationalization (I18N). Because XML not only allows but also *requires* full Unicode support [UNICODE], an XML document can appear in any combination of languages. For example, a single document might have an Urdu element name, a Japanese attribute name, and an Arabic attribute value.

5.1.2 Transparency

The advantage of transparency applies as much to XML networking as to other areas of XML use. Because XML is plaintext, it is easy to test and debug applications that use it. This advantage becomes important for networking because bits on a wire can be particularly difficult to analyze. For a detailed discussion, see Section 7.1.2.

5.1.3 Extensibility

Extensibility has long been an important part of Internet and pre-Internet networking protocols and formats. For example, implementers often add new features by using a distinctive reserved prefix, such as "x-".[3] Typically, applications that do not understand the extensions simply ignore them.

---

[3] This usage will be familiar to many readers from the MIME (Multimedia Internet Mail Extensions) types, such as "video/x-msdownload," and e-mail headers [RFC 822], such as "X-Mailer."

5.1 Advantages of XML Networking

This kind of extensibility is much simpler with high-level text-based protocols, such as HyperText Transfer Protocol [HTTP], than with low-level binary protocols using fixed-length fields, such as the Transmission Control Protocol [TCP] or the Internet Protocol [IP]. Even there, though, the protocols are designed to allow a certain amount of extensibility: Both the IP and TCP have room for new option types to be defined in the future.

The Internet culture of easy extensibility can be traced back in a large part to John Postel's 1981 *Robustness Principle,* included in RFC 793 [TCP], Section 2.10: "TCP implementations will follow a general principle of robustness: be conservative in what you do, be liberal in what you accept from others." People quickly extended this principle to other areas of Internet work and often emphasized the second part—"be liberal in what you accept from others"—over the first. In the 1990s, the idea of extensibility jumped from Internet protocols to Web formats: The Hypertext Markup Language (HTML) required Web browsers to ignore *any* markup they did not understand rather than only specially flagged markup. This approach led to major headaches for Web designers and became ammunition for both sides during the browser wars of the 1990s, but it also allowed experimentation and innovation, moving HTML from a simple specification for sharing research papers in 1990 to the rich visual medium that caught the world's attention and enabled global online communication by 1995.

Ironically, despite the fact that the *X* in *XML* stands for *extensible,* XML itself (Section 1.2) deliberately violates Postel's robustness principle in its definition of the term *fatal error*:

> After encountering a fatal error, the processor MAY continue processing the data to search for further errors and MAY report such errors to the application. In order to support correction of errors, the processor MAY make unprocessed data from the document (with intermingled character data and markup) available to the application. Once a fatal error is detected, however, the processor MUST NOT continue normal processing (i.e., it MUST NOT continue to pass character data and information about the document's logical structure to the application in the normal way).

In other words, an XML parser is not allowed to try to recover from, say, an omitted end tag and continue normally: It has to be conservative rather than liberal in what it accepts. In fact, XML *is* extensible, but its extensibility comes at a higher level.

The design of XML makes it easy to add new element and attribute types to any format, as in HTML, but the XML Namespaces specification [NAMESPACES] goes further by making it possible to avoid naming collisions between extensions from different sources. The ability to add new fields and complex structures to protocols without breaking existing software is one of XML networking's greatest strengths, even if it does come to Postel's principle by an indirect route.

5.1.4 Compatibility

XML networking provides compatibility in two ways.

1. XML itself ensures that information is compatible with any application, operating system, or hardware: There are no byte-order issues, line-end problems, or any of the other small snags that can create big bugs and portability headaches.

2. HTTP, the most popular transport in XML networking, ensures that XML-based network protocols are compatible with existing Web hardware and software, including firewalls, which typically allow HTTP traffic through with no extra configuration required.

Only the end points—the computers sending and receiving XML networking messages—require any special software. Everything else—firewalls, routers, switches, caches, multiplexers, and all the other bells and whistles of the Internet—will simply work. (Note that many people consider the firewall compatibility to be a security flaw, as discussed in Section 5.2.2).

5.1.5 Network Resources

People have concerns about how XML networking will perform once it is in widespread use, but XML networking brings big performance advantages in one area: Because it can contain arbitrarily complex structure, an XML document can batch up information and reduce the number of network transactions required. For example, a hypothetical accounting server with an XML networking interface might allow a client to request information about multiple accounts with a single XML document sent over HTTP, as in Listing 5-1.

Listing 5-1   XML Batch Request
```
<balance-request>
  <account ref="assets.current.accounts-receivable"/>
  <account ref="assets.current.petty-cash"/>
  <account ref="liabilities.current.accounts-payable"/>
  <account ref="income.professional-services"/>
</balance-request>
```

The server could respond with all the information also in a single XML document, as in Listing 5-2.

Listing 5-2   XML Batch Response
```
<balance-info>
  <balance
    account="assets.current.accounts-receivable">144298.00</balance>
  <balance
    account="assets.current.petty-cash">2119.16</balance>
  <balance
    account="liabilities.current.accounts-payable">89376.78</balance>
  <balance
    account="income.professional-services">2033945.39</balance>
</balance-info>
```

In a non-XML system, the same information could require many request/response exchanges, and the extra latency would create major slowdowns for an application. More advanced distributed-computing protocols have mechanisms for batching information on the fly—called *marshaling*—but they are complex to implement and have proved less than impressive in the field. Perhaps XML's simple approach will turn out to be more robust and effective.

5.2 Disadvantages of XML Networking

With a few exceptions, such as RSS [RSS], XML networking is still mostly at the early implementation stage, so both the advantages and the disadvantages are anticipated rather than real. People expect to run into trouble with XML networking in two main areas: performance and security. Both are issues in any distributed computing environment, but XML's basis in text amplifies the performance fears, and its frequent reliance on HTTP brings new security concerns.

5.2.1 Performance

Section 5.1.5 explains why XML networking may be faster over the network itself because XML can represent more information in a single transaction, cutting down on the latency involved with many small network exchanges. At the end points—the client and the server—however, performance is likely to be a problem: The recipient of a network message has to parse the XML, convert string data to various formats, build internal data structures, and then process those structures.

In fact, the main challenge with XML networking could be that servers will fall behind the network in trying to process transactions. The problem is even more serious with smart, content-based network appliances, such as switches and routers, which optimize network speed, routing, and prioritization by examining HTTP headers. If they need to look inside XML documents as they pass by, these appliances will need to be able to parse, process, and analyze XML at wire speed, handling at least tens of thousands of documents every second. Networking companies are already starting to release acceleration hardware to help build such appliances, but many technical problems remain to be overcome.

5.2.2 Security

XML networking with HTTP is easy to retrofit on existing systems because most firewalls already allow HTTP traffic through. That is bad news for the people who want to keep networks secure: Often, organizations have strong reasons for trying to prevent non-Web traffic from getting into and out of their private systems. With XML networking hiding inside HTTP request and response packets, it is possible that computers inside their internal network will accidentally or deliberately release sensitive information or will be used as beachheads for attacking the rest of the network. Firewalls will eventually learn to detect and control XML networking traffic, but doing so will be tricky, as it is not always easy to tell XML networking from XML Web browsing without a lot of slow, resource-intensive computation.

The second security concern comes from XML itself. XML parsers have not yet been tested heavily in a high-demand, public environment, and they may have serious security flaws hidden in them, the way that many other pieces of Internet infrastructure have. For example, XML places no size limits on any markup components: What will happen when someone feeds a terabyte attribute name to an XML networking server? Here are the possibilities, from least to worst damaging.

- The server aborts the connection and returns an error once the name passes a predetermined limit.

- The server continues allocating memory for the name until exhausting all available memory and then faults, bringing the server offline.
- The name overflows the buffer in the server's parser, providing an opportunity for an attacker to take control of the server and use it to attack the rest of the internal network.

Obviously, many more vulnerabilities will show up, both specific to individual software components and endemic to XML itself. It will be risky for security-sensitive organizations to commit too heavily to XML networking until the community has had a few years to find and fix the problems in real, large-scale deployments in the field.

5.2.3 State

The last disadvantage of XML networking is a more minor one: the ability to maintain conversational state. HTTP is a stateless protocol.[4] The client sends a request, the server sends a response, and then the client and the server forget about each other and go on to other things. Because they do not have to keep thousands of connections open, HTTP servers run much more efficiently; the problem, however, is that many Web applications *do* need to maintain state over an extended user session. If a customer is shopping at an online store, for example, the server has to keep track of which customer each request belongs to, what is in the customer's shopping cart, and so on. To do this on top of a stateless protocol, Web applications resort to many kinds of kludges, such as HTTP cookies, `GET` parameters, and so on.

Exactly the same situation will likely occur with XML networking. In some cases, it is sufficient for a client and a server to exchange a quick request/response pair and then forget about each other. In other cases, however, the client and the server will want to maintain a long, stateful relationship, negotiating with each other and modifying each other's information. Unfortunately, XML networking with HTTP will be forced to use the same awkward, unreliable kludges that Web applications use.

5.3 XML Networking Styles

The term *XML networking* covers a wide range of styles, such as the following:

- Remote procedure calls (RPC)
- Asynchronous messaging
- Web Services
- Grid computing
- Syndication (publish/subscribe)

---

[4] HTTP 1.0 was a stateless protocol. HTTP 1.1 allows for a TCP/IP connection to stay open for multiple request/response pairs, so it is technically stateful from a networking perspective. From a developer's perspective, however, it is still stateless. (If you have read the footnote this far, you really need to get a hobby outside of computers.)

5.3 XML Networking Styles

All those styles use XML, and most use it in some combination with the HyperText Transfer Protocol [HTTP].

Some criteria are useful for understanding and classifying XML networking initiatives. First, XML networking may be *synchronous* or *asynchronous*. Synchronous networking is similar to blocking I/O on a computer: A client makes a request and then waits, keeping the connection open, until receiving a response from the server. Clients making synchronous requests expect responses quickly, typically within seconds or even milliseconds. Synchronous networking is familiar to most users from Web browsing: The browser requests a Web page from an HTTP server and then pauses, displaying an animation of some sort, until the page arrives.

Asynchronous networking, on the other hand, is similar to nonblocking I/O. The client sends out messages, possibly receiving confirmation of receipt, then normally continues with other work until a response arrives, which may be minutes, hours, or even days later. Asynchronous networking is familiar to most people from e-mail: A user sends an e-mail message and then continues with other activities; the reply, if any, to the message may come hours, days, or weeks later, and replies do not necessarily arrive in the same order that the original messages went out.

A second distinction among networking styles is *unicast* and *broadcast*. A unicast network message goes from a single sender to a single recipient, and the sender often expects to receive a response, either synchronous or asynchronous, from that recipient. Unicast network messages are similar to e-mail messages sent to one person: The sender normally expects the person to read the message and, often, to reply to it.

Multicast network messages, on the other hand, go from one sender to many recipients, and the sender does not necessarily expect a response from all the recipients; in fact, the sender might not even know who all the recipients are. Unicast can be synchronous or asynchronous, but multicast networking is almost always asynchronous by definition, as different recipients may reply at different times. Multicast networking is similar to sending an e-mail message to a mailing list or a newsgroup: Hundreds or thousands of people may read the message, but only a handful might reply.

The third distinction among networking styles is request/response versus publish/subscribe. With request/response, a client sends out a request message to one or more servers and receives replies, either synchronously or asynchronously. With publish/subscribe, a client asks a server to start sending information: the server continues to send it automatically, possibly over many months or years, until the client asks it to stop. Publish/subscribe is, obviously, similar to a person subscribing to a magazine or newspaper. Figure 5-1 shows the difference between publish/subscribe and request/response.

The final distinction for this chapter is between RESTful and non-RESTful networking styles. Representational state transfer (REST) is a term coined by Roy Fielding in his 2000 doctoral dissertation.[5] RESTful Web resources are ones that have unique and persistent identifiers.

---

[5] Fielding's dissertation is available online at http://www.ics.uci.edu/~fielding/pubs/dissertation/top.htm. It is important to note that there is much more to Fielding's idea of REST than what is described in this chapter.

Figure 5-1 Request/response versus publish/subscribe

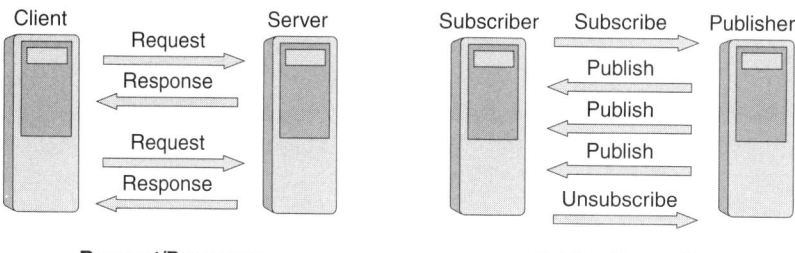

For example, I can type the URL `http://www.phptr.com/ptrbooks/ptr_0136422993.html` into any Web browser and see a Web page describing my book *Structuring XML Documents*. I can bookmark that URL and go back to the same page, or an updated version, 6 months from now. I can e-mail the link to a friend, post it on Yahoo!, and put it in my CV or in this book that you are reading. If someone is searching for information about XML document structure, search engines, such as Google, can return this URL to the person, who can then use it to go to the same page. Most important of all, however, *other* Web pages can use this link to allow people and search engines to find this one. This one little idea—using a unique string for each resource—is, according to many people, the secret formula that made the Web succeed.

It should not be surprising that this approach works; it is the same system that makes the global postal and telephone systems work. My house has an address that is unique in the world, so a properly addressed letter dropped into a mailbox in Japan, Australia, Russia, England, or Cameroon should arrive at my house just as well as one dropped in a mailbox in the same city. My phone line has a phone number that, with area and country code, is also unique in the world, so it is possibly to call me from anywhere linked into the global phone system.

A RESTful networking style, then, is one in which a single identifier—usually a URL or a URN—will consistently refer to the same information. Table 5.1 provides a short, somewhat oversimplified summary of how these four criteria apply to the XML networking styles discussed in this section.

Table 5-1 XML Networking Styles

Style	Synchronous or Asynchronous?	Unicast or Multicast?	Request/Response or Publish/Subscribe?	RESTful?
RPC	Synchronous	Unicast	Request/response	Sometimes
Asynchronous messaging	Asynchronous	Unicast or multicast	Request/response	Not usually
Web Services	Both	Unicast	Request/response	Sometimes
Grid computing	Mainly asynchronous	Mainly unicast	Request/response	No
Syndication	Asynchronous	Multicast	Publish/subscribe	No

5.3 XML Networking Styles

5.3.1 RPC

Normally, computer programs make procedure calls to do much of their work. The computer operating system, such as Linux, Microsoft Windows, MacOS, or PalmOS, provides a basic set of services for reading and writing files, displaying information on the screen, retrieving the date and time, managing network connections, and operating printers and other peripherals. Applications can make procedure calls to the operating system to use these services directly or to higher-level libraries that may then use the operating system's services and provide new services of their own. This model makes a nice, layered stack along the same lines as the OSI networking model described in Section 5.4.1:

- Operating system
- Libraries
- Applications

However, as personal computers became more sophisticated and multitasking, this layered model became inadequate. A user runs several programs at once, such as a word processor, a spreadsheet, and an e-mail client, and those programs might need to communicate with each other rather than only with the operating system. As a result, operating systems introduced *interprocess communications* (IPC) to allow applications to communicate with each other directly.

As the world's computers became better connected through pervasive networking, it appeared that there might be a strong demand for a way for programs to communicate with software running not only on the same computer but also on other computers, using *remote procedure calls*. For example, an application at an automobile manufacturer could use RPC to query the inventory at one of its suppliers and place orders. During the 1990s, three major RPC specifications became prominent: Microsoft's Distributed Component Object Model (DCOM), mainly in the Windows world; Sun's Java Remove Method Invocation (RMI), used exclusively in the Java world; and the cross-platform Object Management Group's Common Object Request Broker Architecture (CORBA). People implemented projects using all three specifications, but all failed to take off in the wider world outside of individual organizations and local area networks. In particular, all were poorly suited for the slower, less reliable network connections that exist once you pass outside a company's firewall.

As XML emerged in the late 1990s, the combination of XML and HTTP seemed an obvious choice for simple, lightweight RPC across the Internet, the same way that the combination of HTML and HTTP had brought in simple, lightweight hypertext a decade earlier. Procedure calls use an invocation and return value, and HTTP uses a request and a response: Both fit the synchronous, unicast, and request/response criteria. Furthermore, the HTTP request and response packets can both contain any arbitrary content, so it is simple to attach an XML description of a procedure call to the request package and an XML description of the return value to the response packet. Listings 5-3 and 5-4 show how the procedure call `getTemperature_degC` (`"us.ny.watertown"`) returning the integer value `-18` might work using HTTP and XML.

Listing 5-3 RPC Invocation Using HTTP and XML

```
POST /rpc/server HTTP/1.0
User-Agent: ACMERPC/1.0
Host: rpc.megginson.com
Content-Type: text/xml
Content-length: 192

<?xml version="1.0"?>
<methodCall>
  <methodName>getTemperature_degC</methodName>
  <params>
    <param>
      <value><string>us.ny.watertown</string></value>
    </param>
  </params>
</methodCall>
```

Listing 5-4 RPC Return Value Using HTTP and XML

```
HTTP/1.1 200 OK
Connection: close
Content-Length: 138
Content-Type: text/xml
Date: Sun, 11 Jan 2004 20:00:00 GMT
Server: ACMERPC/1.0

<?xml version="1.0"?>
<methodResponse>
  <params>
    <param>
      <value><i4>-18</i4></value>
    </param>
  </params>
</methodResponse>
```

In fact, these examples follow the XML-RPC [XML-RPC] specification for remote procedure calls, which really is this simple. XML-RPC has not gained widespread acceptance, but its simplicity has made it popular in certain communities, especially the Web log community.

5.3.1.1 RPC and REST How RESTful is XML-based RPC? For the examples given so far, not at all. Take another look at the first line of Listing 5-3: POST /rpc/server HTTP/1.0. The URL for this imaginary remote procedure call to get the temperature in Watertown, NY, USA, would be something like http://rpc.megginson.com/rpc/server. The URL for the remote procedure call to get the temperature in Reading, UK would be the same.

5.3 XML Networking Styles

In fact, the URL to get the population of Auckland, New Zealand, might also be `http://rpc.megginson.com/rpc/server`, simply using a different method name, such as `getPopulation`, in the content of the HTTP packet.

In other words, the URL by itself is nearly useless because there is no longer a single string that identifies the information. There is nothing that I can save as a bookmark, mail to a coworker, or get as the result from a search engine. There is no way to create a simple link to such information as "the current temperature in Watertown" or "the population of Auckland." Without an ability to share that information, any kind of network effect is unlikely: The information is simply too difficult to find, catalog, and navigate compared to normal HTML Web pages.

Listing 5-5 shows a different style of remote procedure call, also allowed by SOAP 1.2 but not by XML-RPC. Note that this example contains no XML at all, but it does contain a URL:

```
http://rpc.megginson.com/rpc/server/temperature?city=us.ny.watertown
```

This URL uniquely identifies the information being retrieved. If the call were retrieving the temperature in Reading or the population of Auckland, the URL would be different. In fact, the URL is *all* you need to get the information. I could e-mail this URL to another person, who could use a different SOAP client to retrieve the temperature of Watertown as easily as I could.

Listing 5-5   SOAP 1.2 GET Request
```
GET /rpc/server/temperature?city=us.ny.watertown HTTP/1.1
User-Agent: ACMERPC/1.0
Host: rpc.megginson.com
```

In other words, Listing 5-5 is RESTful: A single string uniquely and persistently identifies the information being retrieved, and that string can be saved as a bookmark, e-mailed to a friend, indexed by a search engine, and so on. On the other hand, it is awkward, but not impossible, to use this approach to pass complex data structures as arguments to the remote procedure call. For example, consider the simple XML markup in Listing 5-6.

Listing 5-6   Human Resources Data
```
<employees>

  <employee id="e1001">
    <name>Jane Smith</name>
    <department>Software Engineering</department>
    <salary currency="USD">80000</salary>
  </employee>

  <employee id="e1002">
    <name>John Doe</name>
    <department>Support Services</department>
```

```
    <salary currency="USD">40000</salary>
  </employee>

</employees>
```

If someone wanted to use a remote procedure call to add these two employees to a database, a RESTful URL for the action might look something like the one in Listing 5-7, which would be a single line but has new lines added here for readability. If that does not look bad enough, imagine adding 100 new employees instead of merely two.

Listing 5-7   A RESTful URL?
```
http://rpc.megginson.com/server/employees/add
?employee_1_id=e1001&amp;employee_1_name=Jane%20Smith
&amp;employee_1_department=Software%20Engineering
&amp;employee_1_salary_currency=USD&amp;employee_1_salary=80000
&amp;employee_2_id=e1002&amp;employee_2_name=John%20Doe
&amp;employee_2_department=Support%20Services
&amp;employee_2_salary_currency=USD&amp;employee_2_salary=40000
```

But then, why *would* anyone need to make a RESTful URL for a remote procedure call adding new employees to a database? What could anyone you e-mailed the URL to do with it except add the same employees to the database all over again? What would be the point of bookmarking this action and coming back to it six months from now? Anything that is an action—"add these employees to the database," "buy this book and charge it to my credit card," "transfer $200 to my savings account," "shut down the reactor," and so on—is by its very nature a single-shot event. In such a case, using a RESTful approach—with a URL that automatically repeats the action—could even be harmful—say, when 200 copies of *Lord of the Rings* arrive at your door from Amazon.com, together with a notice from your credit card company.

So how well do XML-based RPC and REST go together? The problem is that you can use RPC both to retrieve information—the equivalent of a `GET` function—and to perform actions, such as `SET` or `PROCESS`. The RESTafarians—or REST zealots—are probably right that a RESTful approach is best for retrieving information, but it is obviously inappropriate whenever the remote procedure call has side effects. SOAP 1.2 would seem to have the advantage over XML-RPC in this respect, as SOAP supports both HTTP `POST` (non-RESTful) and HTTP `GET` (RESTful) RPC.

5.3.1.2   SOAP   Listings 5-3 and 5-4 both used the XML-RPC [http://www.xmlrpc.com/] specification to demonstrate an XML-based remote procedure call and its return value inside HTTP packets. XML-RPC is simple and thus suitable for illustrating the basic concept of XML+HTTP, but the best-known XML-based RPC specification is SOAP.

SOAP [SOAP] used to stand for *Simple Object Access Protocol,* but because the protocol is not simple any more, the acronym no longer has an official expansion. The basic idea of SOAP is

5.3 XML Networking Styles

the same as that of XML-RPC—XML information stashed in HTTP packets—but SOAP adds many additional features, such as extensibility, complex data structures, advanced error reporting, and the ability to use protocols other than HTTP. You can learn most of XML-RPC in a few minutes; SOAP requires days of study even for the most talented implementer.[6] Even so, SOAP messages do not have to be significantly more complex than XML-RPC. Compare Listings 5-8 and 5-9 with Listings 5-3 and 5-4.

Listing 5-8   RPC Invocation Using HTTP and SOAP

```
POST /rpc/server HTTP/1.1
User-Agent: ACMERPC/1.0
Host: rpc.megginson.com
Content-Type: application/soap+xml; charset="utf-8"
Content-Length: 351

<?xml version='1.0'?>
<env:Envelope xmlns:env="http://www.w3.org/2003/05/soap-envelope">
  <env:Body>
    <m:getTemperature_degC
       env:encodingStyle="http://www.w3.org/2003/05/soap-encoding"
       xmlns:m="http://rpc.megginson.com/ns/ipc/">
      <m:location>us.ny.watertown</m:location>
    </m:getTemperature_degC>
  </env:Body>
</env:Envelope>
```

Listing 5-9   RPC Return Value Using HTTP and SOAP

```
HTTP/1.1 200 OK
Connection: close
Content-Length: 350
Content-Type: application/soap+xml; charset="utf-8"
Date: Sun, 11 Jan 2004 20:00:00 GMT
Server: ACMERPC/1.0

<?xml version='1.0'?>
<env:Envelope xmlns:env="http://www.w3.org/2003/05/soap-envelope">
  <env:Body>
    <m:temperature_degC
       env:encodingStyle="http://www.w3.org/2003/05/soap-encoding"
```

---

[6] Ironically, given the different design philosophies, the author of XML-RPC (Dave Winer) was also one of the original authors of SOAP, although he was not involved with the latest SOAP versions, reportedly because of the growing complexity.

```
        xmlns:m="http://rpc.megginson.com/ns/ipc/">-18<
      /m:temperature_degC>
  </env:Body>
</env:Envelope>
```

The big difference between the XML-RPC and SOAP examples is the fact that the markup in the main XML-RPC message has a predefined meaning, whereas contents of the main SOAP message body can be any arbitrary XML. This difference gives SOAP more flexibility at the cost of more complex implementation. (An XML-RPC library can hide XML structure completely, whereas a SOAP library has to expose some of it to the application.) Because it uses arbitrary XML markup, SOAP also uses XML Namespaces to avoid naming collisions. Otherwise, however, the XML-RPC and SOAP examples are not significantly different in their core structure: Using SOAP or XML-RPC, XML-based RPC looks pretty much the same, although SOAP messages are capable of becoming baroquely complex if someone cares to make them that way.

Neither XML-RPC nor SOAP has widespread implementation, but SOAP has strong corporate backing from Microsoft, IBM, and others and generates enormous investor interest; XML-RPC has neither major corporate backing nor investor money but does have a dedicated group of uses in the Web log community. Until people start implementing a lot of XML-based RPC—rather than simply talking about it and collecting investor money—it will be impossible to predict whether XML-RPC or SOAP, if either, will succeed.

5.3.2 Asynchronous Messaging

Synchronous RPC using XML and HTTP was a fairly obvious step: The HTTP specification and various implementations already took care of the tricky networking parts, so it was simply a matter of defining XML payloads and error-handling mechanisms to get a simple, portable, and, ideally, robust RPC system. Asynchronous messaging, on the other hand, is much more difficult to design and implement, as much of the work needs to be done from scratch. With asynchronous messaging, a client sends out a message to one or more servers, and replies arrive at a future time. This kind of networking requires more complex coordination than RPC, as reponses may arrive late, out of order, in duplicate, or not at all. Error handling is also tricky, especially if the message goes out to more than one server: Some servers may report errors, whereas others send normal responses. If the client application requires only a single response, the protocol will have to include a way to arbitrate among candidates in a multicast environment so that more than one does not try to answer.

The higher-level Internet protocols—above TCP/IP—are, almost without exception, synchronous. Although the human side of sending and receiving e-mail may be asynchronous, for example, the Simple Mail Transfer Protocol [SMTP], which moves a message from one point to another, is simply another synchronous file transfer protocol. Internet e-mail protocols have no provision for tracking replies; ensuring final delivery, unless the user opts in to e-mail receipts, which most do not; checking whether replies come within a specified time; or any of the other basic components of reliable messaging.

5.3 XML Networking Styles

Does asynchronous messaging matter? And if so, does it matter enough to justify going to all this trouble? That remains an open debate in the XML and networking communities, and it will not be resolved until we have gained real-world experience with the protocols. A typical use case for asynchronous messaging is a request for bids: A client computer at a shoe company, for example, might want to order a new batch of grommets, so it sends out an XML message to 50 suppliers, requesting bids within 3 days. The computer then goes on to other tasks. Over the next 3 days, 15 bids arrive in response to the original message, and the computer then analyzes them, chooses the most attractive bid, and sends a second asynchronous message to that supplier, offering a contract with a 2-day time limit. A day later, the supplier sends back a message accepting a contract.

That example closely mirrors how people ask for bids and arrange a contract using e-mail or telephone today, but in this hypothetical example, all is automated. In fact, although the business process itself is asynchronous, it could also be built on top of a synchronous request/response model, such as simple RPC: The shoe company sends out the request for bids and receives as a reply an acknowledgment that the bid was received; later, the supplier sends out a request containing a bid, and the shoe company sends back a reply confirming that the bid was received. Keeping track of what bid goes with what initial request is then a problem for application logic rather than protocols, and that approach may be more in the Internet spirit of keeping basic protocols simple.

Although XML-RPC is strictly synchronous, newer versions of SOAP do support asynchronous transport, and vendors and free-software developers will all, no doubt, soon support it. Other specifications in the Web Services forest address asynchronous-messaging issues, including competing reliability specifications from OASIS and the WS-I.

5.3.3 Web Services

Web Services is the XML-networking area that has grabbed the most attention in recent years. The area defined by the term *Web Services* seems to have flexible boundaries that can stretch and contract, depending on each organization's needs. At its core, most activities the term describes share the following characteristics:

- Exchanging information using remote procedure calls—in practice, that means SOAP—or, sometimes, asynchronous messaging
- Having a facility for interface definition and discovery (WSDL)
- Building further layers on top of the basic RPC and interface definition for such functions as security, reliability, and quality of service
- Exchanging information *outside* of the local system: among partners, between consumers and companies, or among parts of a larger organization or company

The political struggles of the bodies writing Web Services specifications are at least as interesting as the specifications themselves, but this book describes those struggles in Chapter 1, not here. This section provides an overview of the Web Services specifications and how the designers think people might use them.

Aside from SOAP, described in Section 5.3.1, the most important specification in the Web Services world is the Web Services Definition Language [WSDL]. A WSDL document describes and defines a collection of services in a way that machines can understand, although it can also contain human-oriented documentation. For example, consider again a simple Web Service providing the temperature for a location. On the most basic level, querying the temperature requires transmitting two messages: the *query* (What is the temperature?) and the response (Here is the temperature). WSDL can define the two messages as shown in Listing 5-10.

Listing 5-10   WSDL Message Definitions
```
<message name="getTemperature_degC_Input">
  <part name="location" element="xsd:string"/>
</message>


<message name="getTemperature_degC_Output">
  <part name="result" type="xsd:float"/>
</message>
```

Next, the WSDL document combines the two messages into a *port type* or, in plain English, a procedure call, as illustrated in Listing 5-11.

Listing 5-11   WSDL Port Type Definition
```
<portType name="TemperaturePortType">
  <operation name="getTemperature_degC">
    <input message="m:getTemperature_degC_Input"/>
    <output message="m:getTemperature_degC_Output"/>
  </operation>
</portType>
```

So far, this procedure call is still abstract: We know that it exists, but there is no information on how to make the call. To provide that information, the WSDL document defines a *binding,* as shown in Listing 5-12.

Listing 5-12   WSDL SOAP Binding Definition
```
<binding name="TemperatureBinding" type="m:TemperaturePortType">
  <soap:binding style="rpc"
    transport="http://schemas.xmlsoap.org/soap/http"/>
  <operation name="getTemperature_degC">
    <soap:operation
      soapAction="http://rpc.megginson.com/rpc/server"/>
    <input>
      <soap:body use="encoded"
        namespace="http://rpc.megginson.com/ns/ipc/"
```

5.3 XML Networking Styles

```
          encodingStyle="http://schemas.xmlsoap.org/soap/encoding/"/>
      </input>
      <output>
        <soap:body use="encoded"
          namespace="http://rpc.megginson.com/rpc/server"
          encodingStyle="http://schemas.xmlsoap.org/soap/encoding/"/>
      </output>
    </operation>
</binding>
```

This binding connects the abstract idea of the `getTemperature_degC` port type—method call—with the specific SOAP implementation of it. Finally, the WSDL document defines a service, which in this case consists of only the one binding, as shown in Listing 5-13.

Listing 5-13 WSDL Service Definition
```
<service name="TemperatureService">
  <documentation>Current temperature in any city.</documentation>
  <port name="TemperaturePort" binding="m:TemperatureBinding">
    <soap:address location="http://rpc.megginson.com/rpc/server"/>
  </port>
</service>
```

All this makes for a fairly long and complex document, even for only one procedure call. The entire WSDL document, including the top-level `definitions` element and the namespace declarations, appears in Listing 5-14. Compare it to the equivalent Java code for declaring a local method call (Listing 5-15). It is obvious why many people complain that WSDL is ridiculously complex and verbose for its intended task.

Listing 5-14 Complete WSDL Document
```
<?xml version="1.0"?>
<definitions name="StockQuote"
targetNamespace="http://rpc.megginson.com/ns/ipc/"
xmlns:m="http://example.com/stockquote.wsdl"
xmlns:xsd="http://www.w3.org/2000/10/XMLSchema"
xmlns:soap="http://schemas.xmlsoap.org/wsdl/soap/"
xmlns="http://schemas.xmlsoap.org/wsdl/">

<message name="getTemperature_degC_Input">
  <part name="location" element="xsd:string"/>
</message>

<message name="getTemperature_degC_Output">
  <part name="result" type="xsd:float"/>
</message>
```

```xml
<portType name="TemperaturePortType">
  <operation name="getTemperature_degC">
    <input message="m:getTemperature_degC_Input"/>
    <output message="m:getTemperature_degC_Output"/>
  </operation>
</portType>

<binding name="TemperatureBinding" type="m:TemperaturePortType">
  <soap:binding style="rpc"
    transport="http://schemas.xmlsoap.org/soap/http"/>
  <operation name="getTemperature_degC">
    <soap:operation
      soapAction="http://rpc.megginson.com/rpc/server"/>
    <input>
      <soap:body use="encoded"
        namespace="http://rpc.megginson.com/ns/ipc/"
        encodingStyle="http://schemas.xmlsoap.org/soap/encoding/"/>
    </input>
    <output>
      <soap:body use="encoded"
        namespace="http://rpc.megginson.com/rpc/server"
        encodingStyle="http://schemas.xmlsoap.org/soap/encoding/"/>
    </output>
  </operation>
</binding>

<service name="TemperatureService">
  <documentation>Current temperature in any city.</documentation>
  <port name="TemperaturePort" binding="m:TemperatureBinding">
    <soap:address location="http://rpc.megginson.com/rpc/server"/>
  </port>
</service>

</definitions>
```

Listing 5-15 Equivalent Java Interface

```
package com.megginson.temperature;

public interface Temperature
{
public float getTemperature_degC ();
}
```

Such a criticism is not entirely fair, however. Working in a distributed, multilanguage, cross-platform environment is inherently more complex than working in a local, monolingual virtual machine, so any distributed-computing discovery mechanism will be at least slightly more verbose. Furthermore, WSDL is designed to handle more than simple request/response method calls; it can also handle push, which it calls *solicit/response;* one-way broadcast; and notification patterns. WSDL is also designed to handle any arbitrary type of transport, including basic HTTP PUT and GET; SOAP is only one optional binding, although it is the one that almost everyone uses. But even with these mitigating factors, WSDL is not a simple format, and it, rather than SOAP, may be the biggest stumbling block to the adoption of Web Services.

The other core Web Services specification is *Universal Description, Discovery, and Integration of Web Services* [UDDI]. UDDI is a registry standard for Web Services: whereas WSDL describes what services are available at a specific site, UDDI describes what sites offer a specific service. UDDI is the specification for a Web Services equivalent of Yahoo! or Google: You would use WSDL to find out what Web Services Amazon.com offers but you would use UDDI to find out what sites offer Web Services for purchasing books in the first place. Although most Web Services people pay lip service to UDDI, it has remained moribund compared to SOAP and WSDL; Web Service registries have little demand because so few publicly available services exist in the first place.

Beyond WSDL and UDDI come a large collection of Web Service specifications designed for such areas as security, reliability, and quality of service, with new specifications appearing continually. The Web Services community is not taking any risks: To prevent Web Services from going the way of the chaotic, free-for-all Web, they are ensuring that *everything* is specified in advance, sometimes with two or more competing specifications, no less. This approach puts the specification writers far out in advance of the implementers; inevitably, most of these specifications will simply wither and die as people learn from implementation experience what does and does not work. At the time of writing, there is much interest in Web Services among vendors and investors and a more moderate but still measurable amount in interest among potential users. It remains to be proven, however, whether such a complex, heavily specified system can survive and flourish or whether something simpler will come and knock it down, just as the Web knocked down complex, heavily specified document-delivery systems a decade ago.

5.3.4 Grid Computing

Distributed computing means spreading work among more than one computer rather than simply moving information around. For example, several computers might share the work of producing a complex weather forecast, analyzing a gene, or storing a large set of data. One particular type of distributed computing receiving a lot of attention is *grid computing,* which involves using a loosely coupled network of computers to pool their computing or storage resources to act as one big, virtual computer. Unlike cluster computing, grid computing does not require close coupling among the computers and is fault tolerant for systems coming on- and offline. The name *grid* was chosen deliberately, to make users think of the power grid: You plug in and use electricity—or in this case, computer resources—when you need them and unplug when you do not.

Grid computing—originally a general approach to distributed computing rather than a set of specific protocols—developed independently of XML networking, but emerging grid specifications, such as OGSA (Open Grid Services Architecture) and the Open Grid Services

Infrastructure [OGSI] propose a standard, open grid infrastructure built on top of SOAP and Web Services. Grid supporters believe that the loose coupling and cross-platform abilities of XML will more than compensate for the extra overhead of sending text over HTTP connections.

The most popular grid software—the open-source *Globus Toolkit* (http://www-unix.globus.org/toolkit/)—has already added support for OGSI and OGSA, so the transition to SOAP and Web Services will likely be a success. Grid computing originated in the academic and research communities, but as it migrates to XML networking, it has gained enthusiastic backing from IBM and Oracle. It is not yet clear that grid computing can be as successful commercially as it has been inside the universities and research institutes, but it does offer another interesting case study of how people can build complex and powerful systems on top of something as simple as XML and HTTP.

5.3.5 Syndication

Syndication, or publish/subscribe, is an entirely different kind of XML networking. It is fair to argue that grid computing and Web Services are usually nothing more than fancy ways of using remote procedure calls: A client calls a procedure and receives a return value. Syndication involves a different kind of communication: A client, called a *subscriber*, registers with a server, called a *publisher*, to open up an information channel. Whenever new information becomes available, the publisher sends, or *syndicates*, a copy of it to all registered subscribers. The differences are fundamental: RPC is generally synchronous, unicast communication, whereas syndication is generally asynchronous, multicast communication; RPC uses a pull model—the client says "Send me this information"—whereas syndication uses a push model—the server says "Here is some more information for you."

Obviously, both the RPC and syndication approaches are useful for different kinds of information and different contexts. RPC allows the client to request exactly the information it needs from the server, exactly when it needs it; syndication requires the client to accept a continual stream of information that it might or might not need, whenever the server happens to be ready to send it. One classic example for electronic information is the stock quote, and it might be useful to look at how both an RPC and a syndication environment might handle that.

In an RPC environment, such as Web Services, the client typically sends an RPC request whenever it wants to get the current stock price, as shown in Figure 5-2. The server then returns the current price of the stock, either as a simple number or as a data structure containing other information, such as currency and the date and time of the quote. Every client that needs the

Figure 5-2 Stock quotes using RPC

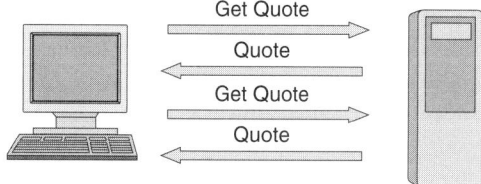

Figure 5-3 Stock quotes, using syndication

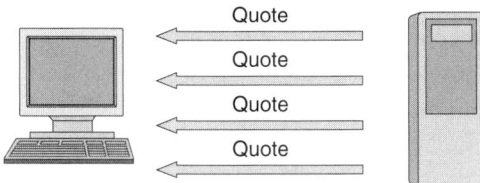

information must open a separate connection to the server, and the server must deal with each request individually, but there is no unnecessary noise: The server sends out information *only* when a client needs it.

In a syndication environment, the subscriber registers once to receive information on the price of the stock MSFT. After that, the publisher sends price information to the server, unrequested, whenever that information is ready for release, possibly every hour, every minute, or hundreds of times every second, depending on the application, as shown in Figure 5-3. At the same time, the publisher's server sends out identical information to every other subscriber that had registered to receive it. The server does not need to manage separate requests from every client, but there is the potential for noise, as every client will not necessarily need to receive every piece of information every time the server sends it.

For financial-planning software, such as a spreadsheet, the RPC model might make the most sense: The software can make a single RPC call to update a stock price at start-up time or when the user requests an update. For a real-time stock ticker or trading software, the syndication model might make more sense: In that case, the software needs to know as soon as possible whenever the stock's price changes.

Many types of information fit easily and naturally into one approach or the other. News, for example, is an obvious candidate for syndication, as publishers need to send out new stories as soon as they become available. Weather bulletins, FAA Notices to Airmen (such as temporary flight restrictions), FBI security alerts, requests for proposals on contracts, virus alerts, and other similar information also fits most naturally into a syndication model. Online purchasing is an obvious candidate for RPC, as buying and selling is usually a one-to-one transaction. Similarly, anything with a side effect, such as bidding on an auction, configuring a Web site, or approving a system design, probably belongs in RPC.

In some cases, however, the fit is not so clear. Consider the sales figures for a division of a large company, for example: Should a client at the head office request the information when necessary, using an RPC-based system, such as Web Services, or should the division syndicate its figures at the close of business every day, possibly to several places within the company? Inventory reports present the same problem: Should a supplier syndicate hourly inventory reports to its customer or instead wait and provide information only when the customer requests it? The answers to both questions will likely vary from system to system, and rules of thumb will emerge once people gain some experience with the two kinds of information sharing.

Here, then, are the two key characteristics of syndication:

1. The publisher initiates the transfer.
2. The publisher sends the same information to multiple subscribers at more or less the same time.

Note that these are conceptual characteristics, not implementation descriptions. The implementation may have the subscriber running a process listening for new information all the time or may have the subscriber polling the publisher periodically to see whether new information is available.

RSS [RSS], the most widely used Internet syndication specification in the world and arguably the most successful XML-based specification of any type, uses polling: Clients, called *feed readers,* or *feed aggregators,* periodically read an XML-based master listing from each publisher to see whether any new information is available. This approach is especially suitable for use by consumers, who are able to tolerate some delay—for example, if they poll every 60 minutes, their news may be up to 60 minutes late—and often have systems that are behind firewalls or do not have permanent network connections.

The news industry, on the other hand, is standardizing on NewsML [NEWSML], which involves pushing an XML file describing each news package out to subscribers. This approach is especially suitable for media companies and other corporate environments, where dedicated computers can be available around the clock to receive new information as soon as the publisher sends it, and a delay of even a minute can be costly.

Another syndication specification, the Information and Content Exchange [ICE], has existed for a few years without finding many supporters. Unlike other syndication standards, ICE is designed not only for delivering information but also for managing subscriptions: subscribing, canceling, looking up catalogs, and so on. ICE or something like it may yet find a niche, as neither of the major syndication specifications includes subscription-management features.

To date, XML-based syndication exists mainly in the Web log community and the news industry, but people may soon find new and creative uses. In many situations, pushing information out to many users is better than the one-to-one connections of Web Services: After all, in the media world, the broadcast television networks still exist years after the arrival of video on demand.

5.3.6 Other Styles

Business-to-business (B2B) networking predates XML; the most common type of B2B networking is electronic data interchange (EDI), used mainly in supply chains. Businesses use EDI to exchange *business documents,* such as purchase orders, price updates, invoices, and requests for quotation: documents that would otherwise be exchanged on paper and then reentered manually at each end. EDI tends to be expensive to implement, and systems are rarely compatible, so EDI communities usually cluster around large companies, such as automobile manufacturers or retailers, so that all the suppliers can implement exactly the same EDI variant that their major customer uses. EDI has not been as effective in more complex relationships between, say,

5.3 XML Networking Styles

multiple suppliers and purchasers, because of the incompatibilities that arise. That means that a supplier with more than one major customer may have to implement and support several parallel EDI systems.

As soon as XML appeared in the late 1990s, people became interested in replacing EDI with some kind of XML for B2B data interchange, hoping to simplify implementations, eliminate incompatibilities, and reduce costs. For example, hundreds of companies belong to RosettaNet [ROSETTANET], a consortium that develops data dictionaries and specifications for business processes and XML-based business messages.

An even more ambitious B2B initiative is ebXML [EBXML] from OASIS and UN/EDIFACT [UN-EDIFACT]. The second sponsor, UN/EDIFACT, also produces the closest thing to an EDI standard, but its creators intend ebXML to do far more than simply replace EDI implementations with XML; instead, they are attempting to automate commerce entirely. In the ebXML vision, company A's computer will go to a registry and look up company B, then retrieve company B's *collaboration protocol profile* from a repository. The collaboration protocol profile contains all the information that company A's computer needs to know to do business with company B:

- What company B offers
- Company B's standard business scenarios, or patterns of doing business
- Company B's supported service interfaces, documentation formats, and technical requirements, such as security

Company A's computer can read and understand this XML-encoded information automatically. If one of the standard business scenarios is appropriate, it can set up a collaboration with company B automatically and start exchanging business documents, placing orders, issuing invoices, and so on.

RosettaNet is an attempt to streamline what people are already doing with EDI; ebXML is an attempt to automate white-collar areas of business, such as procurement, accounts payable/receivable, and even sales, in the same way that machinery automated blue-collar areas, such as shop floors, over the past 200 years. Both of these initiatives started before Web Services began to attract so much attention, but over the past few years, both have made adjustments to accommodate Web Services—and each other—rather than attempt to fight a hopeless battle. RosettaNet and ebXML now both position themselves as ways of *using* Web Services, and OASIS and RosettaNet have been collaborating to start eliminating duplication and make their specifications work together. Unfortunately, this is largely a one-sided exchange: The Web Services groups, being the large gorillas in the relationship, are not reluctant to issue new specifications that encroach on the work of ebXML and RosettaNet.

It is far too early to say whether grand visions, such as RosettaNet and, especially, ebXML, will succeed: The business world is still struggling even with the basic plumbing of Web Services. Nevertheless, once the lower levels of XML networking begin to settle down and companies and organizations have gained implementation experience, successful higher-level specifications of some kind will begin to emerge.

5.4 Special Topics

This section takes brief looks at two special, technical topics related to XML networking: layering models, and switching and routing.

5.4.1 Layering

Successful networking standards, such as TCP/IP or HTTP, create a clean separation between protocol and content. *Protocol* is how information moves; *content* is what information gets moved. In fact, networking engineers often go much farther than that, dividing the networking side itself into multiple layers. The four-layer U.S. Department of Defense (DoD) model is an accurate description of how the Internet works. That model did not catch on, however, perhaps because many telecom and networking companies were dragged kicking and screaming to TCP/IP during the 1990s, and their engineers brought their old way of thinking with them. The four layers in the DoD network model are:

1. Network access: Ethernet, WiFi, and so on
2. Internet: IP
3. Host-to-host: TCP, UDP
4. Process: TELNET, FTP, HTTP, SMTP

Unfortunately, referring to HTTP as "layer 4" would draw nothing but confused stares from networking people, who prefer to work with a model that was never seriously implemented rather than the one that succeeded.

A much more elaborate model is the *Open Systems Interconnection* [OSI] model, which divides networking into seven layers, each one more abstract than the one before it:

1. The physical layer: cables, connectors, and hubs
2. The data link layer: Ethernet
3. The network layer: IP
4. The transport layer: TCP
5. The session layer, usually handled higher up
6. The presentation layer, not usually independent
7. The application layer: HTTP

OSI itself was a set of networking standards that never caught on; ironically, however, although the layers in its model are not a perfect match for the much simpler Internet, the model has lodged itself in people's heads, to the point that networking specialists talk about a "layer-4 switch" or a "layer-7 problem" quite casually. Beyond layer 7 of the OSI model comes whatever

5.4 Special Topics

happens on the application side, such as displaying a Web page in a browser, processing a purchase order,[7] displaying headlines in a blog reader, or playing an MP3 music clip.

Because the networking layers are independent, it is easy to innovate: When you convert your home LAN from Ethernet to WiFi, you do not have to change your computer's network card or install a new browser. Layers 3 and above remain unchanged. At the beginning of the 1990s, introducing HTTP beside existing layer-7 protocols, such as FTP, did not require replacing the TCP/IP Internet with something new, as the lower layers, especially TCP/IP and beneath, do not care what happens at layer 7.

The separation of content from protocol is just as clean as the separation of protocols: People routinely use protocols to move types of content that were invented long after the protocol was designed. For example, in the early years of the Web, when HTTP servers were not yet widely deployed, many Web sites used FTP to deliver their Web pages. Introducing a new type of content, such as XML, does not require changing any of an organization's—or the world's—networking infrastructure.

In that case, why bother with this chapter, when existing network protocols can handle XML as easily as any other content type? First, manufacturers do not always implement the various network protocol layers independently. When a network device, such as a router, knows what kind of content a set of packets represents, it can perform various types of optimizations to move network traffic more efficiently. As a result, it is often useful for a layer-4 router to peek into its packets and figure out whether it is routing, say, e-mail or an HTML page. This behavior is purely an optimization: These devices can handle any kind of content, but by cheating and peeking through the interlayer barrier, they can improve how they handle certain popular kinds of traffic. If some day there is a high volume of XML traffic on networks, it is inevitable that network software and hardware will look at the XML to make routing decisions (see Section 5.4.2).

Next, networking protocols themselves are adding more and more content of their own. A layer-3 IPV4 datagram can hold 20 bytes of data[8] in a few fixed-length fields, 8 bytes of which are taken up just by the sender and receiver IP addresses. In contrast, by the time you move to layer 7, an HTTP packet can contain an arbitrarily long list of plaintext headers. Listing 5-16 shows a basic HTTP 1.1 GET header—to request a Web page—but applications can add any name: value fields they need, as long as they fit on a single line and use only a basic set of ASCII characters.

Listing 5-16   Simple HTTP GET Header
```
GET /foo.html HTTP/1.1
Host: localhost:8080
Accept: text/xml,application/xml,application/xhtml+xml,\
  text/html;q=0.9,text/plain;q=0.8,image/png,image/jpeg,image/gif;\
  q=0.2,*/*;q=0.1
```

---

[7] The purchase order is probably the most painfully overused example in XML networking discussions.

[8] There is a way to add additional information to an IPV4 datagram, but it is not in common use.

```
Accept-Language: en,fr;q=0.8,de;q=0.6,es;q=0.4,it;q=0.2
Accept-Encoding: gzip,deflate
Accept-Charset: ISO-8859-1,utf-8;q=0.7,*;q=0.7
Keep-Alive: 300
Connection: keep-alive
```

People use HTTP headers to add hints for routers, to manage load balancing, and even to direct business information inside an organization. For example, censorship software might add a header `X-Content-Rating: mature` to flag the content in an HTTP packet as inappropriate for younger users. It is inevitable that people would eventually want to add more information to networking protocols than they could conveniently fit in an HTTP header, and this is the second place where XML and networking meet: Using XML as *part of* a networking protocol rather than simply as the content payload can allow allow for much more sophisticated kinds of networking.

It would be possible to invent an entirely new layer-7 networking protocol that used XML natively, but because HTTP is so common and is allowed through most company firewalls, people tend to define new networking protocols as a layer above HTTP, creating what some people call *layer-8* protocols, as if the seven OSI layers were not already too many. Essentially, the XML protocol information is the direct content of the HTTP packet, and then the XML protocol information either contains or refers to the actual content.

5.4.2 Switching and Routing

Since the crash that followed the 1990s Internet and fiber-optic booms, the surviving networking and telecommunication companies have become increasingly interested in XML. Although most people working with XML networking are concerned with the end points—the client and the server, or the publisher and the subscriber—these companies are concerned with the infrastructure in between: How can major organizations and carriers implement and manage large, complex XML-driven networks? How can they perform computationally intensive tasks, such as encryption, validation, and transformation, at line speed?

As a part of this work, some companies and researchers are exploring XML-based switching.[9] Regular TCP/IP networking involves sending information directly from one host to another, based on network addresses. For example, a system might send a SOAP request to `rpc.megginson.com` via HTTP. With content-based switching, networking hardware decides where to send information, based on the information itself. For example, all purchase orders for shoes might go to the clothing department, whereas all invoices might go to accounts payable.

A significant advantage of this approach is that outsiders do not need to know information about the internal network of an organization. For example, people can send information of any kind to `acme.com` without worrying about what department or person should handle it; a content-switched network will send it to the right place automatically.

---

[9] For an overview of work in the field, see the papers describing the YFilter (http://www.cs.berkeley.edu/~franklin/Papers/yfilterDEBull03.pdf) and XTrie (http://www.bell-labs.com/user/minos/Papers/icde02-cam.pdf) algorithms.

Large organizations are already doing this kind of switching—XML-based or otherwise—using metadata hidden in custom HTTP headers, but the approach is awkward, as it relies on the sender's generating and inserting the correct headers *in addition to* the main content. Examining the content eliminates the problem of mislabeling and eliminates the need for special arrangements with people sending the information.

Most of the researchers and organizations working with content switching have settled on the XPath [XPATH] language for specifying patterns in content. For example, a particular department wanting to handle all purchase orders coming from ACME would register an XPath expression, such as `/purchase-order//supplier[text()="ACME"]`, with the content-based network. A similar approach might work for publish/subscribe; thousands of subscribers might register to receive any information that matches certain XPath expressions, such as `//stock[@ticker="MSFT"]`.

An approach like this has obvious advantages and disadvantages. The advantage is flexibility: Companies are free to reorganize their internal networks and even management structures without affecting communication with the outside world. The disadvantage is inefficiency: Compared to switching and routing IP packets, processing XML content is not fast, even in hardware, so a certain loss of speed will be inevitable. Whether XML content switching succeeds or fails, it makes an interesting case study of how XML networking innovation can develop without the assistance or interference of standards writers.

5.5 Final Words on XML Networking

At the time of writing, XML networking is hot, attracting not only attention but also major investment from the largest software and networking companies on the business side, the major news providers on the media side, and many millions of enthusiastic bloggers on the user side. Each of these groups, however, is doing something fundamentally different.

- The software and networking vendors are trying to build a complex distributed-computing and messaging network for automating business processes now done by people.
- The media companies are trying to replace their outdated wire services with channels for providing better content more quickly to news outlets and other subscribers.
- The bloggers are trying to find the simplest way possible to share information with one another directly, without having to go through large businesses or media outlets.

The major difference is how these parties approach complexity. The companies and organizations prototyping with Web Services, ebXML, RosettaNet, and other business initiatives emphasize completeness over simplicity: They will almost always accept increased complexity in return for more features or more complete coverage. The Web log community takes exactly the opposite approach, emphasizing simplicity over completeness, and will usually reject more features if they add to overall complexity. The media people fall somewhere in the middle: They already have decades of experience with helping their customers to deal with their news feeds, and they try, not always successfully, to strike a balance between offering features and keeping things simple.

These areas are not in direct competition, but it is worth asking which approach is likely to be most successful. Previous approaches to distributed networking that aimed for completeness rather than simplicity—CORBA springs immediately to mind—failed to find widespread implementation and eventually drowned in their own seas of specifications, so there is a very strong risk that the Web Services people have failed to learn history's lesson.

Even if the excessive complexity of Web Services and, possibly, grid computing, ultimately leads to failure, however, can excessive simplicity win? While the mind-numbingly simple RSS specifications have clearly succeeded in the syndication world, XML-RPC has not gained widespread implementation in the RPC world, despite its own simplicity. Perhaps the ultimately successful XML-based RPC or asynchronous messaging specification is still to come.

PART THREE

Special Issues

This final part of the book examines special decision and implementation issues that cross over the document/data/networking dividing lines described in Part Two. The problems and techniques described here are part of the toolkit of any experienced XML specialist.

Chapter 6 examines one of the main justifications for XML: the ability to perform intelligent searches of data and documents. The chapter discusses how useful—and how difficult—XML searching is, as well as various design and implementation strategies to make it work.

Chapter 7 looks at what happens when XML runs into the real world, with its thousands of legacy data formats and protocols. Moving information into XML from less structured legacy formats is difficult, but XML can also be part of the solution, serving as a facade to make older information more accessible and manageable.

Chapter 8 confronts XML's hidden weak spot: performance. XML-based systems can be slow to the point of uselessness, but they do not have to be. The problems are often hidden in libraries, toolkits, and popular methodologies that add multiple layers of inefficiencies to the simple XML processing model. In short, Chapter 8 shows how to speed up XML.

CHAPTER 6

XML Searching

Search engines turned out to be one of the few successful businesses on the Web: Millions of people visit search sites, such as Google, every day, often using them as the starting point for their Web browsing, and those visits bring in advertising revenue for the search engines' providers. As search engines have become faster and more accurate, it is possible to argue that they have become the hub of the Web.

XML and its predecessor, SGML, were designed with searching in mind, long before search became the hottest thing online. For all their sophistication, Web search engines are still mainly *full-text* engines: They search for strings of characters. XML markup, on the other hand, can identify precisely whether a word is a part name, a stock ticker symbol, or a geographical area; can specify the currency used for prices and the language used for individual words; and can distinguish book and movie titles from regular text, personal names from common nouns, and part numbers from telephone numbers. If search engines can take advantage of all this contextual information, they will manage more sophisticated searches and return more accurate results.

Is all this possible, though, or even desirable? This chapter looks in detail at the technical and business issues involved in searching and querying XML-encoded information, starting with an overview of its disadvantages and advantages.

6.1 The Advantages of XML Searching

XML markup makes searching smarter by adding contextual information and makes it possible to correlate information from more than one document. Any serious Internet user is familiar with searches that do not work: The words are too common or have too many different meanings for any search engine to return useful results, or perhaps the information is spread among several pages. Solving these problems was one of the initial goals of XML's creators.

6.1.1 Context

Much of the time, full-text search engines do a good job, but they sometimes fall flat. Consider, for example, the difference between *Bush* the U.S. president and *bush* the shrub, or *Washington* the U.S. state and *Washington* the U.S. city. If you were trying to find information on bush pilots flying out of Washington State, you might try the search "bush pilot washington." In late 2003, Google's first ten results were as follows:

1. A site selling a book about a Canadian bush pilot (no connection to Washington)
2. Two newspaper stories about the U.S. Navy naming an aircraft carrier after President Bush Sr.
3. A 2002 *USA Today* story about a small plane violating airspace near President Bush Jr.
4. A 2000 *Washington Post* story about President Bush Jr.'s service in the Texas Air National Guard
5. A 2001 *Pravda* story critical of President Bush after the midair collision between a Chinese fighter jet and a U.S. surveillance plane
6. The Amazon.com page for a biography of an Alaskan bush pilot, published by University of Washington Press
7. Two pages from *FlyRod & Reel* magazine: one stating that it has no listings for Washington and another listing angling retailers in the state
8. A 2003 news story from the *Washington Times* about a U.S. Navy pilot being held by the Iraqi government

I choose Google for this example precisely because it is a very good full-text search engine: It infers the relevance of information on a Web page not only from the text on the page but also from the other pages that link to it, the pages that link to those pages, and so on. With this difficult example, the first slightly relevant result is the twenty-third, which mentions a bush pilot who did fly once in Washington State; after that, the matches revert mainly to politics.

An experienced search-engine user could work around the problem by adding more words to the query. For example, bush pilots in Washington State have to deal with a lot of mountains, and the query string "bush pilot washington mountains" returns fewer political hits. Even better, a search string that contains specific aircraft types used in bush plane flying, such as "bush pilot washington cessna 180" returns almost all relevant matches. Most of the population is not that adept with search-engine query strings, however, and would likely give up on the whole thing; furthermore, these more specific queries would miss pages that do not happen to mention mountains or Cessna 180 airplanes.

Although homographs, such as *Bush* and *bush* can make full-text searches difficult, an even trickier problem comes when the search results depend more on context than on the individual words. For example, consider trying to find Web pages that discuss the history of the word *sex*, without hitting thousands of pornography sites. Unless the decades-old dream of full machine artificial intelligence finally shakes off its dust and comes true, these are searches that will continue to flummox traditional full-text search engines.

As long as artificial intelligence remains a distant dream, we need to concentrate on getting plain old human intelligence into our XML documents, and that is precisely what XML-based markup languages do. The following News Industry Text Format [NITF] fragment shows how news providers can tag articles to avoid confusing search engines.

```
<p>Today in <location><city>Seattle</city>,
<state>Washington</state></location>, <person>President
Bush</person> opened a new museum.</p>
```

6.1 The Advantages of XML Searching

The markup represents added human intelligence from the news reporter or editor: *Washington* represents a state, not a city, and *Bush* represents a person, not a shrub. The XML document contains not only the news story itself but also what the author knew about the news story. As this information survives all the way to the final document, search engines require no special artificial intelligence to use it.

Similarly, several markup languages, including DocBook [DOCBOOK] and the Text Encoding Initiative [TEI] define markup for talking about the history of words. Following is a DocBook example:

```
<para>The word <wordasword>sex</wordasword> has gradually come
to mean not only gender, but the physical act of procreation, and,
eventually, all physically-intimate acts.</para>
```

The `wordasword` element makes it clear that this paragraph discusses the word *sex* rather than the act: A search engine could easily pick out this contextual information to return exactly the pages the user wanted.

XML markup is information that a document's creator knew but could not put in the main text. Because this information is available, search tools could potentially use it to return far more accurate results.

6.1.2 Correlation

In addition to basic context, XML markup also makes it possible to correlate information, matching instances of the same thing described in different ways and converting among different representations. To start with a simple example, consider only a few of the many ways documents might refer to British Prime Minister Tony Blair:

- Tony Blair
- Prime Minister Blair
- the British Prime Minister
- the prime minister
- the P.M.
- Mr. Blair
- Blair

Given this variety, searching for information about Prime Minister Blair is difficult, and the work is made even worse by the fact that many of these phrases can apply to other people: for example, in a different context, "the prime minister" could refer to the prime minister of Australia, Canada, India, or many other countries.

How is it possible to define a Web in which people can easily search for information about Prime Minister Blair no matter how he is described? One possibility is always to normalize the name when it appears; unfortunately, if people are forced always to write "British Prime Minister

Tony Blair," text will become awkward and unnatural, and even that might not be sufficient if another person named "Tony Blair" became British prime minister in the future.[1]

Using XML markup, however, it is a simple matter to attach a unique identifier to every location that mentions Prime Minister Blair. As long as the identifier is well known, search engines can look for it rather than for the text it contains, as shown by the following markup fragments:

```
<person ident="ps10563blair">Tony Blair</person>

<person ident="ps10563blair">Prime Minister Blair</person>

<person ident="ps10563blair">the British Prime Minister</person>

<person ident="ps10563blair">the Prime Minister</person>

<person ident="ps10563blair">the P.M.</person>

<person ident="ps10563blair">Mr. Blair</person>

<person ident="ps10563blair">Blair</person>
```

If in the future, another person shared the same name and title, that person would have a different identifier, so search engines would not return false hits.

Most things in the world—people, concepts, historical periods, and so on—do not yet have standard, universally accepted identifiers, so this is more than a markup problem. However, many identification schemes do exist, such as stock market symbols; publication identifiers, such as ISBNs; social security numbers, phone numbers, postal codes, and country, language, and currency codes. The following example shows the use of a stock ticker symbol for identifying a company:

```
<p>Today, <company symbol="NASDAQ.MSFT">Microsoft</company>
announced a new software strategy.</p>
```

Even limiting searching to current widely accepted identifiers, XML markup can make it significantly easier to correlate information described in various ways.

Now, consider a more difficult problem than simple identification: a search for world government spending programs that cost more than USD 1 billion. This kind of a search is far beyond the capabilities of current full-text search engines, but XML markup can add hints to help future search engines do the work. The following example uses News Industry Text Format [NITF] markup once again:

```
<p>Today, Congress approved an additional <money unit="USD">3
billion</money> in education spending.</p>
```

---

[1] This risk is not far fetched: Consider the phrase "U.S. President George Bush."

The `money` element makes it clear that this article is referring to "3 billion" in currency, and the `unit` attribute indicates that the currency is U.S. dollars, using a code from the ISO 4217 standard for identifying world currencies [ISO-4217]. A search engine would still use full-text searching algorithms to determine that the article dealt with government spending, but then the tagging would help it determine the amount. Even more interestingly, the `money` element adds enough intelligence that the search engine could return correct results for pages using entirely different currencies; at the time of writing, the money in the next example is less than USD 1 billion, so it should not return a hit:

```
<p>The Canadian federal government committed an additional <money
unit="CAD">1.1 billion</money> in health-care spending.</p>
```

Automatic currency conversion during searching—based on intelligent tagging like this—could be especially useful for financial institutions and others mining large international document repositories for information. Many other types of conversion and substitution are also possible with markup, including dates and times, language conversion and recognition of synonyms, subsets, and supersets. (For example, a search for information about New England should return pages that mention Vermont.)

Obviously, a lot of infrastructure is required before search engines can work like this. But it does provide an intriguing view of a future that markup might help to enable, where people and programs can search for and find the precise information they need, relying on intelligence encoded in XML markup.

6.2 The Disadvantages of XML Searching

Despite the optimistic view of many people in the XML community, the XML searching problem is complicated, from both technical and business perspectives. In some situations, XML-based contextual searching can be a major advantage; in others, it can be an unnecessary cost; in yet others, it can make the search engine's results worse. This section introduces some of the problems with the very idea of XML-based searching.

- XML searching may be too complex for most users.
- Documents on the Web can use deceptive markup to raise their ranking in a search.
- XML documents are generally not interoperable in the same search environment, because of all the different, incompatible vocabularies.

6.2.1 Usability

Tim Bray, cofounder of Open Text, which ran an early Web search engine, and coauthor of the original XML specification [XML], wrote the following passage in a Web log (http://www.tbray.org/ongoing/When/200x/2003/06/17/SearchUsers):

> Nobody Uses Advanced Search . . .
>
> Every search engine has an "advanced search" screen, and nobody (quantitatively, less than 0.5% of users) ever goes there. This drove us nuts back at Open Text, because our engine was very structurally savvy and could do compound/boolean queries that look like what today we'd call XPath. But nobody used it.
>> What most people want is to have a nice simple field into which they will type on average 1.3 words and hit Enter, and have the result come back to them. So anyone who's building search needs to focus almost all their energy on doing an as-good-as-possible job given those 1.3 words and no other inputs.

This observation does not bode well for XML searching. If users are unwilling to use even relatively simple full-text techniques, such as Boolean or proximity searches, how much hope is there that they will be willing to formulate the complex queries that can take advantage of XML markup? Fortunately for the future of XML searching, Bray does go on to qualify that observation:

> . . . Except the People who Do
>
> Of course, the people who do use Advanced Search are your most fanatical users, the professional librarians, spooks, and private investigators. And the ones who will do what it takes to find out everything about research on the rare disease their child just got diagnosed with. These people tend to be loud-mouthed and aggressive and will get in your face if you don't have advanced search or it's not real good.

Presumably, these same kinds of people would be the ones using XML context in their searches. Others of Bray's "fanatical users" might be academics preparing papers, journalists researching news stories, and software agents collecting and amalgamating information for politicians and managers. This last example, in fact, may point to the real potential users of XML searching: not people but software. People other than governors and CEOs need to make decisions in their own lives, from changing jobs to buying new clothes, and software agents that find information for people—say, for price comparison—could benefit greatly from the extra information provided by XML markup, assuming, of course, that vendors were willing to encode their pricing information in a standard format and accept the transparency that comes with that.

And that leads to another usability problem: XML searching requires people or software to know a *lot* about the structure of the documents they're searching. If all XML documents shared a single, global vocabulary, searching would be relatively straightforward, at least for power users: Every price would appear inside a `price` element, every bar code would appear inside a `upc` element, every person's name would appear inside a `person` element, and so on. This is unlikely ever to happen, for two reasons:

1. No single, accepted authority could impose a common vocabulary on all users.
2. XML documents can encode a potentially infinite variety of information, so a common vocabulary would always be incomplete.

6.2 The Disadvantages of XML Searching

Some XML-related specifications are designed to work around these problems, at least partly—see Section 6.3.3 for more information—but in reality, if a large amount of XML markup did appear on the Web today, generalized XML searching would be almost useless, given the hundreds of incompatible XML-based vocabularies. The best people can hope for is specialized searching inside repositories or across Web collections in which all XML documents share a common type: Conceptually, this is the equivalent of a site search engine rather than a Web search engine, and it falls far short of a revolution in Web searching. Even then, searching will be more complex than the most difficult "advanced search" page currently available on full-text Web search engines. Either users will have to become experts in XML structure, or they will have to limit themselves to a few precooked searches, such as "Search for a person" or "Search for a part number," through Web sites that can construct an XML query for them.

In the end, XML searching may be useful for specific project applications. But usability issues alone make it seem unlikely that XML will ever cause the social revolution in Web searching that some supporters hoped for when the specification first appeared.

6.2.2 Trust

HTML already supports adding some information to Web pages to improve search results, using the HTML `meta` element. Listing 6-1 contains a header for a hypothetical HTML page describing bush planes in Washington:

Listing 6-1   HTML `meta` Element
```
<head>
  <title>Flying in the mountains</title>
  <meta name="description" content="Bushplane flying in the Cascades
    during the 1950s and 1960s"/>
  <meta name="keywords" content="washington state aviation bushplane
    bush pilot"/>
</head>
```

A regular Web search engine could use this information to return much more useful results for the sample "bush pilot washington" query from Section 6.1.1. In fact, the entire tag set from the Dublin Core Metadata Initiative [DUBLIN-CORE] is available for use in HTML `meta` elements (this example omits `title`, as it is redundant with the HTML `title` element. Listing 6-2 contains a selection of Dublin Core elements in an HTML page header.

Listing 6-2   Dublin Core in HTML `meta` Elements
```
<head>
  <title>Flying in the mountains</title>
  <meta name="DC.creator" content="One-armed Joe Conner"/>
  <meta name="DC.subject" content="aviation"/>
  <meta name="DC.description" content="Bushplane flying in the
    Cascades during the 1950s and 1960s"/>
  <meta name="DC.publisher" content="Bush Flying Enthusiast Club"/>
```

```
<meta name="DC.contributor" content="Jane Scudrunner"/>
<meta name="DC.date" content="1999-01-15"/>
<meta name="DC.type" content="http://purl.org/dc/dcmitype/Text"/>
<meta name="DC.format" content="text/html"/>
<meta name="DC.language" content="en-US"/>
<meta name="DC.rights" content="Copyright (c) 1999 by the Bush
  Flying Enthusiast Club"/>
</head>
```

This functionality has been available for many years. Some Web search engines will make limited use of the non-Dublin Core `description` and `keywords meta` elements, but over time, they have learned to give even those very little weight. At the time of writing, no leading search engines support the Dublin Core element set.

This omission seems curious at first. Competition in the search-engine market is fierce, and the main competitive advantage is to return more accurate results. Surely, using this kind of metadata from Web pages could improve search results significantly.

The problem with this approach is that a large number of Web pages, quite simply, lie. In the late 1990s, when search engines did give some weight to the `keywords meta` element, many sites—especially those pushing pornography, financial scams, or other borderline products and services—would deliberately add misleading keywords to ensure that their sites appeared near the top of search-engine rankings, even if the site had little to do with the search. In fact, even mainstream companies paid specialists—and still do—to help them get higher search rankings.

As a result, search engine developers have learned to mistrust self-proclamations, such as keywords, and to focus more on external evidence. Most famously, Google weights search results based on how many other relevant Web sites link to a page, but even there, people are continually trying to find ways to abuse the system, such as putting up farms of bogus Web pages linking to other pages or adding links to Wiki sandboxes.

So where does that leave XML markup for searching on the Web? If Web search engines today cannot trust simple HTML `meta` elements to provide honest information about resources, how will XML search engines of the future be able to trust much more elaborate XML markup? Surely, there will still be a strong incentive to cheat and deceive. Search metadata and markup have had some success inside closed environments, such as universities, corporations, and governmental organizations, in which the incentives to cheat are lower, and it is possible to weed out and eliminate cheaters. On the Web, where the incentives to cheat are high and there is no effective way to police information publishers, lack of trust may destroy the usefulness of XML searching even if no technical problems get in the way.

6.2.3 Interoperability

People have proposed hundreds of vocabularies based on XML, and they are nearly all incompatible with one another. Consider again the markup used by a few popular XML document types to refer to the title of a book, movie, or similar resource, repeated from Chapter 1:

Document Type	Markup
XHTML	`cite`
DocBook	`citetitle`
NITF	`object.title`
TEI	`title`
Dublin Core	`Title`

Even more confusingly, some document types use the same element name for different purposes. In TEI, `title` refers to the title of something the text is referring to, such as *Gone with the Wind;* in DocBook, `title` refers to the heading of a chapter, section, or other division in a text; in XHTML, `title` is text to be displayed at the top of a browser window or in a list of search results. Of course, there are hundreds of other document types, with more appearing all the time, and future XML-based document types could arbitrarily assign an element name for a title, such as `título` or `n3`. If there were hundreds of millions of XML documents on the Web, how could anyone do a smart search for the word *wind* in a title, for example? See Section 6.3.3 for some partial solutions to this problem.

6.3 Markup Considerations

Markup can be added to a document for many reasons besides searching. For example, markup can provide targets for cross-references, information on data typing, ranges where formatting can be applied, and so on. This section, however, deals specifically with the use of XML markup to enable more intelligent searching, leaving aside other issues.

When using XML markup to add information for searching, the main choice is between searching *in-line markup* or *external metadata*. Both approaches have their advantages.

- In-line markup makes it easy to identify a precise location inside a resource.
- External metadata does not require converting all information to XML and works with both text and binary data, such as video or audio.

This section also looks at the roles of XML schemas and namespaces in searching, as they can provide extra annotation on top of regular XML markup.

6.3.1 In-Line Markup

XML promises the ability to add intelligence to documents, making searching easier and more effective. That intelligence comes mainly in the form of *in-line markup*: The tags and attributes add structure and descriptive information to the flat text. Every piece of markup is like a tiny note, an extra bit of information to let a machine or a person understand the text better. In that respect, the XML markup is similar to marginal notes in a book or to a director's commentary on a DVD. Following is a paragraph with a lot of in-line markup:

```
<p><chron norm="2004-01-12">Today</chron>, <person
gender="female">Jane Smith</person> announced that <org>ACME
Widgets</org> will be relocating its head office to <location>
<city>Albany</city>, <state>New York</state></location>.</p>
```

This paragraph contains a lot of information beyond the straight text: The markup makes it explicit that *today* means January 12, 2004; that *Jane Smith* is a female person; that *ACME Widgets* is an organization; that *Albany* is a city; that *New York* is a state; and that "Albany, New York" together describe a location. A search engine that used XML markup could take advantage of all this information to return more precise search results.

All this leads to a compelling vision of a future Web, where search engines can use extra intelligence added to XML documents to refine and improve search results, so that people can find the information they're looking for quickly and easily. Unfortunately, in-line markup also has its limitations for searching.

First, indexing and retrieving information from in-line markup requires parsing an entire document. Not only can that be a time-consuming process, especially if many documents change frequently, but also it involves issues of security and intellectual property. Many document publishers want to make their documents available to be indexed by search engines but do not want to publish them to the world at large: For example, an investing site might want public search engines to return hits for its articles but limit full access to paid-up members. Furthermore, making extra intelligence available in the document makes it easier for others to steal that intelligence and remarket it without permission from the original information provider.

Second, in-line markup needs to be standardized—and its content needs to be normalized—for searching to work properly. If one document uses `person` to tag a person's name and a second document uses `name`, how will search engines be able to work out which is which? (See Section 6.2.3 for further discussion.)

Third, in-line markup works naturally only for one-to-one relationships: It is awkward to tag the same kind of information in two different ways in an XML document, but information often exists in more than one real-world context. For example, the same thing can be both a book title and a product for sale, so either of the following XML fragments could make sense:

```
<p>In <booktitle>The Two Towers</booktitle> ...</p>
```

```
<p>In <productname>The Two Towers</productname> ...</p>
```

People have contrived various ways to work around this kind of problem. One possibility is to nest the elements:

```
<p>In <productname><booktitle>The Two
Towers</booktitle></productname>...</p>
```

6.3 Markup Considerations

However, that approach can get increasingly complex—and lead to complex DTDs and schemas—as the layers get deeper. The second alternative is to move all but one of the classification hierarchies from the element name to attributes:

```
<p>In <productname type="booktitle">The Two Towers</productname>
   ...</p>
```

Again, this approach can get fairly complex with multiple layers of markup.

Fourth, in-line markup requires that information be in an XML format: New information needs to be created in XML, and old information needs to be converted to XML. Both of these requirements can be expensive and difficult undertakings, and the benefits of smarter searching might not justify the costs in software development or acquisition and in staff training. See Chapter 7 for more discussion.

To summarize, in-line markup has four major problems.

1. Software needs access to the entire document during searching or indexing.
2. The document content must be normalized.
3. In-line markup is optimized for a one-to-one relationship between content and meaning.
4. Converting old content to XML and creating new content in XML both require significant investments in software and training.

Nonetheless, in-line markup brings some significant advantages for searching. First, in-line markup anchors search results against a location in a document. Someone searching legislation, for example, would like to see the specific paragraph and clause that matches the search criteria, not simply an entire bill or law. If a target document contains a fragment like the following, a search for the city "Toulouse" will be able to take the user to precisely the point that mentions the city:

```
<listitem><city>Toulouse</city><listitem>
```

That level of granularity does not matter much when documents are short, but it is very useful for displaying results from, say, a 40-page report.

Second, in-line markup does not require a separate production step: The same in-line element that tags *Bush* as a person in a news story, for example, allows a publishing system to generate a special typeface, a hyperlink to a background page, or even an index entry in a printed book. In this regard, rather than creating extra work, in-line markup saves the authors work: They simply have to identify, once, what the word *Bush* represents, and all the rest can happen automatically.

Third, in-line markup keeps everything conveniently in one place: In 20 years, a separate XML metadata file might be lost, but in-line markup in the document or data will still be available. Furthermore, someone revising a file has all the information—content and markup—on the screen at the same time. Although it is possible to produce and maintain complex tools to keep multiple files in sync and to display them simultaneously, even a simple text editor, such as Notepad or vi, can keep a single XML file with in-line markup up to date.

Fourth, although adding extra markup makes more work for the author, in many cases, the author is the person most qualified to do that work. In-line markup allows authors to add intelligence while the content is still fresh in their minds, rather than requiring them or someone else to come back later and perform a second step. Consider the following:

```
<step>Insert <consumable>XTC-453</consumable> as required.</step>
```

Was *XTC-453* a consumable or a nonconsumable? When writing the original step, the author almost certainly knew. But will the author remember 3 weeks later when creating an external metadata file? How long would it take a different person, such as an editor, to look up the information and find out?

In the end, using in-line XML markup for searching and retrieval makes sense when

- It is critically important to capture intelligence from authors at authoring time
- All the information to be searched is, or can be, in XML
- Search results need to point to specific locations inside large documents
- Searching and publishing can use the same markup for different purposes
- The cost of software and training, and the time required for indexing and searching, are not serious concerns

Detailed, in-line XML markup is costly in many ways, but the more of these criteria that apply to a project, the more likely it is that the cost will be justified. On the other hand, if few or none of these criteria apply to a project, using external XML metadata might be a better choice.

6.3.2 External Metadata

XML documents are designed to contain rich contextual information in elements and attributes mixed in with the content. This approach allows the same markup to be used by formatting tools, search engines, and many other types of software. In practice, however, in-line markup has not been very popular for searching: Despite all its advantages, companies that have made markup-aware search engines for SGML and later XML for more than a decade have not found a big market.

Outside of specialized applications, such as academic research, people don't ordinarily need or want to specify searches in terms of complex XML structure (see Section 6.2.1). For example, if I am looking for analysts' reports on Microsoft, I am not likely to care whether the word *Microsoft* appears within a `company` element as the second child of a `paragraph` element. In fact, context is not always as important as people claim. The careful reader might have noticed that Section 6.1.1 kept coming back to the same few examples of ambiguous search terms: *Bush*

6.3 Markup Considerations

and *Washington*. That repetition is not simply a result of my laziness; it is, in fact, difficult to think of searches that do not work well with modern full-text search engines, such as Google, and examples that demonstrate the need for XML often end up looking contrived.

After user testing, it turns out that, in many projects, people need to perform only a few types of contextual searches. For example, maintenance engineers searching a manual for farm machinery might want to use contextual searches for part numbers and, possibly, tool names, but for nearly everything else, a full-text search will be sufficient. It is unlikely that they will need to search for the word *carburetor* only within a `step` or `warning` element and even less likely that they will care about the parents of those elements. The users will probably be happy with a search form containing a few dedicated buttons with such labels as Search all, Search only Part Numbers, and Search only Tool Names. Similarly, unless someone is doing very specialized research, a document base of novels for university students can probably get away with a few contexts, such as Search in Titles, Search in Text Body, and Search in Dialogue.

In such situations, implementers can often save the cost of an elaborate markup-aware search system and simply write a script to pull the special context out and put it into a database or index file. For example, the implementers could create one database table for part numbers and one for tool names, and each table could reference the appropriate part of the text; for the rest, an off-the-shelf full-text search engine would be appropriate. A database table for part numbers could be as simple as the following:

```
Partno       Docref       Pos

2576-01      doc47856     29847

7703-91      doc28882     195

0056-22      doc00267     4599
```

In this example, the `Docref` column is a foreign key pointing into a separate table listing all the documents in the repository. A slightly fancier implementation might also use XPaths rather than byte positions, storing the path for each element in yet another table, but that would depend on the availability of a specialized XML viewer for the client. Alternatively, searches might always point to markup at a predetermined level—say, `task` or `article`—using an identifier rather than an XPath or position.

This kind of arrangement is especially powerful because it works for non-XML and even nontextual content. For example, the `partno` database table can point to PDF files, images, or videos, as well as to XML documents.

The problem with this approach is exchanging metadata in a database or index file. If one organization shares its content with another, it is difficult to move the metadata to the new system: The second organization might use a different database layout or a different search engine, for example. Moving binary information across CPUs can cause byte-order problems and many other challenges.

This is where XML comes back into play. If the metadata is in a separate XML document instead of a database table or index file, it becomes software and hardware independent: You can exchange, archive, and search it just like the primary content itself. Using the Resource Description Framework [RDF], the fragment pointing to part numbers might look like Listing 6-3.

Listing 6-3   External XML Metadata
```
<metadata>
  <partno>
    <value>2576-01</value>
    <doc ref="docs/service/abc.xml"/>
  </partno>
  <partno>
    <value>7703-91</value>
    <doc ref="docs/installation/def.xml"/>
  </partno>
  <partno>
    <value>0056-22</value>
    <doc ref="docs/troubleshooting/ghi.xml"/>
  </partno>
</metadata>
```

Different organizations using different hardware and software platforms can exchange the metadata in a portable way. Of course, a simple XML-encoded index file will not usually make sense, as it can be regenerated from the original XML documents automatically. The most valuable kind of metadata for searching is metadata that adds information to the original document, as in Listing 6-4, an RDF fragment using the Dublin Core 1.0 [DUBLIN-CORE].

Listing 6-4   RDF Metadata, Using the Dublin Core
```
<rdf:Resource about="hamsters.xml">
  <dc:title>All about Hamsters</dc:title>
  <dc:creator rdf:resource="http://www.hamster-u.edu/"/>
  <dc:description>Care, feeding, and training of small, aggressive
    rodents.</dc:description>
  <dc:date>2002-01-01</dc:date>
  <dc:subject>rodents</dc:subject>
  <dc:subject>hamsters</dc:subject>
  <dc:subject>pets</dc:subject>
  <dc:language>en-US</dc:language>
  <dc:rights>Free redistribution permitted.</dc:rights>
</rdf:Resource>
```

This information represents a human analysis of the document rather than a computer analysis. For example, the words *cage, shavings,* and *seeds* may appear more often in the Web page than the word *hamster,* but the human who designed the metadata knew that hamsters were the subject; likewise, the word *pets* might not appear at all on the page, but the human knew that *pets*

6.3 Markup Considerations

was a relevant subject word. The last-modified date for the Web page might be 2003-06-06—perhaps when it was restored from a backup—but the metadata author knows that the page was written on 1 January 2002.

In this example, note the use of both standard structures, the `rdf:Resource` container with a pointer to the resource being described, and standard descriptive fields: `dc:title`, `dc:creator`, and so on. Both types of standardization are important for metadata to be effective, but the first one has value independently of the second. A standard structure lets an indexing or search engine, as well as other types of software, understand what *kind* of information the metadata document contains; in this case, the `rdf:Resource` element is a container holding the description of a resource, `hamsters.html`, and the various `dc:*` elements hold individual pieces of information about that resource. A computer program can determine all that without even knowing what the `dc:*` elements mean.

So XML metadata will work best when it uses standard structures to mark up metadata components. Even if it does not have any information about the specific names used in an XML document, the searching, or other, software can still understand what names represent classes and what names represent properties, and it can map the relationships among different objects. RDF, XML Topic Maps [XTM], and NewsML [NewsML] are the three best-known examples of this kind of standardized metaformat; they are data-oriented layers on top of XML, the way that TCP is a transaction-oriented layer on top of IP.

Despite all these advantages, external metadata is not always the most appropriate approach. As mentioned in Section 6.3.1, external metadata requires managing at least two separate files: one for the main content and a second for the metadata. It is also difficult to use external metadata files to point *into* resources rather than *at* them, especially if the resource is not an XML file. The ISO *HyTime* specification [HYTIME] attempted to provide a standard mechanism for pointing into arbitrary kinds of resources—using SGML, but by extension, available to XML. However, HyTime never caught on, suggesting that the demand for that sort of generalized referencing did not yet exist.

Nonetheless, external metadata files have one enormous advantage: They *do* work with non-XML content. An RDF file can just as easily add metadata to an Excel spreadsheet, a video clip, or an MP3 audio file as to an XML file. There is no need to convert all content to XML to take advantage of external XML metadata files for smart searching and querying. For many applications in many organizations, external XML metadata will be the way to get 80 percent of XML's advantages with only 20 percent of the work.

For example, the same RDF metadata structure used earlier can apply to a photograph, as in the fragment in Listing 6-5.

Listing 6-5 External Metadata for a Photograph
```
<rdf:Resource about="hamsters.jpg">
  <dc:title>Hamster at play</dc:title>
  <dc:creator rdf:resource="http://www.hamster-u.edu/"/>
  <dc:description>Young hamster running in a wheel.</dc:description>
  <dc:date>2002-01-01</dc:date>
```

```
    <dc:subject>rodents</dc:subject>
    <dc:subject>hamsters</dc:subject>
    <dc:subject>pets</dc:subject>
    <dc:language>en-US</dc:language>
    <dc:rights>Free redistribution permitted.</dc:rights>
</rdf:Resource>
```

Listing 6-6 shows how similar metadata could be applied to a computer game.

Listing 6-6 External Metadata for a Computer Game
```
<rdf:Resource about="hamsters.exe">
    <dc:title>Find the Hamster!</dc:title>
    <dc:creator rdf:resource="http://www.hamster-u.edu/"/>
    <dc:description>Find the hamster hiding in its cage. For children
      aged three to five.</dc:description>
    <dc:date>2002-01-01</dc:date>
    <dc:subject>rodents</dc:subject>
    <dc:subject>hamsters</dc:subject>
    <dc:subject>pets</dc:subject>
    <dc:subject>games</dc:subject>
    <dc:language>en-US</dc:language>
    <dc:rights>Free redistribution permitted.</dc:rights>
</rdf:Resource>
```

With external metadata, the same software can index and search HTML documents, JPEG images, and DOS executable programs. There is no need to convert the original resources to XML, and the person creating the metadata does not even need write access to the original content. Figure 6-1 shows how a search system can use external XML metadata to provide uniform access to all content: XML and non-XML. That opens up one of the most intriguing possibilities of external metadata for searching and indexing. Instead of simply being an add-on for the main content—extra information to improve search and retrieval—metadata can become a commodity in itself.

Companies exist that collect and sell information about books, music, video, and other consumer products to vendors, including retail chains and online stores. XML metadata files make it easier to exchange that kind of information, and as the exchange becomes easier and cheaper, other markets may open up. For example, instead of simply a wrapper around their news stories, major news providers could package and sell as a separate product their enormous amount of internal information about important people, places, and companies.

In the end, both internal markup and external metadata have their advantages. Internal markup is especially effective if you are searching within individual XML documents that you control, whereas external metadata is especially effective when searching many different kinds of XML and non-XML documents and other resources that you may not control. In many cases, the

6.3 Markup Considerations

Figure 6-1 External metadata for searching

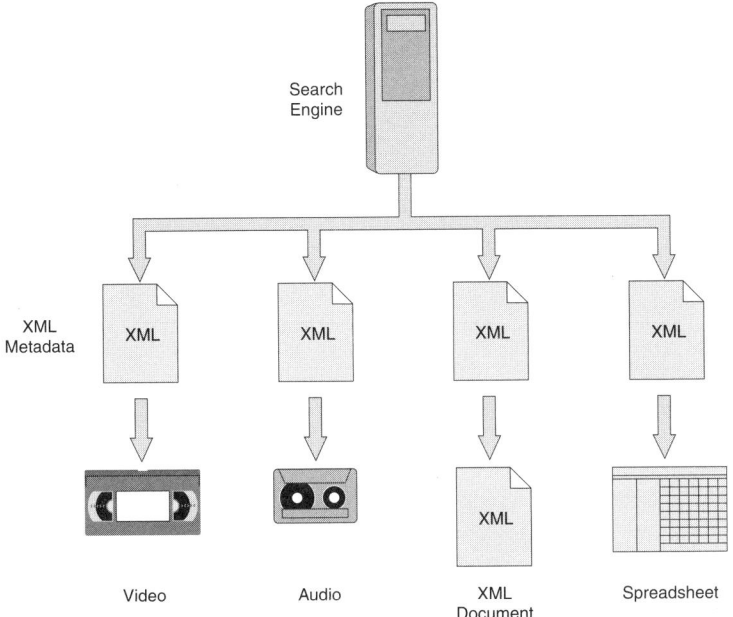

two can be complementary, with the external XML metadata leading the way to the individual resources and the internal markup adding extra value to the resources that happen to be XML documents.

6.3.3 Namespaces, Schemas, and the Semantic Web

As discussed in Section 6.2.3, XML markup can improve the quality of search results only if someone, somewhere, knows what the markup means. Inexperienced people writing about XML often claim that DTDs or schemas can provide this meaning, but they are wrong. In some special cases, this claim has a very small amount of truth, such as RDF Schema [RDF-SCHEMA]; in general, however, DTDs and schemas allow software only to check structure and add default content. Consider the simple DTD in Listing 6-7.

Listing 6-7 Simple DTD for searching

```
<!ELEMENT bibliography (title, biblio.entry+)>

<!ELEMENT title (#PCDATA)>

<!ELEMENT biblio.entry (author+, booktitle, publisher, year)>

<!ELEMENT author (#PCDATA)>
```

```
<!ELEMENT booktitle (#PCDATA)>

<!ELEMENT publisher (#PCDATA)>

<!ELEMENT year (#PCDATA)>
```

What can general-purpose XML searching and indexing software, with no built-in knowledge about this document type, do with the DTD that it could not do without it? Listing 6-8 contains an invalid XML document that references the DTD.

Listing 6-8 Sample Document for Searching

```
<?xml version="1.0"?>

<!DOCTYPE bibliography "bibliography.dtd">

<bibliography>
  <title>References Cited</title>

  <biblio.entry>
    <author>Jane Smith</author>
    <booktitle>History of ACME Widgets</booktitle>
    <year>1999</year>
  </biblio.entry>

</bibliography>
```

The indexing engine can apply `bibliography.dtd` to the XML document and determine that the document is not valid, because of the missing `publisher` element, but still does not know anything about the document's meaning; computers do not understand natural languages, so element names, such as `author`, have no special meaning. To see a DTD as a computer sees it, you need to make all the element names into meaningless strings, as in Listing 6-9.

Listing 6-9 Sample DTD for Searching, with Opaque Names

```
<!ELEMENT e1 (e2, e3+)>

<!ELEMENT e2 (#PCDATA)>

<!ELEMENT e3 (e4+, e5, e6, e7)>

<!ELEMENT e4 (#PCDATA)>

<!ELEMENT e5 (#PCDATA)>
```

6.3 Markup Considerations

```
<!ELEMENT e6 (#PCDATA)>

<!ELEMENT e7 (#PCDATA)>
```

Without the natural-language element names, which carry information for humans but not for computers, it should be very obvious how little use a DTD or a schema is in determining the meaning of the document in Listing 6-10.

Listing 6-10   Sample Document with Opaque Names

```
<?xml version="1.0"?>

<e1>
  <e2>References Cited</e2>

  <e3>
    <e4>Jane Smith</e4>
    <e5>History of ACME Widgets</e5>
    <e6>ACME Press, Inc</e6>
    <e7>1999</e7>
  </e3>

</e1>
```

Somewhere in the search process, then, a human has to intervene to add intelligence. That process can take place in any of several stages.

- The computer programmers can build that knowledge into the code, as might happen with a search engine designed for a single document type, such as XHTML.
- System integraters or support staff can add that knowledge into a runtime configuration file, as might happen with a general-purpose XML search engine's being installed and configured for a single XML project.
- Interface designers can add that knowledge to a front end that converts simpler queries, possibly using menus and forms, to XML search criteria.
- The end users performing searches can add the knowledge in the searches they specify.

No matter how the knowledge is added, the problem is made much more difficult by the lack of standardized names and structures in XML vocabularies (see Section 6.2.3). For example, consider two organizations publishing information on the Web in XML: The first one, a sports publisher, creates an element called score to encode the final standing in a professional sports match, such as a hockey game (Listing 6-11); the second one, a lobby group, creates an element called score to encode how friendly newspaper and magazine articles are to its cause (Listing 6-12).

Listing 6-11 Using `score` for Sports

```
<game type="hockey">
  <date>2008-01-04</date>
  <team>Big City Marauders</team>
  <team>Smalltown Hicks</team>
  <score>3:1</score>
</game>
```

Listing 6-12 Using `score` for Ranking

```
<review>
  <publication>Canoes everywhere!</publication>
  <title>The case for the freedom to canoe</title>
  <score>8</score>
</review>
```

What should a search engine or a crawler do when it finds an XML element named `score`? Sometimes, it will be possible to guess, based on context: In this case, the `score` inside a `game` element is the result of a sports competition, whereas the `score` inside a `review` element is a rating applied to a publication. In other cases, XML-aware search engines could try to infer meaning from the surrounding text and linking pages, the way that full-text search engines do today. In all cases, though, there is very little improvement over non-XML-based searching.

This is the specific problem that the XML Namespaces specification [NAMESPACES] addresses. An XML Namespace concept should be familiar to many computer programmers, as it works similarly to a Java or Perl package or to a C++ namespace. An XML Namespace makes element and attribute names globally unique by attaching a URI, such as a Web URL, to each one. In the earlier example, the sports publisher would use a different namespace from the lobby group, so there would be no chance of confusing the two `score` elements:

http://www.sportsnet.com/pubs/ns/ `score`
http://www.airlobby.org/namespace/ `score`

Nearly all XML libraries and applications support namespaces like these. Still, even with namespaces, an intelligent search engine cannot tell what either name *means* but can only avoid false positives: It knows that the two are not the same. There is no risk of confusing the two `score` elements, but there is also no way of knowing that a third element, named `ranking`, is a synonym for one of the `score` elements.

The only way for search engines to determine the full meaning of XML elements and attributes automatically is to implement the kind of full artificial intelligence that has been eluding computer scientists for decades. However, the W3C, led by Sir Tim Berners-Lee, the originator of HTML and the Web, is working on a solution that might be more technically realistic. The *Semantic Web* [SEMANTIC-WEB] uses XML together with RDF to relate specific concepts to

6.3 Markup Considerations

more general concepts. The simplest type of relationship is the inheritance relationship, in which X is a kind of Y. For example, someone might set up an inheritance chain like this:

a `stock-price` is a kind of `price`
a `price` is a kind of `monetary-value`
a `monetary-value` is a kind of `number`

Given this information, a searching and indexing engine that finds an XML document like the one in Listing 6-13 could fall back through the inheritance chain until it finds something that it recognizes. For example, it does not know what `stock-price` means, so it moves one step up the inheritance tree and finds `price`. When it has no luck with that, it moves up one more level and tries `monetary-value`. If the search engine does happen to know about `monetary-value`, it can now proceed to work with the element at this level of abstraction: It does not know that it is a stock price or even a price, but it does know that it's a currency value. Some information is lost, but some meaning survives.

```
Listing 6-13   Stock Price in XML
<stock-quote>
  <stock-id>ABCD</stock-id>
  <date>2004-02-16</date>
  <stock-price currency="USD">13.41</stock-price>
</stock-quote>
```

In real life, of course, these examples would need to use namespaces, they would need to be in RDF rather than vanilla XML, and most important, they would need an RDF schema to inform the search engine about the inheritance pattern. Schemas are the key to the Semantic Web: Listing 6-14 shows an example of an RDF schema defining all three properties.

Listing 6-14   RDF's Property Inheritance
```
<rdf:RDF
    xmlns:rdf="http://www.w3.org/1999/02/22-rdf-syntax-ns#"
    xmlns:rdfs="http://www.w3.org/2000/01/rdf-schema#">

  <rdfs:Property ID="stock-price">
    <rdfs:label>Stock Price</rdfs:label>
    <rdfs:range
        rdf:resource="http://www.w3.org/2000/01/rdf-schema#Literal"/>
    <rdfs:subPropertyOf rdf:resource="#price"/>
  </rdfs:Property>

  <rdfs:Property ID="price">
    <rdfs:label>Price</rdfs:label>
    <rdfs:range
```

```
            rdf:resource="http://www.w3.org/2000/01/rdf-schema#Literal"/>
     <rdfs:subPropertyOf rdf:resource="#monetary-value"/>
  </rdfs:Property>

  <rdfs:Property ID="monetary-value">
     <rdfs:label>Monetary Value</rdfs:label>
     <rdfs:range
            rdf:resource="http://www.w3.org/2000/01/rdf-schema#Literal"/>
  </rdfs:Property>

</rdf:RDF>
```

Note that the schema *still* cannot specify what the properties mean, only that they are related: A price is a more general equivalent of a stock price, and a monetary value is a more general equivalent of a price. If the application does not already know the meaning of a monetary value, this inheritance chain will be of little use. To try to add some more value to this schema, the W3C has developed the Web Ontology Language [OWL], on top of RDF schema to provide more detail about relationships than the simple specific/general distinction of inheritance. For example, OWL can specify that one property is the inverse of another and can express cardinality restraints, among other features.

In fact, the W3C is designing the Semantic Web to deal with relationships more sophisticated than simple inheritance, in the hope that softwarelike search engines will be able to start with a simple set of base types, such as the ubiquitous *Dublin Core,* and use those to understand a wide variety of information on the Web. From a security perspective, the Semantic Web would, obviously, be extremely vulnerable to the problem of trust (see Section 6.2.2). From a design perspective, the Semantic Web is far more similar to the failed, overdesigned hypertext systems of the 1980s than to the simple World Wide Web that pushed them all aside.

Finally, from a social perspective, the Semantic Web may require too much central planning and central control to be practical. Beyond the minimum necessary infrastructure, such as allocation of domain names and IP addresses, the Internet and the technological world in general tend to resist centralization, elaborate interrelationships, and complex design, all of which are necessary ingredients for a Semantic Web. Nevertheless, it is possible that some useful tools and information will come out of the project and that those will help us to improve XML searching and indexing generally, even if the Semantic Web itself does not succeed.

6.4 Final Words on XML Searching

When designing an XML project, you need to make two important decisions about XML searching. First, you need to decide whether it's necessary at all: For many projects, full-text searching may be enough, especially if the full-text engine also supports simple fielded searches. If you decide that users are not likely to take advantage of the full XML structure, you can design or choose an XML document type with much less dense markup; using less markup will lower costs and speed up production throughout the project's development and implementation.

6.4 Final Words on XML Searching

If something more than full-text searching is required, the main choice will be between in-line markup and external metadata. If your searching requirements involve locating a precise spot inside a document; if the same tagging can be used for more than one purpose, such as searching and formatting; and if all your information is in XML or can be converted to XML, in-line markup might make more sense. On the other hand, if you need to manage many different information formats, such as pictures or video, or you want to share metadata for searching without sharing the objects themselves, external metadata will be a better choice for your project.

The fact that XML-aware search engines have had trouble finding a market while the major database vendors enthusiastically add more and more XML features suggests that many more XML implementers are choosing external metadata of some sort, possibly using a database rather than an XML file. In the future, external metadata may become a commodity: Companies already sell databases of car parts, books, music, video, and all kinds of other information. Using XML will make that information much easier to buy and sell, and standard metadata formats, such as RDF, could open a new market for XML work.

CHAPTER 7

XML and Legacy Information

If you have been reading this book from the beginning, you might be a little tired of XML, so this chapter begins with a not entirely irrelevant historical digression. Under the Roman Empire in southeastern Europe, the Middle East, and northern Africa, Greek *koine* was a common language that people from various nations used to communicate, share literature, and do business. For most of these people, *koine* was not their native language: They necessarily had to give up some of their expressive ability for the chance to communicate more widely.

For example, consider the collection of Greek *koine* letters and narratives that were later collected into the Christian *New Testament*. For the most part, these documents were written by people who did not speak Greek as their first language, and as a result, few critics hold them up as models of great classical literature. On the other hand, many people were able to read them easily over many centuries and in a wide geographical area, from Augustine of Hippo in north Africa to the early Christian congregations in what are now Turkey, Greece, and Italy.[1] A common language was not only useful for literature and religion, however, but also made it possible for people to do business and run government without the need for interpreters and with a reduced risk of misunderstandings.

In contemporary times, we have a similar need for communication in large organizations, which typically have dozens or hundreds of different computer systems, some new and some decades old, trying to communicate using many different formats and protocols. Most of those technical languages were once optimized for the individual systems, giving them great expressive power, but only when communicating with other systems of the same type. Over time, these legacy systems have become more and more isolated from newly developing networks: Other systems do not understand their language or understand it only with great difficulty. Sometimes, the legacy systems are almost completely cut off, holding potentially valuable data or performing useful computations that almost no one can get to, barely connected, if at all, to the larger computer network.

As Greek *koine* did for the peoples of the Roman Empire 2,000 years ago, XML can bring these systems together by giving them a basic common language. It will not be perfect, of course: Like *koine,* it will be a second language for most of the systems, reducing their expressive power but bringing them into contact with many more systems than they could otherwise reach.

---

[1] Greek *koine* is still the language of Eastern Orthodox Christianity. Note that many other religions at various times have also recognized the value of a common language, such as Arabic for Muslims—even in non-Arab countries, like Turkey or Iran—vulgar Latin for Roman Catholics until the last century, Sanskrit for Hindus, or Hebrew for modern Jews.

This chapter introduces the ideas and issues involved with using XML as a *koine* for legacy systems. This process is not always easy, because conversion from other formats to XML is not simply a matter of adding tags and rearranging information. Sometimes, required information will not be present, and human intervention will be necessary. Sometimes, conversion to XML is not economical, and other strategies, such as XML metadata (Section 7.3.2) will make more sense. This chapter begins with the most obvious advantages of using XML as a *koine* for interoperability.

7.1 Advantages of XML for Legacy Information

The advantages of using XML for legacy information are compelling.

- XML can wrap the interfaces of old systems and allow them to interact with more modern systems.
- XML can make information and protocols transparent, to simplify debugging and implementation.
- XML can reduce the amount of code that system integrators have to maintain.

In many ways, the advantages of XML for information are similar to those of TCP/IP for networking. Some of the many different kinds of physical network transports have abilities beyond TCP/IP, but it was not until everyone agreed to start using TCP/IP that worldwide networking really took off. Like TCP/IP, XML has the potential to help everyone: Developers end up with simpler, more robust systems to build and maintain, whereas managers and executives end up with more and better information to help them make decisions.

7.1.1 Interfaces

Legacy interfaces are a problem in many larger organizations. Computer systems built from the 1960s to the early 1990s have few standard methods for communicating, often relying on custom protocols over slow serial interfaces. Interfacing with each one is a custom job, and the complexity can quickly spread over an entire project, as illustrated in Figure 7-1.

One of the best practices for solving this problem of system integration is to come up with a common communication protocol or interface, then implement a *facade* in front of each legacy system to act as a translator, as illustrated in Figure 7-2. XML is not necessary: Any popular RPC protocol, such as CORBA, DCOM, or Java RMI, will work. XML-based remote procedure calls, such as SOAP or XML-RPC, introduced in Chapter 5 bring some additional advantages, however.

- Unlike Java RMI or Microsoft DCOM, XML over HTTP has no language or operating system dependencies, making it useful for heterogeneous environments.
- XML and HTTP can get through firewalls easily, when necessary, and can work well with HTTP-aware networking software.
- XML provides loose coupling, making future extension easier.

7.1 Advantages of XML for Legacy Information

Figure 7-1 Communication using legacy interfaces

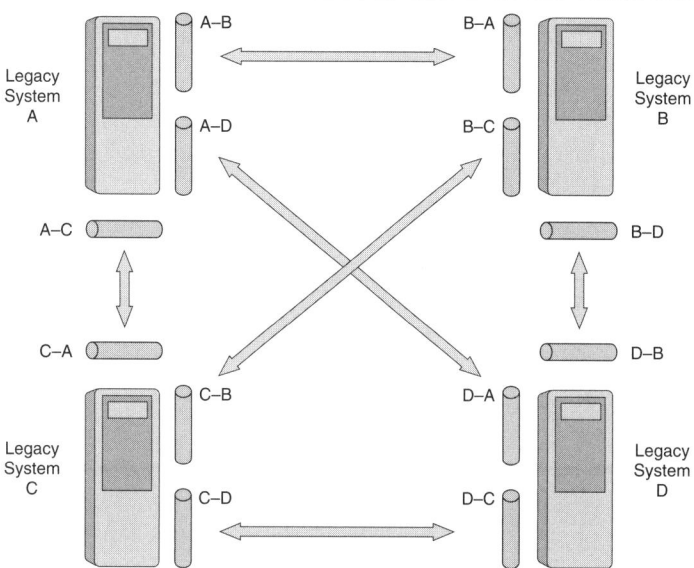

- XML is already internationalized with Unicode, eliminating many low-level problems, such as byte order and character encoding.
- XML and HTTP can be RESTful, with all the accompanying advantages (see Section 5.3).
- XML payloads are human readable and easy to simulate and debug.

Figure 7-2 Common facades over legacy interfaces

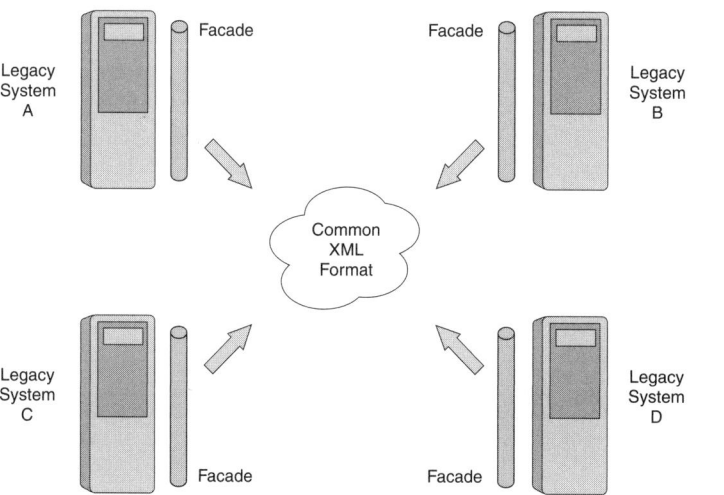

For examples of how XML over HTTP can work, see Section 5.3.1.

7.1.2 Transparency

XML information is transparent: It is in plaintext with, usually, natural-language labels for elements and attributes, so a person who has no prior knowledge of an XML-based data format still has at least a fighting chance of figuring out what is going on. To understand the importance of transparency, consider the data record in Listing 7-1.

Listing 7-1   Data in Fixed-Length Format

```
0x00  0x00  0x53  0x46  0x4f  0x03  0x00  0x00  0x00  0x00  0x00  0x00
NUL   NUL   S     F     O     ETX   NUL   NUL   NUL   NUL   NUL   NUL

0x00  0x53  0x41  0x4e  0x20  0x46  0x52  0x41  0x4e  0x43  0x49  0x53
NUL   S     A     N           F     R     A     N     C     I     S

0x43  0x4f  0x66  0x05  0x02  0x42  0xe7  0x99  0x9a  0x00  0x28  0x42
C     O     f     ENQ   STX   B     ç     ---   ---   NUL   (     B

0x16  0x7a  0x5a  0xc2  0xf4  0xbf  0x6f  0x00  0x0d  0x41  0x88  0x02
SYN   z     Z     Â     ô     ¿     o     NUL   CR    A     X     STX

0x0c  0x41  0x71  0xe3  0x54  0x55  0x53  0x00  0x43  0x41  0x4b  0x43
NP    A     G     ã     T     U     S     NUL   C     A     K     S

0x46  0x4f
F     O
```

Imagine that, as often happens in real life, you are working with an old database and have no documentation for the format: The owner uses an ancient, proprietary, closed-source library from a company that is no longer in business and now wants to retire the last computer that can run that library. The library is a fixed-length database: Every record is 62 bytes wide, and each field starts at the same position and uses the same number of bytes in the record. With a little work, the record in Listing 7-1 should not be too difficult to crack. The customer confirms for you that SFO is in fact a navigation aid identifier, so you assume, until proved wrong by another record, that the first field is five characters for the identifier, null-padded on the left. If the designer was consistent, all text fields will be null-padded on the left, so you can make out a 20-character field containing SAN FRANCISCO, probably the navaid name, as well. Other possible strings, such as AX, AG, TUS, and CAKSFO are inconclusive. After a chat with some subject-matter experts, you discover that KSFO is the identifier for San Francisco airport, so the airport identifier is probably a 4-byte field at the end of the record. Before that, you notice CA, which is the abbreviation for California, making it likely that the US before it is a country abbreviation for the United States. After a fair bit of time has elapsed, you will start to discover that some of the bytes are IEEE 754 float-

7.1 Advantages of XML for Legacy Information

ing-point numbers. (You are very lucky that an old database used that format.) Other bytes are integers: With that, you will probably be able to puzzle out most of the rest of the record. In real life, things are often even more complicated than this.

Fortunately, newer databases are likely to make information available in much simpler formats. For example, Listing 7-2 contains the same information as Listing 7-1 but uses a tab-delimited format, split here into three lines for readability.

Listing 7-2   Data in Tab-Delimited Format
```
SFO      VOR      SAN FRANCISCO      2002-05 low      115.8 40      \
37.619483         -122.373892        13      17.001   15.118 US     \
CA       KSFO
```

There are no more binary numbers to puzzle out here, and enumerated values have been replaced with short strings. It is fairly easy to guess what most of the record means at only a quick glance: `VOR` is the navaid type, `2002-05` is probably the date the record was updated, `37.619483` is probably the latitude, and so on. However, even if you did know the format in advance, it might be difficult to remember which field was which: In fact, the record from which this example was derived had more than twice as many fields, many of them nonobvious. For example, was `40` the range or the elevation? If it's the range, is it in kilometers, statute miles, or nautical miles?

Listing 7-3 is much longer but also much easier to read. It labels every field explicitly with a human-readable word or phrase, such as `identifier`; groups related information in the `specifications` and `location` subgroups; and explicitly provides units of measurement where needed.

Listing 7-3   Data in Human-Readable Form
```
<navaid>
  <identifier>SFO</identifier>
  <type>VOR</type>
  <name>SAN FRANCISCO</name>
  <cycle-date>2002-05</cycle-date>
  <specifications>
    <type>low</type>
    <frequency unit="MHz">115.8</frequency>
    <nav-range unit="nm">40<nav-range>
  </specifications>
  <location>
    <latitude unit="deg">37.619483</latitude>
    <longitude unit="deg">-122.373892</longitude>
    <elevation unit="ft">13</elevation>
    <twist dir="east">17.001</slaved-var>
    <magnetic-variation dir="east">15.118</mag-var>
    <country>US</country>
```

```
    <state-prov>CA</state-prov>
    <nearest-airport>KSFO</nearest-airport>
  </location>
</navaid>
```

In this case, a developer who is working on a script or debugging a message has less need to look at documentation to discover what is what. If in 50 years the documentation is lost, it will take at worst hours rather than days or weeks to crack the format. In fact, a format like this makes debugging not only easier but also less common: Programmers are less likely to introduce bugs when the data is self-labeling, as they do not have to rely on their memory of how fields are arranged.

7.1.3 Code Reduction

One advantage of using a common information format—XML or otherwise—is a reduction in the amount of code required. Consider, for example, a company that has one legacy system handling human resources, one handling sales, and one handling customer data. If the chief financial officer wants information on payroll, the information systems (IS) department will write a program to extract and analyze data from the human resources computer; if the vice president for sales wants information on channels, the IS department will write a program to extract and analyze data from the sales computer and another program to extract and analyze data from the customer computer and will then try to collate the results. The company ends up with hundreds of small, special-purpose programs all over the place, many of them undocumented.

A common XML format offers a better solution. Once each legacy system has a converter attached, special code is no longer required to use it; instead, all business analysis and reporting logic can live in a single, central location, if desired, where it is easy to document and maintain. Because each system no longer has a separate reporting program, less code needs to be maintained, and so, less can go wrong with the system in the future.

7.1.4 Network Effect

Despite the promises of enterprise-software vendors, much of the information in corporate or government computers is isolated in old systems with proprietary interfaces, allowing access only in limited ways. A government department may have a database of taxpayers and a database of corporations, but if the two databases are on old systems, it may be impossible to link them.

A common XML data format with centralized analysis and reporting, as described in Section 7.1.3, gives an organization an exponential increase in the way that information can be combined and cross-referenced. For example, if eight systems all use the same information format, their information can be combined and compared in reports and analyses in more than 250 ways, compared with perhaps four or five hard-coded methods that existed before.

Not all of those reports and analyses will be useful, of course, but the ability to combine information quickly and easily can be a powerful business tool. A trucking company, for example, might find a correlation between the time needed to collect its accounts payable and the amount of container traffic in a specific state, spotting trends that were too difficult to find before.

7.2 Disadvantages of XML for Legacy Information

This effect is very similar to what happens on a computer network: The network becomes exponentially more valuable as more users join it. In this case, it is information rather than people joining a network.

7.2 Disadvantages of XML for Legacy Information

Despite the advantages of using XML formats and interfaces for legacy information, some serious drawbacks can easily compromise a project:

- A large, up-front investment in analysis
- Mismatches in granularity, making automated conversion difficult or impossible
- Bloat in the size of information objects because of the verbosity of XML markup
- Versioning issues as the system grows, increasing the difficulty and disadvantages as each new component is added

These problems are not enough to destroy the usefulness of XML for wrapping legacy interfaces—people are already building those interfaces successfully in the field and will likely build many more of them in the future, whatever happens with Web Services and other trends. But people should keep their expectations realistic. Unifying information with XML can save money, but doing so requires a reasonably large up-front investment and a lot of performance tuning to make it work. If you are interested in a way to get most of the rewards of XML for a significantly smaller investment, you might want to skip ahead to Section 7.3.2.

7.2.1 Analysis

Section 7.1.2 showed how much easier it is for people to analyze an XML-based information format than the traditional fixed-length field or delimited-text data formats. But legacy-data projects always have to start with the data in its original format, so however much easier XML may make the work of future analysts, the current analysts will have to deal with information formats like the one in Listing 7-1, which was deliberately simplified; the ones that analysts encounter in the wild are typically much, much more opaque.

In the best case, complete and accurate documentation is available for all the legacy formats. More typically, the documentation was never available, because the format was proprietary to a vendor that supplied software to use it, or was lost, or else the documentation is inaccurate because of subsequent ad hoc changes to the data format. As a result, the analysts have to begin the equivalent of a large-scale decryption exercise, examining hundreds or thousands of legacy data records in detail in order to isolate the patterns in them. Even then, exceptions may show up in isolated records weeks or months later. This kind of work can be a lot of fun for people like me who enjoy puzzles and code breaking, but it is expensive for the people paying their salaries or fees, especially as it is difficult to predict how long the work will take.

The legacy-format analysis, however, is only the first step. After that, technologists have to find a way to convert the legacy formats, which may number dozens, to the common XML format and back again. This step involves overcoming both technical problems, such as the one described in Section 7.2.2, and political problems: It might be necessary to leave out some less-important information for the sake of compatibility, and different stakeholders will have different opinions about the meaning of *less important*.

A reasonably large corporate or government legacy data project can expect this step to occupy several senior analysts for anywhere from 3 to 12 months; it will also require frequent meetings with managers and stakeholders during that time. In some cases, the expected advantages of a common XML interface will not be enough to justify the large, up-front expenditure.

7.2.2 Granularity Mismatch

Once the initial analysis is complete, legacy-data projects usually have to face the problem of granularity mismatch. To take an extremely simple example, consider how systems store names. One legacy system might store names in a single field, for coarse granularity:

```
Name            Dr. Jean M. Smith
```

Another legacy system, however, might decompose the name slightly, separating the surname to enable sorting, for intermediate granularity:

```
Surname         Smith
GivenNames      Dr. Jean M.
```

Meanwhile, a third system might decompose the name in excruciating detail and include a pre-formatted display version, for fine granularity:

```
Honorific       Dr.
GivenName1      Jean
GivenName2      M.
Surname         Smith
DisplayName     Dr. Jean M. Smith
```

If a single XML interface needs to work for all these systems, the designers are left with some complex choices. In general, down conversion—from finer to coarser granularity—can be handled automatically, but up conversion—from coarser to finer granularity—cannot. If the shared XML interface will be used for reading from the legacy systems, it will be necessary to use coarse granularity in the XML, as the systems using finer granularity can down convert to the coarse version.

```
<name>Dr. Jean M. Smith</name>
```

7.2 Disadvantages of XML for Legacy Information

On the other hand, if the shared XML interface will be used for writing to the legacy systems, it will be necessary to use fine granularity, as shown in Listing 7-4 in the XML, as the systems using the coarser granularity can down convert from the fine version.

Listing 7-4 Fine Granularity in XML
```
<name>
  <honorific>Dr.</honorific>
  <given-name>Jean</given-name>
  <given-name>M.</given-name>
  <surname>Smith</surname>
  <display-name>Dr. Jean M. Smith</display-name>
</name>
```

Now, what happens if the XML interface will be used for reading *and* writing? This is where legacy-data projects typically stumble, especially because the granularity mismatches tend to be far larger and more complex than the simple examples in this section. Typically, people end up taking one of two approaches. either loosening the XML structure to allow variations in granularity or retiring some of the legacy systems after manually converting their data.

The first alternative kills off much of the advantage of a shared XML interface, as the XML information is no longer consistent or predictable; the second alternative implies a significant escalation in the project's cost. Unfortunately, the problem of granularity mismatch often does not surface until well into a legacy project, after a company or organization has already invested a large amount of money, but it should be predictable: Nearly every project wrapping XML interfaces or formats around legacy data from multiple sources is going to encounter this problem eventually.

7.2.3 Bloat

Section 7.1.2 demonstrated how XML makes information much more transparent, but that transparency comes at a cost: XML can be significantly more verbose than some optimized binary formats; to put it more bluntly, XML can be bloated.

Once again, compare Listings 7-1 and 7-3. The fixed-length example uses 62 bytes to represent a record, whereas the XML example uses 635 characters for the same information, which could represent from 635 to 2,540 bytes, depending on the character encoding in use. The XML example could be modified to make it somewhat shorter, and many binary formats—most notoriously, Microsoft Word documents—can be much more bloated than XML, but on balance, an order-of-magnitude inflation for transparently tagged XML is not unusual.

Of course, networks are fast, disk storage is cheap, and many XML documents can compress down to less than 30 percent of their uncompressed size, but in some applications, the extra verbosity of XML is simply unacceptable. For example, embedded or portable devices may have restricted storage, or even a large system may need to capture and archive huge amounts of data from sensors or push data very quickly for real-time stock market or other information. In time, computer hardware will likely become fast enough, and storage large enough, that XML works well even for these applications, but it is not there yet. A big niche still exists for hand-optimized, non-XML data formats for real-time networking or large-scale data storage.

7.2.4 Growth and Versioning

The final drawback of using a common XML format or interface for legacy data comes not from XML, but from the very problem of maintaining common interfaces. This problem creeps up on a project, seeming minor at first but sometimes suffocating a project completely during later stages.

A typical project might start with a proof of concept by implementing an XML interface to one legacy system. After completing the analysis (Section 7.2.1) and implementation, the technologists design an XML format that matches the legacy system's needs fairly closely and that allows for future additions for other systems. Although it might take a little more time and money than initially expected, the proof-of-concept project is successful, so the team proceeds to extend the XML interface to a second legacy system, using the same XML format. After completing an analysis, it becomes clear that the second system's information needs do not fit well with the first XML format, possibly because of granularity mismatches (Section 7.2.2), so the team goes back and redesigns the format, testing it against both systems; writes an XML interface for the second system to support the new, second version of the XML format; and then rewrites, retests, and redocuments the interface for the first legacy system so that it also supports the second version of the XML format.

At this point, the project has two legacy systems working through the same XML interface, bringing in many of the advantages described in Section 7.1. The project is a bit more over time and over budget, but it is clearly working, and management decides that the project team has likely learned enough from the first two implementations that it will be able to go more quickly through the remaining systems.

Unfortunately, management turns out to be wrong. Each new legacy system added forces more and more extensive changes to the shared XML format, and each time, *all* the existing XML interfaces need to be rewritten. Eventually, the cost of adding one more legacy system to the project is prohibitively expensive because of the amount of recoding that will be required for all the other systems; in short, the granularity mismatches become so severe that it is no longer possible to design a common XML format that brings any real benefits.

Unfortunately, this versioning problem is common in attempts to use XML as a *koine* to allow legacy systems to communicate. XML provides a useful low-level data format, but it cannot automatically make incompatibilities between information systems disappear, any more than other proposed solutions, such as the overhyped enterprise resource planning (ERP) software could. This problem suggests that once a network of legacy systems connected via a common XML format reaches a certain size, it is incapable of growing further. In other words, it can solve problems in a department but not, perhaps, across an entire enterprise. For that, other solutions, such as XML metadata (Section 7.3.3) might be a more practical solution.

7.3 Special Topics

The topics in this section cover some of the more technical issues of using XML with legacy information. First is the problem of conversion (Section 7.3.1): The information is in a legacy format of some sort and needs to end up in XML. What is the best way to get it there? The answer depends largely on the nature of the information and the way people will use it. Legacy tabular data, for example, can often be converted to XML automatically and on the fly, whereas legacy documents may require a lot of manual intervention.

Section 7.3.2 examines a programming technique that is very common in the XML community, which this book calls *virtual XML*. Instead of converting information to XML documents, you can often simply make it available through a standard XML parsing interface, such as the DOM or SAX. This trick can speed up processing and simplify code.

Section 7.3.3 introduces an alternative to converting legacy data: metadata. For many users, metadata gives nearly all the advantages of legacy data conversion at only a tiny fraction of the cost. A company or an organization starting to implement XML should consider this approach first, at least to gain experience, before committing to a major legacy-data conversion project.

7.3.1 Conversion Strategies

OK, so Section 7.1 convinced you of the advantages of using XML as a *koine* for all your legacy data, and you're confident that you can overcome the disadvantages (Section 7.2). Now it's time to start converting the legacy data to XML. You can classify any conversion as one of four types.

1. *Down conversion:* The result of the conversion—XML, in this case—contains less structure or information than the legacy data.
2. *Cross-conversion:* The result contains exactly the same structure and information as the original, although possibly in a different, predictable, arrangement.
3. *Up conversion:* The result contains more structure or information than the original document.
4. *Mixed conversion:* The result contains some structure or information that was not present in the original but also omits some structure or information that *was* present in the original.

You should always be able to automate down conversion and cross-conversion: In general, computers are better at discarding or rearranging information than they are at creating it. That is very important for systems that process a lot of high-speed streaming information, for which human intervention would be too slow or too expensive. It is also useful for converting large collections of legacy data, significantly reducing the costs.

Up conversion and mixed conversion, on the other hand, are extremely difficult to automate. Sometimes, it is possible to use heuristics, such as pattern matching,[2] to infer some of the missing

---

[2] Because of its pattern-matching capabilities, the Perl programming language is very popular for legacy-data conversion.

structure, but that approach is not entirely reliable. A human nearly always has to intervene afterward and fix problems in the resulting XML.

In fact, automatic up conversion is the XML community's equivalent of the *philosopher's stone*. As noted in Chapters 2 and 3, one of the biggest obstacles to XML's acceptance in documentation environments is the editing tools: If only, people assume, it were possible to allow authors to work in their familiar word processor—usually, Microsoft Word—and convert the result to XML, the barriers to entry for XML documentation projects would be much lower. As a result, over the history of SGML and XML, vendors have repeatedly announced and released tools promising the ability to convert word processor documents to XML automatically. These tools generally rely on the authors' using specific word processor styles, either voluntarily or enforced by plug-ins. Of course, these tools do not work outside of simple demos or highly constrained samples, but new hope springs every time someone announces yet another tool that can supposedly convert base legacy documents into XML gold.[3]

In addition to the quality of conversion, you also have to consider the direction:

- *One-way:* The information will be converted only from the legacy data, in this case, to XML but never back again.
- *Round-trip:* The information will be converted to XML, modified, and then converted back to the legacy format. Any changes to the XML are expected to make their way back to the original.

Round-trip conversions are much more difficult than one-way conversions. If *either* direction is an up conversion or a mixed conversion, you will not be able to automate the process at all. As a result, only a cross-conversion will work for round-tripping, without ongoing, and expensive, human intervention.

Why would anyone want to round-trip information, however? Why not simply convert everything to XML once and be done with it? In fact, many legacy systems are well debugged and very good at what they do: Replacing them completely would be expensive and risky. The whole point of an XML interface is that a company or an organization can keep its existing technology investments and use the XML as a facade to allow old systems to interoperate better with newer components, not so that everything can be unplugged, thrown away, and replaced with shiny, new XML-based systems.

For example, an investment bank might have a mainframe that has been programmed and debugged over many decades to deal with complex international financial transactions. Building a new system from scratch would cost tens or hundreds of millions of dollars, and it would take years before the bank had tested the new system thoroughly enough to trust it with multibillion-dollar transactions daily: Clearly, the mainframe is there to stay. However, the investment bank then acquires another, smaller financial institution, which also has a mainframe that has been

---

[3] I once worked at a company that produced perhaps the *least-unsuccessful* attempt at an automated up-conversion plug-in for Microsoft Word, although I was not directly involved with the product's development.

programmed over many decades to deal with a slightly different set of regulations and requirements for its different customer base. It does not make any sense to unplug either computer; at the same time, however, the merger will show benefits only if there is a way for the two computers to talk to each other, sharing the information that they usually keep locked up in their internal proprietary formats. This is precisely where XML round-tripping is essential: When the first legacy system produces XML, the second has to be able to read it; when the second makes changes and regenerates the modified XML, the first legacy system has to be able to read that and find the changes.

In general, this kind of work, although challenging, is manageable. Tabular or hierarchical information inside old systems is usually well-enough structured that, after a fair bit of analysis and design, it is possible to come up with a shared XML-based format that allows cross-conversion. Legacy documentation systems, on the other hand, pose a much greater problem: The structure of their documents is generally loose and oriented toward formatting, like the text in Listing 7-5.

Listing 7-5   Typical Legacy Document

```
/P /B TASK 3/eB
/P /B Step 2:/eB
/P Attach part number 3004-555 /I Case Cover/eI to the case using
   four 1//2 inch #6 Phillips screws.
```

This example uses formatting codes, such as `/P` for paragraph breaks, `/B` and `/eB` for boldface, and `/I` and `/eI` for italics, but contains no generic structural information. The XML, on the other hand, might look like Listing 7-6.

Listing 7-6   Typical Converted XML Document

```
<task>
  <step>
    <p>Attach <part no="3004-555">Case Cover</part> to the case
     using four <part>1/2 inch #6 Phillips screws</part>.</p>
  </step>
</task>
```

This is obviously an up conversion and will require a lot of manual intervention. Pattern matching and other heuristics can help to reduce the work. For example, a Perl program could guess that the word `step` followed by a number and colon, in boldface, always represents the beginning of a `step`, but there are bound to be exceptions that a person will have to clean up.

So, as a general rule, it is fair to say that converting legacy data to XML can often be a cross-conversion or a down conversion, as long as there are no granularity mismatches (Section 7.2.2), but converting legacy documents to XML can often be an up conversion or a mixed conversion. That implies that it is reasonable to put an XML interface in front of a legacy data system but that a legacy document system, up to and including modern word processors, will need to be replaced with an XML system.

7.3.2 Virtual XML

Many XML components and applications communicate with parsers through standard interfaces, the most popular of which are the tree-based Document Object Model [DOM] and the event-based Simple API for XML [SAX]. For example, consider the trivial XML document in 7-7.

Listing 7-7 Trivial XML Document for Parsing
```
<greeting>
  <recipient>Frank</recipient>
  <sender>Sally</sender>
  <message><emphasis>Hello</emphasis>, Frank!</message>
</greeting>
```

An XML parser—usually in a library—will process the XML markup and then make it available to the application through either a tree of DOM nodes, as illustrated in Figure 7-3, or a stream of SAX events, as shown in Listing 7-8. (Both options are simplified to remove unwanted whitespace.)

Listing 7-8 Stream of SAX Events
```
startDocument()
startElement("greeting")
startElement("recipient")
characters("Frank")
endElement("recipient")
startElement("sender")
characters("Sally")
endElement("sender")
startElement("message")
```

Figure 7-3 Tree of DOM nodes

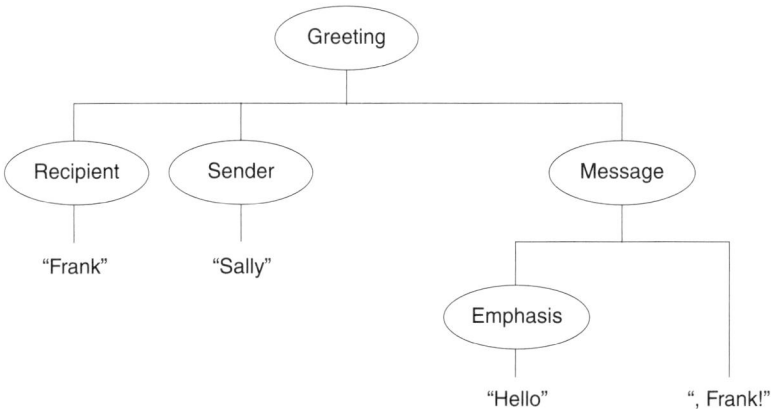

7.3 Special Topics

```
startElement("emphasis")
characters("Hello")
endElement("emphasis")
characters(", Frank!")
endElement("message")
endElement("greeting")
endDocument()
```

Higher-level applications, such as XSLT engines, query engines, browsers, and database interfaces, typically read XML exclusively through these interfaces rather than look at the XML text directly. This fact leads to a neat trick: If it is possible to do an automated conversion (see Section 7.3.1), instead of having the conversion produce XML markup for other applications to parse, the conversion can simply deliver DOM nodes or SAX events directly to other XML-aware components. For example, consider the following simple legacy data table:

sales region	1999	2000	2001	2002	2003
east	10.5	9.3	3.8	2.5	5.0
central	7.2	6.1	5.0	4.9	4.1
west	20.8	21.1	7.6	6.8	6.9

As an XML document, this same information could be very long, depending on the markup used. Listing 7-9 shows only the first entry in XML.

Listing 7-9 XML Sample for Legacy Data Table
```
<sales region="east">
  <sales-millions year="1999">10.5</sales-millions>
  <sales-millions year="2000">9.3</sales-millions>
  <sales-millions year="2001">3.8</sales-millions>
  <sales-millions year="2002">2.5</sales-millions>
  <sales-millions year="2003">5.0</sales-millions>
</sales>
```

As an alternative to producing the XML, the conversion application could simply pose as an XML parser and deliver the events through a SAX interface, as in Listing 7-10. (Note that whitespace between elements is omitted, so this is not exactly the same as Listing 7-9.)

Listing 7-10 SAX Events for a Virtual Document
```
startDocument()
[...]
startElement(sales, [region="east"])
startElement(sales-millions, [year="1999"])
characters("10.5")
```

```
endElement(sales-millions)
startElement(sales-millions, [year="2000"])
characters("9.3")
endElement(sales-millions)
startElement(sales-millions, [year="2001"])
characters("3.8")
endElement(sales-millions)
startElement(sales-millions, [year="2002"])
characters("2.5")
endElement(sales-millions)
startElement(sales-millions, [year="2003"])
characters("5.0")
endElement(sales-millions)
endElement(sales)
[...]
endDocument()
```

To an XSLT engine, an XML database, a query engine, or any number of other popular XML-aware components, it will make no difference that these events did not come from an XML document: The application simply saves the step of writing XML text out to disk and then reading it in again through a parser.

This strategy can also be useful as the first part of a conversion. For example, you can begin by writing a parser that generates events for legacy data in its current format and then pass the information through a series of transformations—using standard XML tools—until it ends up in its final format.

7.3.3 Metadata

Conversion to and from XML makes sense for wrapping an interface around legacy systems or for updating a large legacy repository of documents, but it can be a large and expensive project, especially for an organization that is new to XML. Conversion is also impractical for non-text-oriented information, such as video.

In these cases, one useful approach is to use external XML metadata as the equivalent of a library's card catalog, with descriptions, summaries, keywords, and other relevant information for each resource. For example, the record in Listing 7-11 describes a document stored in a word processor format.

Listing 7-11 XML Metadata for a Document

```
<document id="doc809985">
  <title>Project Report: X300-381</title>
  <location code="0010">professional services</location>
  <filename>\reports\2000\x300-381 Report.doc</filename>
  <format>application/x-ms-word</format>
  <date>2000-11-10</date>
  <author>Henry Waller</author>
```

7.3 Special Topics

```xml
    <class code="0528">project report</class>
    <subjects>
      <subject code="1007">networking</subject>
      <subject code="1720">security</subject>
      <subject code="2019">customer: Maple Leaf Networks</subject>
      <subject code="4551">project: Maple Leaf Networks
        firewall</subject>
    </subjects>
    <description>
      Final report on a project to implement advanced firewall support
      for Maple Leaf Networks' new facility. The project cost a total
      of CAD 250,000 to implement over 18 months, coming in CAD 10,000
      over its initial budget but on time.
    </description>
</document>
```

The XML metadata is not the document itself—that lives in file x300-381 Report.doc—but rather information about the file that people can index, search, exchange, archive, and even sell. If two companies are working together, this information can easily be stored in a shared repository. If a senior executive is flying across the Pacific Ocean for 18 hours, this information can be copied onto a notebook computer or CD-ROM and sent along. Once someone identifies that the file is of interest, the person can obtain the complete, non-XML, file and examine it. Listing 7-12 contains a similar metadata record for another bit of information: a video clip.

Listing 7-12   XML Metadata for a Video Clip

```xml
<document id="vid0027811">
  <title>Promo: We Deliver</title>
  <location code="0018">marketing</location>
  <filename>\clips\promos\we-deliver.mov</filename>
  <format>video/quicktime</format>
  <date>2001-01-12</date>
  <author>Justine LaGuarde</author>
  <class code="0997">promotional material</class>
  <subjects>
    <subject code="7002">multimedia</subject>
    <subject code="8001">branding and public awareness</subject>
  </subjects>
  <description>
    Video for conferences and the Web site, promoting the skills and
    diversity of our company. The video emphasizes our successes
    and the youth and energy of our employees (all real employees,
    not actors or models), and encourages potential customers to
    trust us to help them build solutions.
  </description>
</document>
```

The XML metadata describing a video looks essentially the same as the metadata describing a document: The same applications can process both. A search for "youth" in the company search engine would return the information for the video in Listing 7-12, whereas a search for "security" in the same search engine would return the information for the document in Listing 7-11.

7.4 Final Words on XML and Legacy Information

It is important to distinguish two different ways of using XML with legacy information:

1. Wrapping a data interface in XML without modifying the legacy system
2. Converting a repository of information to XML, usually permanently

Wrapping an interface in XML RPC (see Chapter 5) can bring significant interoperability benefits for relatively little work. There is a speed cost, however, so extremely high-speed environments, such as trading systems, might not want to use this approach. For everyone else, XML-based interfaces can avoid the need to maintain old client libraries and infrastructures on many different systems, centralizing them all at a single conversion point. The information in the legacy system becomes more transparent and cross-platform, so that many kinds of computers can access the information.

Converting a large information repository to XML can be much more difficult and typically requires a lot of manual intervention, especially if the repository contains loosely structured documents rather than tightly structured data tables. Vendors and consultants are often overly optimistic about the costs of converting old information, so customers should proceed with caution.

Sometimes, conversion is too expensive for the benefits it might realistically bring. Typically, there are two good reasons for converting old information to XML.

1. The information is still live and needs to be updated and maintained in a new, XML-based system.
2. There are explicit data-format requirements for search, query, or sharing information with partners.

In many cases, however, it is best to start by leaving old information in its original format and simply using XML metadata to share information *about* information, rather than the information itself. Metadata in the form of XML documents is easy to share, archive, copy, search, and analyze and is typically much less expensive to produce.

CHAPTER 8

XML Performance and Size

XML has a reputation for being big and slow.

- An XML document is often larger—sometimes *much* larger—than equivalent files in other formats, requiring more memory, disk storage, and network bandwidth.
- XML files need to go through complex parsing and transformations, which can take up considerable processing power and time.

An XML document can be larger in two ways: (1) in its proper XML form, requiring more storage space and bandwidth; and (2) in its compiled, in-memory form, requiring more computing resources.

Sometimes, XML deserves this reputation. Building a Document Object Model [DOM] tree, for example, or performing an XSLT [XSLT] transformation can use up a surprising amount of time and memory. Often, developers miss these problems while building a proof of concept but then run into them hard while building a production system with a full traffic load.

XML's very nature causes some of these problems—a plaintext format with frequent and repeated labels is bound to be a bit big and a bit slow—but XML's designers decided that it was worth trading some size and efficiency for the advantages of a portable, transparent information format. This has been a winning tradeoff in the past: Most of the popular Internet formats, such as SMTP, FTP, HTTP, POP3, and TELNET, also use plaintext, and their transparency and simplicity caused them to win out over more optimized but less transparent competitors.

On the other hand, many of the worst performance problems people run into with XML are a result of the tools and libraries they choose and the way they use them. Toolkits often hide large size and performance costs behind a simple interface: One or two function calls can trigger an exponential time and space explosion behind the scenes. When this happens, developers do not have to give up on XML, but they sometimes have to abandon their toolkits and do more work by hand. This chapter introduces some of the tips and tricks to work around XML's imperfections in a high-performance environment.

8.1 Advantages of XML for Size and Performance

Because XML markup is text, some developers assume that it will always be more verbose and slower to process than binary format. In fact, an optimized binary format can be efficient when the data structure is highly consistent, but when structure varies—for example, with optional or repeatable fields or hierarchical relationships—a binary format can end up as large as an XML file, sometimes even larger.

Likewise, people assume that parsing XML will always be slower than parsing a binary format, but in practice, tool support sometimes cancels out that different: Because XML is so widely used, many free-software developers and commercial vendors have put a lot of time into profiling and optimizing the programs that do low-level XML parsing.

8.1.1 Space Efficiency

When data is in a highly consistent, predictable format, such as a table (see Section 4.3.1), it is possible to build efficient binary formats for storing it. For example, a binary file containing a table of 1,000 rows of 8 short integers will require only 16 octets for each row, or 16,000 octets in total, or even less with some compression schemes. Compare that with a row with typical XML markup in Listing 8-1.

Listing 8-1   A Row of Integers in XML

```
<row>
   <num>18</num>
   <num>11</num>
   <num>64</num>
   <num>23</num>
   <num>5</num>
   <num>65</num>
   <num>2</num>
   <num>10</num>
</row>
```

Even using fairly succinct XML names, such as `row` and `num`, the XML example requires 130 octets for each row, or eight times as much storage space as the binary format.

The binary format is space efficient because it can make assumptions about the data: There is no need to label rows or items, because a new item will start every 2 octets, and a new row will start every 16 octets. But what happens if the data is not *quite* so regular? The binary format will have to start adding extra information.

- If the rows have variable lengths—that is, items can be omitted from the end—the binary file will have to store the length of each row, adding an overhead of 1 or 2 octets for each row.
- If individual items have variable lengths, such as textual data, the binary file will have to store the length of each item, adding an overhead of 1 or 2 octets for each item.
- If items can be omitted or repeated in the middle of rows, the binary file will have to label each item so that it will be clear what has been repeated or omitted, adding an overhead of typically 4 octets for each item, assuming pointers into a name table.
- If the data is not simple rows of items but can have a more complex structure of nodes, the binary file may have to maintain navigational points, such as parent, first child, and next sibling, adding typically 4 octets for each node.

8.1 Advantages of XML for Size and Performance 187

- If leaf and branch nodes can be mixed at the same level, as in XML or HTML mixed content, nodes will require type information, adding typically 1 octet for each node.

Accordingly, Table 8.1 shows that the memory requirement for item, or node, is now 17 octets, excluding the overhead of keeping one unique copy of each element name in a lookup table. By comparison, an item as an XML element can take as few as 4 octets `<a/>`, depending on the name length and encoding.

Even when both the start and end tags appear and the name is longer, such as `table`, the overhead for the start and end tags will be only twice the name length plus 5 octets in UTF-8 encoding, or, in this case, 15 octets, still shorter than the overhead in the binary format. Furthermore, the binary format does not yet have any mechanism for representing the equivalent of XML attributes, which would add yet more pointers and other overhead to it.

In the end, then, it is not the fact that XML is a text-based format that makes it verbose; rather, it is the fact that XML can encode very complex structure. When that extra structure is not necessary, an XML document can also be concise:

```
<r>1 2 3 4 5 6 7 8</r>
```

The 22 octets required for that data row in XML compare favorably to the 16 octets required for the data row in binary format. In fact, if the individual numbers were 4-octet integers, the efficient binary encoding would require 32 octets, whereas this particular XML row would still require only 22 octets. It is possible to tune a binary format to use a little less space, say, by stemming, but it is important to recognize that XML itself, text-based as it is, does provide a relatively efficient way to represent complex structures.

8.1.2 Software and Hardware Support

The text-based protocols used on the Internet—SMTP for sending e-mail, HTTP for retrieving Web resources, FTP for downloading files, and TELNET for connecting to remote machines—are all text based, like XML, and they have suffered from the same complaints that XML faces. Because they are text, they require an initial parsing step that slows down processing.

Table 8-1   A Binary Node

Property	Length (octets)
Type	1
Name pointer	4
Parent pointer	4
Next-sibling pointer	4
First-child pointer	4
Total	17

However, as the Web grew in popularity, individual developers and networking companies started to make software and hardware especially designed to work with these higher-level protocols. For example, many, if not most routers, can read and understand HTTP as well as the lower-level TCP and IP protocols and can make more intelligent routing choices as a result. Hardware acceleration is available for creating and managing HTTP, and networking libraries are efficient and well debugged. It does not matter so much that HTTP adds a little parsing overhead, because modern software and hardware support more than cancels out that disadvantage.

The same process is starting to take place with XML. Although higher-level tools, such as XSLT engines, remain slow, the low-level tools, especially XML parsers, have become fast and robust. Someone parsing an XML file is taking advantage of thousands of hours of experimentation, debugging, profiling, and optimizing that highly competitive XML parser providers—both vendors and free-software developers—have put into their products. Compared to custom-designed code to read a binary format, an XML parser is less likely to crash or fall into performance traps, such as unintentional buffer copying, and more likely to run fast and efficiently.

Furthermore, like HTTP, XML is starting to get hardware support. Several vendors, such as DataPower, Sarvega, and Reactivity, are releasing products for low-level XML parsing and, sometimes, for such higher-level operations as XSLT. This hardware still needs to be proven in the field and the market, but it suggests that the processing inefficiencies particular to XML will matter even less in the future than they do now.

8.2 Disadvantages of XML for Size and Performance

Despite the advantages mentioned in Section 8.1, XML does sometimes cause a significant increase in data size and processing time. These disadvantages are the result of design decisions and tradeoffs made by XML's original designers. For example, to make XML fully internationalized, the designers chose to require Unicode support, which can increase the memory required for processing and storing information from XML documents. The designers also chose the robustness of redundant labels in start and end tags, increasing the amount of space XML requires in disk storage or the amount of bandwidth for moving it over a network. The most serious performance risk, however, is one that people do not often worry about: XML's ability to include external resources.

8.2.1 Repetition

XML repeats every element and attribute name for every element and attribute instance: In fact, it repeats the element name *twice* for every instance. If a long XML document contains 20,000 nonempty elements named `maintenance-entry`, the string `maintenance-entry` will appear in the document 40,000 times, consuming between 680,000 and 2,720,000 bytes of storage space, depending on the character encoding.

For loosely structured XML, such as human-readable documents (see Chapter 3), this overhead is often not a problem, but for highly structured XML, such as a database dump, these repeated names represent a significant overhead. There is a temptation to use short, cryptic element

8.2 Disadvantages of XML for Size and Performance

and attribute names, such as `c183`, instead of `workflow-approval`, destroying XML's advantage of transparency. There is also a temptation to reduce the amount of tagging, using whitespace and line ends to delimit some fields. These solutions are not particularly good, but they do show the desperation people face when dealing with enormous XML data files.

8.2.2 Encoding

Sometimes, text can be more efficient than binary representations: For example, the long integer "1" requires 1 byte to represent in text using UTF-8 text encoding but 4 bytes to represent in a typical binary encoding. More often, however, the XML textual representation is longer: For example, the short integer "15,383" requires between 5 and 20 bytes in text, depending on character encoding, but only 2 bytes in binary form.

In fact, character encoding itself can cause an enormous size increase for XML documents, both in memory and on disk. The Unicode UCS-4 encoding, which, fortunately, almost no one uses, requires 4 octets for each character, so 100,000 characters become 400,000 bytes of storage. UTF-16, which is more common, requires 2 bytes for most characters. UTF-8 requires only 1 byte for ASCII characters but as many as 6 bytes for some Asian characters.

8.2.3 External References

The biggest performance risk for XML comes not from the fact that it is text based, that it is parsed, or that it can use Unicode but from the fact that XML documents can include external files. To make things worse, the inclusion can take place in the lowest-level XML parsing layer, where it is completely hidden from—and sometimes outside the control of—the application developer. For example, consider Listing 8-2.

Listing 8-2   Referencing an External DTD

```
<!DOCTYPE doc SYSTEM "http://www.example.org/dtds/doc.dtd">

<doc>
...
</doc>
```

By default, almost all validating XML parsers will go to `www.example.org` and download `doc.dtd` every time they parse this document, leading to some serious performance problems.

- Even with a fast network connection, each document will likely require seconds rather than milliseconds to parse.
- If `www.example.org` is slow, possibly because of a heavy network load, parsing will slow down even further, possibly on the order of minutes for each document.
- If `www.example.org` goes offline, parsing will fail completely.
- If `www.example.org` has a security breach, an intruder could modify the DTD to cause denial of service or include false information in XML documents referencing it.

External DTD subsets are the greatest danger, but they are not the only way XML documents can cause files to be downloaded automatically during processing: The documents can also use external parameter entities in the DTD subset and external text entities in the document itself. Some XML parsers will also automatically download schemas, such as XML Schema [XML-SCHEMA] or RelaxNG [RELAXNG], referenced from inside a document.

Organizations can work around this problem by always parsing inside a sandbox that prohibits or limits external network access, providing local copies of required files, such as schemas. Many developers do not consider this step at first, however, and when looking over HTTP server logs, it is not uncommon to see some sites hitting the same online DTD file hundreds or thousands of times a day, almost certainly because of automatic downloading by XML parsers.

8.3 Processing Performance

One of XML's great strengths is the enormous selection of libraries, applications, toolkits, and frameworks available to developers in nearly every programming language and on nearly every platform. Sometimes, especially in the case of such low-level components as parsers, this software has been heavily optimized for size or performance. In other cases, however, publicly available XML software is optimized instead for ease of use; when that happens, the software can hide design choices that trigger enormous size or performance hits while processing XML.

When a high-level component, such as an XSLT engine, becomes an efficiency bottleneck, developers need to understand how their tools work and where the costs come from. This section describes some of the optimizations available to developers to improve XML performance for parsing, querying, and transforming XML and then introduces the technique of XML pipelines.

8.3.1 Parsing Interfaces

Although people have come up with some innovative ideas for XML parsing interfaces, such as pull parsers and query-based parsers, nearly all XML parsing interfaces in common use fall into one of two groups:

1. Tree-based interfaces, such as the Document Object Model [DOM]
2. Event-based interfaces, such as the Simple API for XML [SAX]

DOM-like interfaces allow applications to navigate and modify an XML document in much the same way that they navigate and modify a file system, by moving up and down various branches. As a matter of fact, some XML user interfaces even present XML documents using file system iconography, with folder icons for elements and file icons for text.

Unfortunately, the ease of use of DOM-like interfaces comes at a high price: An XML document's entire structure must be available for random access. In practice, that means that the structure must be in a database or, most commonly, in computer memory. During batch processing, building that in-memory data structure requires a time for allocating objects[1] and memory for

---

[1] Tree-based interfaces often require several objects for each markup component.

keeping them, typically five to ten times the size of the original XML document. For a desktop application, these requirements are not usually a problem: A user editing a 2MB XML document will not mind waiting a few seconds for the document to load and can easily spare 20MB of memory to edit it. However, on a system handling hundreds or thousands of XML documents simultaneously and quickly, such as a server or high-speed information system—or even worse, a network appliance—the memory and time overhead are entirely unacceptable.

In these cases, switching to an event-based interface, such as SAX, may be a good choice. SAX-like interfaces do not allow random access to an XML document—although a DOM-like interface is similar to a hard drive, a SAX-like interface is more similar to a tape drive—but the SAX-like interface uses near-constant memory no matter how large an XML document may be[2] and tends to use very little processing time, as it does not need to allocate new objects during its run.

Unfortunately, programming with a SAX-like parsing interface is considerably more complicated than programming with a DOM-like interface. The application needs to capture and store any information it requires as the information streams past, and there is no way to follow backward references in a document. When ease of implementation is the priority, a DOM-like interface makes sense; when performance is the priority, a SAX-like interface makes sense.

Often, applications parsing data-oriented XML documents build their own, in-memory data trees.

- An accounting application might build a tree of ledgers, accounts, and entries.
- A geodata application might build a tree of polygons and points.
- A graphics program might build a tree of shapes and lines.

An application that builds a specialized data tree using a DOM-like XML parsing interface takes a double hit: First, the parser uses a lot of time and memory to build a parse tree of the XML document, and then the application uses more time and memory to build its own tree before discarding the parser's tree. In such a case, simply switching to an event-based interface can reduce an application's time and memory requirements for XML processing to a fraction of what they originally were.

Another place that tree-based interfaces often hide performance is in transformations, discussed in Section 8.3.3.

8.3.2 Queries

Sometimes, an application reads an XML document simply to extract a small bit of information hidden somewhere inside it. A bibliographical application might need to extract only the title and the author's name from an XML-encoded research paper, like the one in Listing 8-3.

---

[2] Memory requirements vary with maximum element nesting depth, not document length: Typically, even long XML documents have elements nested only a few levels deep.

Listing 8-3 Bibliographical Information in a Research Paper
```
<article>
  <articleinfo>
   <title>Frog populations in Frontenac County</title>
   <author>
     <honorific>Dr.</honorific>
     <firstname>Jose</firstname>
     <surname>Schmidt</surname>
     <affiliation>
       <orgdiv>Department of Biology</orgdiv>
       <orgname>King's University</orgname>
     </affiliation>
   </author>
  </articleinfo>

 <sect1>
 <title>Introduction</title>

 <para>During the summers of 1999 and 2000, a team of researchers
    [...]</para>

 [...]

 </sect1>

 [...]

</article>
```

If the paper were 100 pages long, building a DOM tree of the entire XML document simply to extract the title and author information would be extremely wasteful. It is much better to write a short, perhaps 50-line, program in Perl, Java, Python, C, or C++ to extract the required information from an event stream provided by a SAX-like interface. In fact, the application can terminate parsing as soon as it has all the required information, so the parser will not need to read most of the document at all, much less build it into an in-memory tree.

Unfortunately, custom programming is not always a practical solution: Many people need to extract information from XML documents in a more generic way that does not require hard-core computer programming skills. For situations like these, the XML community has largely settled on XPath [XPATH] as a simple query syntax for XML documents.[3] For example, the following

---

[3] At the time of writing, the XQuery [XQUERY] specification was not yet complete. XQuery builds on top of XPath, making it into a proper, full-featured query language. It is not yet clear whether XQuery will gain the kind of widespread acceptance that XPath has.

8.3 Processing Performance

XPath expressions select the element containing the article title and the subtree containing the author's name:

```
/article/articleinfo/title
/article/articleinfo/author
```

A general-purpose query application can use these expressions to return matching fragments from an XML document, the same way that the UNIX `grep` command uses regular expressions to return matching fragments from a text file. An interactive XML editor or browser can use these expressions to bring the cursor to the matching points in a document.

Unfortunately, it is necessary to have random access to the original XML document to support all of XPath, and that, once again, requires a DOM-like interface. In a high-speed environment, in which predictable, consistent performance is important, it may be necessary to restrict queries to the subset of XPath that *can* be supported by a streaming interface. Both of the previous XPath expressions, for example, could be resolved by an application using a SAX-like parsing interface, as they do not require any backward references.

The XPath 1.0 expressions that can be matched most efficiently—for time and memory—are the ones that limit themselves mostly to context on the element stack, particularly parent, child, ancestor, and descendant relationships. For example, all the following XPath expressions could be matched against output from an event-based XML parser, such as a SAX parser, storing no context except for a stack of elements and their attributes up to the root element and the index of each element in the stack relative to its siblings:

```
//caution
/book//chapter/title[contains(string(), "Crimson")]
//section[@id="preface"]//character[string()="Joseph"]
```

- The first XPath expression simply requires matching the `caution` element, with no additional context.
- The second expression requires matching the current element against `title` and examining the element stack to ensure that the parent element is `chapter` and that the root element is `book`, then testing whether the string `"Crimson"` appears in the element's content.
- The third expression requires matching the current element against `character`, testing whether that `section` element with the `id` attribute equal to `"preface"` appears anywhere in the element stack, and testing that the element's content is exactly the string `Joseph`.

These are all queries that will use near-constant memory no matter how long an XML document is, as none requires random access. The following inefficient expressions, on the other hand, do require random access to a document or else the caching of a large part of a document's contents:

```
//caution[../para[contains(string(), "oil")]]
/book//chapter[following-sibling:chapter/title[string()="Crimson"]]
//link[id(@ref)/@status="modified"]
```

- The first XPath expression matches any `caution` element that has a sibling named `para` containing `oil` in its content. As a result, a query engine will have to save the content of every `caution` element until the parser has finished reporting all its siblings.
- The second expression matches any chapter that appears before a chapter with the title `"Crimson"`. As a result, the query engine will have to cache the content of all chapters until the parser is finished processing the parent element.
- The third expression is the most inefficient: In the worst case, it will require the query engine to cache every link element until the end of the document.

Fortunately, the efficiency concerns for XPath expressions are not so serious, because many technical specialists, not to mention ordinary users, will find such expressions anywhere from excessively complicated to baffling. Limiting a high-performance query engine to efficient expressions still provides a respectable amount of query capability while also allowing an application all the advantages of a SAX-like interface (see Section 8.3.1): Modifying an application to use only this subset, together with a SAX-like parser, can bring significant speed and memory improvements to an XML application.

8.3.3 Transformations

Performance problems with transformations are closely related to the problems with parsing interfaces (Section 8.3.1) and queries (Section 8.3.2). The most popular specification for transforming XML documents into XML or another format is XSL Transformations [XSLT], but because XSLT supports the full XPath specification, XSLT also requires random access to the original XML document. Therefore, XSLT engines typically use a DOM-like interface with all the extra time and memory overhead.

XSLT's expressive power, and the fact that it is a template language, make it ideal for complex structural transformations; in those cases, extra time and memory might be a reasonable tradeoff for rapid development. On the other hand, many transformations are small and do not require the ability to restructure a document extensively. In these cases, the significant overhead of using XSLT processors other tree-based transformation tools is unacceptable.

Before considering alternatives, this section takes a quick look at the efficiency of XSLT engines. XSLT engines read an XML document as input and create a new document, possibly XML, as output. Although the engines require random access to the input document, they have no such requirement for output, so there is no need to build a *second* in-memory document tree. Command line XSLT utilities are generally well-enough designed that they do not build a second DOM tree, or the equivalent, but simply write out the result as a stream, However, if an XML project happens to use an XSLT library, a developer could end up using the library to generate a DOM tree, for XML, before writing any output. This is, obviously, a bad idea when memory is at

8.3 Processing Performance

a premium, and fixing this problem is an easy way to halve the memory consumption of any project that uses XSLT.

A second optimization is possible with XSLT, but to date, no one seems to have taken advantage of it. XSLT requires random access to the input document but does not modify the original document; as a result, it is possible to parallelize XSLT processing, assigning different processors to perform different parts of the transformations on the input document.[4] This approach will not solve the memory problem but could bring significant speed improvements for large input documents or complex transformation rules.

As mentioned earlier, however, XSLT's ability to access the input document randomly using XPath expressions is not necessary for many kinds of transformations, and an application working with an event stream, such as SAX, can run much faster, using very little memory. SAX-like transformations are complicated or impossible when the transformation requires major structural changes, but such transformation works well in three cases:

1. Adding information to a document
2. Removing information to a document
3. Modifying information in place, such as renaming elements and attributes or changing text

Many typical transformations fall into these categories. For example, one common transformation for technical and sales publications is adding live data from a database at publication time. The original XML markup might look like that in Listing 8-4.

Listing 8-4   Catalog Entry before Transformation
```
<item>
 <source>Henrickson</source>
 <name>Acoustic Guitar</name>
 <description>This guitar includes a mahogany fret board, gold-plated
  tuning pegs, and a solid top.</description>
 <price dbref="g3905778/price"/>
</item>
```

The transformation engine executes a database query based on the value of the `dbref` attribute in the `price` element and replaces it with the latest price information, as shown in Listing 8-5.

Listing 8-5   Catalog Entry after Transformation
```
<item>
 <source>Henrickson</source>
 <name>Acoustic Guitar</name>
```

---
[4] Thanks to Ken Holman of Crane Softwrights for pointing this out to me.

```
<description>This guitar includes a mahogany fret board, gold-plated
  tuning pegs, and a solid top.</description>
<price>
  <status>sale</status>
  <expiry-date>2005-01-01</expiry-date>
  <currency>USD</currency>
  <amount>1999.00</amount>
</price>
</item>
```

A tree-based transformation engine, such as XSLT, brings little advantage to this kind of work. In fact, because XSLT does not specify a standard method for database access, any XSLT template would not be portable anyway, even if the engine did support database access. On the other hand, using Perl, Python, or Java, a transformation like this is trivial for an experienced developer.

8.3.4 Pipelines

Another performance problem that can creep into an XML processing system is duplicated parsing. An XML document will often pass through several components in a chain from the point it enters a system to the point it leaves; if the XML is written to disk and then reparsed into memory each time a component touches it, a system might slow down.[5] The solution to this problem is to use a processing pipeline like the one in Figure 8-1.

The XML document enters the pipeline through the parser on the left, which converts the document to a series of SAX or SAX-like events. The parser then passes the events on to the first component, which manipulates them as necessary—say, by adding or removing information—then passes the modified events on to another component. The second component knows nothing about the first component: As far as it is concerned, the events could be coming directly from a parser. The second component makes further changes to the event stream and then passes the modified events on to the third component, and so on. At the end of the chain is a component that simply writes the events back out to disk or sends them out over the network in XML format. The alternative to this pipeline would be to parse and rewrite the XML document for each processing component, as in Figure 8-2: Note all the extra work required for processing.

Figure 8-1 XML processing in a pipeline

---

[5] Notwithstanding this problem, XML parsing is normally very fast: Speed problems typically come from higher-level processes, such as tree building, querying, and transformation, not from the low-level parsing. The fastest software-based XML parsers can read thousands of short documents every second, even on a low-end desktop computer.

Figure 8-2 XML processing without a pipeline

The pipeline concept works with both DOM-like interfaces and SAX-like interfaces. For DOM-like interfaces, the components all work on the same in-memory tree in sequence, making changes and then passing the tree on to the next component. The beginning of the pipeline is also a parser—and tree build, in this case—and the last component is also a writer.

Aside from the fact that, for efficiency, the components need to run on the same system, this approach has one problem: Without XML to examine between each component, it can be difficult to find and fix problems. Fortunately, however, the pipeline components are modular, so it is easy to fit in extra debugging components to write out the events as XML at various points in the processing.

The pipeline model is the most common one used by skilled XML developers working with SAX and other event-based interfaces, and it has proved itself in high-speed, high-demand environments. The model is not quite as common with the DOM and other tree-based interfaces, as people tend not to use those in high-speed environments in the first place, but it can work equally well.

8.4 Size

This section describes some ways to work around XML's size problems, both with XML markup and with internal representations of parsed XML documents.

8.4.1 Unicode and Character Size

XML documents can use many different character encodings, and those affect the size of a document on disk, through the network, and in memory. Choosing the right character encoding for a project can be the cheapest and easiest kind of compression.

Because the W3C designed XML for international use, all XML parsers are *required* to support the standard Unicode encodings UTF-8 and UTF-16. Many XML parsers also accept other popular encodings, such as ASCII, ISO-8859-1—the ISO Latin 1 alphabet, sometimes informally called *8-bit ASCII*—and Shift-JIS. Other than the Unicode UTF and UCS encodings, no character encodings support the entire Unicode character set: For example, ISO-8859-1 does not support Japanese characters, and Shift-JIS does not support accented European characters. In XML document instances, however, it is possible to include characters outside the current character set by using character references; the following example includes the Russian word *мир* in an ASCII-encoded XML document:

```
<?xml version="1.0" encoding="US-ASCII"?>

<trivia>The Russian word <q>&#x43c;&#x438;&#x440;</q>
means both <q>world</q> and <q>peace</q>.</trivia>
```

If space and bandwidth are at a premium, then, it is possible to save some space by choosing the right XML character encoding.

- With UTF-16, all characters—at least, all the ones you're likely to use—require 2 octets, so the phrase "Hello, world!" will use 26 octets to store 13 characters.
- With UTF-8, basic ASCII characters require only 1 octet, so "Hello, world!" would use only 13 octets to store 13 characters; however, Cyrillic or accented European characters require 2 octets each, and other characters for other languages can require up to 6 octets.
- With the ISO-8859 character encodings, each character requires only 1 octet, even accented European characters, but any characters not in the set require XML character references, such as `&#x43c;`.

Of course, many other character encodings are available, but the tradeoffs should be obvious. XML documents containing English-language documents and computer programming code will be smallest with UTF-8 and generally twice as large with UTF-16; non-English European languages will be smallest with one of the ISO-8859 alphabets, if available, and only slightly larger with UTF-8. Many other world languages, such as Chinese, will be smallest with UTF-16 or a specialized encoding and can grow considerably larger with UTF-8. In most cases, where storage space is not severely constrained and every millisecond of bandwidth doesn't count, choosing either UTF-8 or UTF-16 and sticking with it may be the best choice; if size is critical, choosing the right encoding for storage can bring considerable savings.

The second Unicode-related size issues come when the XML document has been parsed and read into the computer: Typically, parsers will convert the original XML document's characters into a standard internal encoding for processing, almost always UTF-8 or UTF-16, so that any Unicode characters can be included. The same size advantages and disadvantages for various languages apply here: English and European languages will generally use less space with UTF-8, whereas nonalphabetic languages, such as Chinese, will use less space with UTF-16. There are also processing considerations: UTF-8 works better with older libraries in some programming languages, such as C and C++, but string manipulation can be tricky because characters do not have a fixed width. UTF-16 gives all characters a fixed width and works well with modern programming languages, such as Java, but it can be difficult to use in older libraries and programming languages.

8.4.2 Internalization

Internalization is a useful trick from older programming languages, such as LISP. Because the same symbol, such as `list`, can appear frequently in a LISP program, implementers can save space if they put exactly one copy of each symbol in a lookup table and always point to that one location, rather than copying the symbol over and over again and wasting memory.

Many, if not most, XML parsers internalize element and attribute names in the same way, as a name may appear hundreds or thousands of times in an XML document. In Listing 8-6, the element name `list` appears twice, and the name `item` appears eight times, but the XML parser would allocate only a single instance of each in memory.

8.5 Size

Listing 8-6   Repeated Names
```
<list>
  <item>100</item>
  <item>200</item>
  <item>300</item>
  <item>400</item>
</list>
```

In general, parsers do not internalize other strings, such as attribute values and character data, as they are much less likely to be repeated, and internalizing adds some processing overhead. However, an attribute value or character data content in XML documents is sometimes limited to a set of enumerated values: For example, the status of a task entry in a dictionary might be `"draft"`, `"pending"`, `"approved"`, or `"released"`. Because the value must be one of these and no other, an application can internalize the value of the element or attribute holding the information, as the values are very likely to repeat. Sometimes, XML schemas and DTDs can provide hints to XML processors about what values are enumerated, but applications should pay attention to internalization opportunities as well, as they can provide important memory savings.

8.4.3   Compression

If an XML document is going out over the network or being kept in long-term storage, brute-force compression is sometimes a much better choice than any of the other techniques in this section. XML is text with a lot of repetition, so it compresses surprisingly well. For example, at the point that I'm writing this paragraph, the XML manuscript for this book is 440,320 bytes long. Simply running the manuscript through the UNIX `bzip2 -9` command reduces its size to 98,815 bytes, or only 22 percent of the original. If you are willing to trade a bit of processing time for the sake of reducing storage or network bandwidth requirements, straightforward compression will save far more space than any of the other techniques in this section and will outperform almost any optimized binary format as well.

Unfortunately, brute-force compression is not always the answer. Compressed XML needs to uncompressed before it can be used in any way, and it is virtually useless for in-memory processing. In these cases, specialized compression techniques, such as internalization, can bring some savings, but they are much less dramatic.

8.5   Final Words on Performance and Size

For many XML projects, performance is not as important as people think. Parsing an XML document takes very little time, often a millisecond or less. Typically, an application will spend several orders of magnitude more time processing the information than parsing it, so even a 1,000 percent improvement in parsing time would speed up the typical application too little to matter.

Parsing time does start to matter for applications that need to run at I/O speed, however, and it matters greatly for network appliances that need to run at wire speed. These applications may need specialized solutions, such as XML parsers burned into silicon. Such components are starting to appear, but it will take time before they have an opportunity to prove their performance and value in the field.

For everyone else, the most important optimizations for size and speed come not in XML parsing but in how applications work with the information once an XML parser has delivered it and what encodings they use to store it on disk. Few of the techniques introduced in this chapter will magically eliminate all performance and size problems; used together, however, they may make an application fast enough for today's requirements and, perhaps, even for tomorrow's.

CHAPTER 9

Final Words

In the summer of 2004, XML was at a stage both exciting and frustrating. Popular awareness of XML is very high, not only because of hype around Web Services: XML is generally the first choice for anyone implementing a new file format or planning a project to share large quantities of information among organizations. On the other hand, XML is still surprisingly difficult to use. If I want to send someone a collection of data, such as financial projections or part prices, the recipient will be able to use the information far more easily if I encode it in comma-delimited text or Microsoft's proprietary Excel format than in XML. If I want to publish a short story or submit a project proposal, people will be able to use the document far more easily if I encode it in HTML, PDF, or Microsoft's proprietary Word format rather than in XML. Sadly, those points are true even if the people are not running the Windows operating system.

On the other hand, XML does make it some jobs easier: It can represent much more complex data structures than most other formats, and it comes with internationalization and portability for free. If single-source publishing is a real requirement, nothing does it better than XML, once you've spent enough time and money setting up your system. And even if it ends up being slower, XML networking may be the most valuable kind simply because it connects more people and organizations in more different ways. When old, incompatible, proprietary systems are hindering business and draining money, XML can seem like a very cheap solution indeed.

Because XML has the reputation of being difficult to learn and expensive to set up, much XML writing—and indeed, much of this book—concerns itself with XML in the enterprise and government, not XML for the ordinary user. That is not what XML's creators intended. XML came from the World Wide Web Consortium, an organization with a strong focus on ordinary users and usability, rather than from a database or enterprise software group. XML's creators envisioned an information format that would free ordinary people as well as enterprises to share information in any format they would like. In fact, both of the major browsers available today, Mozilla and Microsoft Internet Explorer, support displaying and manipulating *any* XML document on the user's desktop.

Despite the browser support, using XML for Web documents never caught on, but XML has affected ordinary users in other ways: RSS, for example, is the core engine of the Web log movement, the biggest thing since the Web itself. DocBook allows single-source publishing not only from big publishers but also from the individuals who volunteer their time to work on the Linux operating system: I have used some of their tools to write this book and produce interim proofs. Whatever happens with the muddle of higher-level Web Services specifications, SOAP seems to be catching on: Early implementers, such as Amazon.com and Google, have SOAP servers on the public Internet, available to any user, and SOAP will soon open up the Windows desktop for better interaction with the outside world.

What these success stories all have in common is networks of *people,* not of computers. To make XML succeed, people have to get together and form a social network, based on two principles.

1. They will use one or more common formats for information.
2. They will share that information.

If the group sticks to these principles, the expense and difficulty of setting up XML end up being spread out among many people, and XML—at least in one particular flavor—becomes a cheap and easy solution.

It is important to remember that these networks do not form simply because someone has written a specification or because a group of big vendors has formed a consortium but because people decide to do something together with XML. If you are thinking of starting an XML project—ranging from a personal project in your spare time to a multimillion-dollar enterprise information system—looking for these networks is the key. Where they exist, you will find knowledge and software support to help you do your job, and you will find an audience for your work when it is finished. Where they do not exist, you will bear the burden of high costs and uncertain risks, no matter how high the pile of official specifications and endorsements you have sitting on your desk.

The next few years may tell whether XML moves to the forefront, like HTML, or settles down as just one more enterprise and server-side tool, like Java. It should be an interesting ride, and I would like to wish you the best of luck with your own XML work, wherever it takes you.

Glossary

ad hoc standard   A specification that has been widely accepted and implemented without the backing of any standards body, consortium, or similar organization.

asynchronous   A term used, somewhat loosely, in networking to describe exchanges that do not have to happen at the same time or in the same order.

backward compatibility   The ability to support older versions of a specification or format. Typically, if a specification is backward compatible, it is a superset of the previous version.

BLOB   A *binary large object*, such as a picture or a sound clip, stored in a database. *See also* CLOB.

CLOB   A *character large object*, such as an XML document, stored in a database. *See also* BLOB.

cross-conversion   A translation between two information formats that contain the same type and quantity of information.

data   In common XML usage, highly structured repeating information, such as the type that can appear on spreadsheets or in relational databases.

de facto standard   A specification that has become the equivalent of a standard through widespread adoption.

denormalized   *See* normalized.

document   In common XML usage, loosely structured information with mixed content, such as the type that can appear in word processors or on Web pages.

down conversion   A translation to a simpler format, discarding structure content available in the source format. Down conversion is generally the easiest to automate.

EDI (electronic data interchange)   The practice of exchanging machine-readable information electronically with business partners, particularly in a supply chain. EDI software generally has to be customized or custom written for each business network.

entity relationship   Things (entities), information about things (attributes), and connections to other things (relationships). Database designers and object-oriented programmers often start with entity-relationship models, sometimes using a class diagram.

extensibility   In the context of XML, the ability to add new kinds of information without invalidating an existing specification.

forward compatibility   The ability to support *future* versions of a specification or format, typically by identifying and ignoring unrecognized information in a predictable way.

full-text searching   Nonstructured text searching: looking only at textual content, without any kind of markup or other contextual information.

HTTP (Hypertext Transfer Protocol)   The Internet protocol used for requesting and retrieving resources on the World Wide Web. HTTP is also the basis of most XML networking specifications.

legacy information   In XML usage, any information *not* encoded in XML, particularly textual information.

metadata   Information about information. For example, a library card is metadata for a book.

mixed content   Text and subelements mixed together in an element's content.

mixed conversion   A translation between two information formats, each of which contains some types of information not present in the other.

namespace   *See* XML Namespace.

network effect   The theory that the value of a network or specification is roughly proportional to the number of users, squared. This theory explains why people tend to converge quickly around standards once they reach a certain level of acceptance and why crude specifications with many users tend to defeat technically elegant specifications with few users.

normalized   Used loosely, a relational database or other data set in which no information is repeated anywhere in the data set. For example, if two objects refer to the same street address, that address must be made into an object of its own.

primary key   For database specialists, a unique identifier that can be used to retrieve a row of data, roughly corresponding to an object.

publish/subscribe   A type of networking whereby a recipient starts and stops a flow of information from a provider by subscribing and unsubscribing.

remote procedure call   A library, method, or other programming invocation made across machines.

request/response   A type of networking whereby the recipient sends a single query to a server, which sends a reply. HTTP follows the request/response model.

REST   Representational state transfer, a popular rule that every resource available online must have a unique and persistent address.

RPC   *See* remote procedure call

schema   In XML usage, a set of structural rules that can be used either to help authors generate documents or to check documents' validity. Popular schemas are DTDs, W3C XML Schema, and RelaxNG.

SGML   *See* Standard Generalized Markup Language

Glossary

single-source publishing Publishing to multiple formats, such as the Web and print, from a single XML master document.

Standard Generalized Markup Language XML's predecessor, ratified by ISO as a standard in 1986 but now mostly obsolete.

synchronous In networking, a loose term for exchanges that happen close to the same time and in order, such as an HTTP request/response.

transformation Converting information from one structure to another. XML specialists usually use the term *transformation* to refer exclusively to XML-XML conversions and *formatting* to refer to other kinds of conversion.

unicast In networking, sending information from a single source to a single destination.

up conversion Data translation that adds information or structure to the source. This is the most difficult kind of conversion to automate and often needs to be done by hand.

XML Namespace A technique for making XML element and attribute names globally unique, similar to Java and Perl packages.

Bibliography

This short section mentions a handful of somewhat recent XML books that I've found useful or interesting. But these are not the only good books or even necessarily the best. In fact, by the time you read this, the best XML books may be ones that did not exist at the time of writing. Go to your local bookstore, browse a bit, and enjoy. Apologies in advance to my many fellow authors whose work deserves to appear here but does not.

This book deals with XML best practices at a middle level, somewhere between managers and developers. A companion book for developers is Elliotte Rusty Harold's *Effective XML: 50 Specific Ways to Improve Your XML* (Addison-Wesley, 2004), which dives into the low-level details of XML design and processing, such as when to use attributes and elements. You do not necessarily have to agree with Elliotte's opinions on every issue, but knowing what the issues are will help you make your own, informed decisions.

If you use SAX and Java, a good resource is David Brownell's *SAX2* (O'Reilly, 2002), which goes over the SAX specification in detail and introduces various programming strategies for building XML applications on top of SAX. There have been minor changes to SAX since this book came out, but none is very significant.

Two excellent books are available on XSL, written by two of the best-known names in the field. Michael Kay's *XSLT: Programmer's Reference* (Wrox, 2001) is still the first place to go for learning XSLT. The software mentioned in the book is out of date, but the techniques and examples are still useful. Ken Holman's *Definitive XSL-FO* (Prentice-Hall, 2003) is a good, detailed complement for generating formatting print output at the other end of the XSL processing chain.

The W3C XML Schema specification comes with a primer that does a good job of introducing the specification, but when the time comes for you to understand W3C XML Schema in more depth, Priscilla Walmsley's book *Definitive XML Schema* (Prentice-Hall, 2002) is much more readable than the full W3C Recommendation and contains many examples.

Without doubt, many other good XML books are available. Some of my original favorites are now too old to list here, as is my own first book, *Structuring XML Documents* (Prentice-Hall, 1998).

Specifications Referenced

[**ASCII**] *X3.4-1977: American National Standard Code for Information Interchange.* American National Standards Institute (ANSI) Standard, 1977.

[**CALS-TABLE**] Norman Walsh. *XML Exchange Table Model Document Type Definition.* Organization for the Advancement of Structured Information Standards (OASIS) Technical Memorandum TR 9901:1999. Available for free download (http://www.oasis-open.org/specs/tm9901.html).

[**CANONICAL-XML**] John Boyer. *Canonical XML Version 1.0.* World Wide Web Consortium (W3C) Recommendation, 15 March 2001. Available for free download (http://www.w3.org/TR/xml-c14n).

[CSS] Bert Bos, Tantek Çelik, Ian Hickson, and Håkon Wium Lie. *Cascading Style Sheets, Level 2 Revision 1: CSS 2.1 Specification.* World Wide Web Consortium (W3C) Candidate Recommendation, 25 February 2004. Available for free download (http://www.w3.org/TR/CSS21/).

[DOCBOOK] Norman Walsh. *The DocBook Document Type.* Organization for the Advancement of Structured Information Standards (OASIS) Committee Specification 4.2, 16 July 2002. Available for free download (http://www.docbook.org/specs/cs-docbook-docbook-4.2.html).

[DOM] Arnaud Le Hors, Philippe Le Hégaret, Lauren Wood, Gavin Nicol, Jonathan Robie, Mike Champion, and Steve Byrne. *Document Object Model (DOM) Level 3 Core Specification.* World Wide Web Consortium (W3C) Recommendation, 7 April 2004. Available for free download (http://www.w3.org/TR/2004/REC-DOM-Level-3-Core-20040407/).

[DSDL] *ISO/IEC 19757—DSDL Document Schema Definition Languages.* This work is currently under way: There are links to some material on the project home page (http://dsdl.org/).

[DUBLIN-CORE] *Dublin Core Metadata Element Set, Version 1.1: Reference Description.* Dublin Core Metadata Initiative (DMCI) Recommendation, 2 June 2003. Available for free download (http://dublincore.org/documents/dces).

[EBXML] ebXML Technical Architecture Product Team. *ebXML Technical Architecture Specification v1.0.4.* United Nations Centre for Trade Facilitation and Electronic Business (UN/CEFACT) and Organization for the Advancement of Structured Information Standards (OASIS), 16 February 2001. Available for free download (http://www.ebxml.org/specs/ebTA.pdf).

[HTML] Dave Raggett, Arnaud Le Hors, and Ian Jacobs. *HTML 4.01 Specification.* World Wide Web Consortium (W3C) Recommendation, 24 December 1999. Available online (http://www.w3.org/TR/html401/).

[HTTP] *Hypertext Transfer Protocol—HTTP/1.1.* Internet Engineering Task Force (IETF) RFC 2616, 1999. Available for free download (http://www.ietf.org/rfc/rfc2616.txt).

[HYTIME] *ISO/IEC 10744:1997: Information Technology—Hypermedia/Time-Based Structuring Language (HyTime).* International Organization for Standardization (ISO) and International Electrotechnical Commission (IEC), 1977.

[ICE] Jay Brodsky et al. *The Information and Content Exchange (ICE) Protocol.* IDEAlliance Working Draft Version 2.0, 1 December 2003. Available for free download (http://www.icestandard.org/spec/SPEC-ICE-2.0Full.pdf).

[INFOSET] John Cowan and Richard Tobin. *XML Information Set (Second Edition).* World Wide Web Consortium (W3C) Recommendation, 4 February 2004. Available for free download (http://www.w3.org/TR/xml-infoset/).

[IP] Information Sciences Institute, University of Southern California. *Internet Protocol: DARPA Internet Program Protocol Specification.* Defense Advanced Research Projects Agency (DARPA), September 1981. Now Internet Engineering Task Force (IETF) RFC 791. Available for free download (http://www.ietf.org/rfc/rfc0791.txt).

[ISO-639] *ISO 639-1:2002 Codes for the representation of names of languages—Part 1: Alpha-2 code.* International Organization for Standardization (ISO), 2002. Available online (http://www.loc.gov/standards/iso639-2/langhome.html).

[ISO-1000] *ISO 1000:1992 SI units and recommendations for the use of their multiples and of certain other units.* International Organization for Standardization (ISO), 1992.

[ISO-3166] *ISO 3166-1:1997 Codes for the representation of names of countries and their subdivisions—Part 1: Country codes.* International Organization for Standardization (ISO), 1997. Available online (http://www.iso.ch/iso/en/prods-services/iso3166ma/02iso-3166-code-lists/list-en1.html).

[ISO-4217] *ISO 4217:2001 Codes for the representation of currencies and funds.* International Organization for Standardization (ISO), 2001. Available online. (http://www.bsi-global.com/Technical%2BInformation/Publications/_Publications/tig90.xalter).

[MATHML] David Carlisle, Patrick Ion, Robert Miner, and Nico Poppelier. *Mathematical Markup Language (MathML) Version 2.0 (Second Edition).* World Wide Web Consortium (W3C) Recommendation, 21 October 2003. Available for free download (http://www.w3.org/TR/MathML/).

[MIME] N. Freed and N. Borenstein. *Multipurpose Internet Mail Extensions (MIME) Part Two: Media Types.* Internet Engineering Task Force (IETF) RFC 2046. Available for free download (http://www.ietf.org/rfc/rfc2046.txt).

[NAMESPACES] Tim Bray, Dave Hollander, and Andrew Layman. *Namespaces in XML.* World Wide Web Consortium (W3C) Recommendation, 14 January 1999. Available for free download (http://www.w3.org/TR/REC-xml-names/).

[NEWSML] *NewsML Version 1.2 Functional Specification.* International Press Telecommunication Council (IPTC) 10 October 2003. Available online http://www.newsml.org/IPTC/NewsML/1.2/specification/NewsML1.2-spec-functionalspec_7.html).

[NITF] News Industry Text Format (NITF) version 3.2. International Press Telecommunications Council (NITF) 14 October 2003. Available for free download (http://www.nitf.org/specifications.php).

[OGSI] S. Tuecke et al. *Open Grid Services Infrastructure (OGSI) Version 1.0.* Global Grid Forum (GGF), 27 June 2003. Available for free download (http://www-unix.globus.org/toolkit/draft-ggf-ogsi-gridservice-33_2003-06-27.pdf).

[OSI] *ISO/IEC TR 13532:1995 Information technology—Telecommunications and information exchange between systems—Protocol combinations to provide and support the OSI Network Service.* International Organization for Standardization (ISO), 27 December 1995.

[OWL] Deborah L. McGuinness and Frank van Harmelen. *OWL Web Ontology Language Overview.* World Wide Web Consortium (W3C) Recommendation, 10 February 2004. Available for free download (http://www.w3.org/TR/owl-features/).

[PRISM] *PRISM: Publishing Requirements for Industry Standard Metadata Version 1.2(h).* IDEAlliance, 23 September 2003. Available for free download (http://www.prismstandard.org/PAM_1.0/PRISM_1.2h.pdf).

[RDDL] Jonathan Borden and Tim Bray. *Resource Directory Description Language (RDDL).* 18 February 2002. Available for free download (http://www.rddl.org/).

[RDF] Dave Beckett. *RDF/XML Syntax Specification (Revised).* World Wide Web Consortium (W3C) Recommendation, 10 February 2004. Available for free download (http://www.w3.org/TR/rdf-syntax-grammar/).

[RDF-SCHEMA] Dan Brickley and R. V. Guha. *RDF Vocabulary Description Language 1.0: RDF Schema.* World Wide Web Consortium (W3C) Recommendation, 10 February 2004. Available for free download (http://www.w3.org/TR/rdf-schema/).

[RELAXNG] James Clark and Makoto Murata. *RELAX NG Specification.* Organization for the Advancement of Structured Information Standards (OASIS) Committee Specification, 3 December 2001. Available for free download (http://www.relaxng.org/spec-20011203.html).

[RFC822] David H. Crocker. *Standard for the Format of ARPA Internet Text Messages.* Internet Engineering Task Force (IETF) RFC 822, 13 August 1982. Available online (http://www.ietf.org/rfc/rfc822.txt).

[RTF] *Rich Text Format (RTF) Specification, version 1.6.* Microsoft Corporation, 1999. Available online (http://msdn.microsoft.com/library/default.asp?url=/library/en-us/dnrtfspec/html/rtfspec.asp).

[RSS] *See [RSS1.0] and [RSS2.0]*

[RSS1.0] Gabe Beged-Dov et al. *RDF Site Summary (RSS) 1.0.* RSS-Dev Working Group, 9 December 2000. Available online (http://web.resource.org/rss/1.0/spec). *Note: see also [RSS2.0].*

[RSS2.0] Dave Winer. *RSS 2.0 Specification.* Harvard Law, 15 July 2003. Available online (http://blogs.law.harvard.edu/tech/rssVersionHistory). *Note: in this version, "RSS" stands for "Really Simple Syndication"; see also [RSS1.0].*

[SAX] *Simple API for XML, version 2 (SAX2).* Documentation and implementation available for free download (http://www.saxproject.org/).

[SEMANTIC-WEB] *Semantic Web.* World Wide Web Consortium (W3C). Information available online (http://www.w3.org/2001/sw/).

[SGML] *ISO 8879:1986(E). Information processing—Text and Office Systems—Standard Generalized Markup Language (SGML).* International Organization for Standardization (ISO) 15 October 1986.

[SMTP] John Postel. *Simple Mail Transfer Protocol.* Internet Engineering Task Force (IETF) RFC 821, August 1982. Available for free download (http://www.ietf.org/rfc/rfc0821.txt).

[SOAP] Nilo Mitra. *SOAP Version 1.2 Part 0: Primer.* World Wide Web Consortium (W3C) Recommendations, 24 June 2003. Available online (http://www.w3.org/TR/2003/REC-soap12-part0/).

http://www.w3.org/TR/2003/REC-soap12-part1/
http://www.w3.org/TR/2003/REC-soap12-part2/
http://www.w3.org/TR/2003/REC-soap12-testcollection/

[SQL] *ISO/IEC 9075-1:2003 Information technology—Database Languages—SQL—Part 1: Framework (SQL/Framework).* International Organization for Standardization (ISO), 12 December 2003. (ANSI X 3.135-1992 is the widely implemented version of SQL).

[SVG] Jon Ferraiolo, Jun Fujisawa, and Dean Jackson. *Scalable Vector Graphics (SVG) 1.1 Specification.* World Wide Web Consortium (W3C) Recommendation, 14 January 2003. Available for free download (http://www.w3.org/TR/SVG/).

Bibliography

[TCP] Jon Postel. *Transmission Control Protocol DARPA Internet Program Protocol Specification.* Internet Engineering Task Force (IETF) RFC 793, September 1981. Available for free download (http://www.ietf.org/rfc/rfc0793.txt).

[TEI] C. M. Sperberg-McQueen and Lou Burnard. *Text Encoding Initiative: The XML Version of the TEI Guidelines.* Text Encoding Initiative (TEI), 2004. Available online (http://www.tei-c.org/P4X/).

[UDDI] Tom Bellwood et al. *UDDI Version 3.0.1.* Organization for the Advancement of Structured Information Standards (OASIS) Technical Committee Specification, 14 October 2003. Available online (http://uddi.org/pubs/uddi-v3.0.1-20031014.htm).

[UML] *OMG Unified Modeling Language Specification.* Object Management Group (OMG), 3 March 2001. Available online (http://www.omg.org/docs/formal/03-03-01.pdf).

[UNICODE] Joan Aliprand et al. *The Unicode Standard, Version 4.0.* The Unicode Consortium, 2003. Available online (http://www.unicode.org/versions/Unicode4.0.1/).

[URI] Tim Berners-Lee et al. *Uniform Resource Identifiers (URI): Generic Syntax.* Internet Engineering Task Force (IETF) RFC 2396, August 1998. Available online (http://www.ietf.org/rfc/rfc2396.txt).

[URL] Tim Berners-Lee et al. *Uniform Resource Locators (URL).* Internet Engineering Taskforce (IETF) RFC 1738, December 1994. Available online (http://www.ietf.org/rfc/rfc1738.txt).

[VRML] *ISO/IEC 14772 Information technology—Computer Graphics and Image Processing—The Virtual Reality Modeling Language: Part 1: Functional Specification and UTF-8 Encoding.* International Organization for Standardization (ISO), 1997. Available online (http://www.web3d.org/x3d/specifications/vrml/ISO_IEC_14772-All/index.html).

[WSDL] Erik Christensen, et al. *Web Services Description Language (WSDL) 1.1.* World Wide Web Consortium (W3C) Note, 15 March 2001. Available online (http://www.w3.org/TR/wsdl).

[XBRL] Philip Engel et al. *Extensible Business Reporting Language (XBRL) 2.1.* XBRL International Recommendation, 31 December 2003. Available for free download (http://www.xbrl.org/specification/XBRL-RECOMMENDATION-2003-12-31+Corrected-Errata-2004-04-29.pdf).

[XFORMS] Micah Dubinko et al. *XForms 1.0.* World Wide Web Consortium (W3C) Recommendation, 14 October 2003. Available online (http://www.w3.org/TR/xforms/).

[XHTML] *XHTML (TM) 1.0 The Extensible HyperText Markup Language (Second Edition): A Reformulation of HTML 4 in XML 1.0.* World Wide Web Consortium (W3C) Recommendation, 26 January 2000. Available online (http://www.w3.org/TR/xhtml1/).

[XLINK] Steve DeRose, Eve Maler, and David Orchard. *XML Linking Language (XLink) Version 1.0.* World Wide Web Consortium (W3C) Recommendation, 27 June 2001. Available online (http://www.w3.org/TR/xlink/).

[XMI] *OMG XML Metadata Interchange (XMI) Specification, version 1.2.* Object Management Group (OMG), January 2002. Available online (http://www.omg.org/docs/formal/02-01-01.pdf).

[XML] Tim Bray, Jean Paoli, C. M. Sperberg-McQueen, Eve Maler, and François Yergeau. *Extensible Markup Language (XML) 1.0.* (Third Edition). World Wide Web Consortium (W3C) Recommendation, 4 February 2004. Available online (http://www.w3.org/TR/REC-xml/).

[XML-CATALOG] Norman Walsh. *XML Catalogs.* Organization for the Advancement of Structured Information Standards (OASIS) Committee Specification, 24 October 2002. Available online (http://www.oasis-open.org/committees/entity/specs/cs-entity-xml-catalogs-1.0.html).

[XML-ENCRYPTION] Donald Eastlake and Joseph Reagle. *XML Encryption Syntax and Processing.* World Wide Web Consortium (W3C) Recommendation, 10 December 2002. Available online (http://www.w3.org/TR/xmlenc-core/).

[XML-INFOSET] John Cowan and Richard Tobin. *XML Information Set (Second Edition).* World Wide Web Consortium (W3C) Recommendation, 4 February 2004. Available online (http://www.w3.org/TR/xml-infoset/).

[XML-RPC] Dave Winer. *XML-RPC Specification,* 15 June 1999. Available online (http://www.xmlrpc.com/spec).

[XML-SCHEMA] David C. Fallside. *XML Schema Part 0: Primer.* World Wide Web Consortium (W3C) Recommendation, 2 May 2001. (See additional parts at the same location with the normative specification.) Available online (http://www.w3.org/TR/2001/REC-xmlschema-0-20010502/).

[XML-SIGNATURE] Donald Eastlake, Joseph Reagle, and David Solo. *XML-Signature Syntax and Processing.* World Wide Web Consortium (W3C) Recommendation, 12 February 2002. Available online (http://www.w3.org/TR/xmldsig-core/).

[XML-STYLESHEET] James Clark. *Associating Style Sheets with XML Documents Version 1.0.* World Wide Web Consortium (W3C) Recommendation, 29 June 1999. Available online (http://www.w3.org/TR/xml-stylesheet/).

[XPATH] James Clark and Steve DeRose. *XML Path Language (XPath) Version 1.0.* World Wide Web Consortium (W3C) Recommendation, 16 November 1999. Available online (http://www.w3.org/TR/xpath).

[XPOINTER] Steve DeRose, Eve Maler, and Ron Daniel Jr. *XML Pointer Language (XPointer) Version 1.0.* World Wide Web Consortium (W3C) Last Call Working Draft, 8 January 2001. Available online (http://www.w3.org/TR/WD-xptr).

[XQUERY] Scott Boag et al. *XQuery 1.0: An XML Query Language.* World Wide Web Consortium (W3C) Working Draft, 23 July 2004. Available online (http://www.w3.org/TR/xquery/).

[XSL-FO] Sharon Adler et al. *Extensible Stylesheet Language (XSL).* World Wide Web Consortium (W3C) Recommendation, 15 October 2001. Available online (http://www.w3.org/TR/xsl/).

[XSLT] James Clark. *XSL Transformations (XSLT) Version 1.0.* World Wide Web Consortium (W3C) Recommendation, 16 November 1999. Available online (http://www.w3.org/TR/xslt).

[XTM] Steve Pepper and Graham Moore. *XML Topic Maps (XTM) 1.0.* TopicMaps.Org Specification, 6 August 2001. Available online (http://www.topicmaps.org/xtm/).

Bibliography

Organizations Referenced

[**HL7**] *Health Level Seven* (HL7). http://www.hl7.org/.

[**IDEALLIANCE**] *IDEAlliance.* http://www.idealliance.org/.

[**IETF**] *Internet Engineering Task Force (IETF).* http://www.ietf.org/.

[**IPTC**] *International Press Telecommunications Council (IETF).* http://www.iptc.org/.

[**ISO**] *International Organization for Standardization* (ISO). http://www.iso.org/.

[**MOZILLA**] *The Mozilla Foundation.* http://www.mozilla.org/.

[**OASIS**] *Organization for the Advancement of Structured Information Standards* (OASIS). http://www.oasis-open.org/.

[**ROSETTANET**] *RosettaNet.* http://www.rosettanet.org/. (Warning: cookies required.)

[**UN-CEFACT**] *United Nations Centre for Trade Facilitation and Electronic Business* (UN-CEFACT). http://www.unece.org/cefact/.

[**UN-EDIFACT**] *United Nations Directories for Electronic Data Interchange for Administration, Commerce and Transport* (UN-EDIFACT). http://www.unece.org/trade/untdid/welcome.htm.

[**USPTO**] *United States Patent and Trademark Office* (USPTO). http://www.uspto.gov/.

[**W3C**] *World Wide Web Consortium* (W3C). http://www.w3.org/.

[**WS-I**] *Web Services Interoperability Organization* (WS-I). http://www.ws-i.org/.

Index

Abstraction
   data, 81
   standards for, 4, 6–7, 10
Acceleration, 117, 188
ACID (atomicity, consistency, isolation, durability) tests, 103–105
Addressable data, 98
Adobe PostScript language
   as de facto standard, 26
   for printing, 73
Advanced searches, 148–149
Aircraft manuals, 56, 74
American Iron and Steel Institute, 17
American National Standards Institute (ANSI), 11
Analysis of legacy information, 173–174
ANSI (American National Standards Institute), 11
APIs, 22
Application specifications, 24–25
Archiving data
   benefits of, 80
   in XML projects, 34, 36
Artificial intelligence in search process, 162
Associating Style Sheets with XML Documents, 20
Asynchronous networking, 119, 126–127
Atomicity in ACID test, 103
Attributes
   in markup, 64
   in relationships, 87
   repetition of, 188

Auditing data, 80
Authors, in-line markup for, 154
Automated conversions with legacy information, 181
Automation, 77

B2B (business-to-business)
   automation for, 77
   types of, 134–135
Backward compatibility, 44
Base64 encoding, 96
Batch requests, 116
Batch searching, 37
Berners-Lee, Tim, 13, 162
Binary data
   external references, 96
   internal, 96–97
   representations of, 189
   space efficiency in, 186
Binary Large Objects (BLOBs), 34, 36
Binding
   data, 94, 109–110
   programming languages, 22
   in WSDL, 128–129
BIS (Bureau of Indian Standards), 11
Bloat in legacy information, 175–176
BLOBs (Binary Large Objects), 34, 36
Bloomberg service, 38
Boolean searches, 148
Bourret, Ronald, 110
Bray, Tim, 147–148
Broadcast networking, 119

Budgets in XML projects, 46–47
Bureau of Indian Standards (BIS), 11
Business documents, 134
Business-to-business (B2B)
  automation for, 77
  types of, 134–135
bzip2 program, 199

CALS Table Model, 21
Canonical XML, 19
Capitalization, 58–59
Cascading style sheets (CSS), 12
  as filters, 23
  XML support in, 69
CDATA sections, 52
Change markup, 62–63
  custom publishing issues in,
    65–66
  problems from, 63–65
Character large objects (CLOBs), 36
Character size, 197–198
Client-side rendering, 38
Client-side XML, 69
CLOBs (character large objects), 36
Cluster computing vs. grid computing, 131
Code reduction in legacy information, 172
Collaboration protocol profiles, 135
Collections, 98
Common data styles, 81–82
  graph, 85–90
  hierarchical, 90–92
  tabular, 82–85
Common Object Request Broker
    Architecture (CORBA), 121
Compatibility
  networking for, 115–116
  in standards, 27–29
  in XML projects, 44–46
Compressed XML, 107
Compression, 199

CompuServe, 33
Computer games, external metadata for, 158
Concurrent version system (CVS), 36, 74
Consistency
  in ACID test, 103
  in standards, 27–29
Content
  management of, 74–75
  non-XML, 95–97
  vs. protocols, 136–137
Context in searches, 143–145
Converting
  currency, 147
  legacy information, 177–182
  XML to HTML, 38
CORBA (Common Object Request Broker
    Architecture), 121
Core specifications, 18
Correlation in searches, 145–147
Country identification codes, 11,
    100
Cover, Robin, 8, 17, 25
Cover Pages, 8, 17, 25
Creation stage in XML projects, 34–35
Cross-conversions with legacy information,
    177
Currency
  codes for, 11, 100
  converting, 147
Custom coding, transformation for, 37
Custom libraries, reading XML with, 110
Custom programming for queries, 192
Custom publishing, 56, 65–66
CVS (concurrent version system), 36, 74

Data, 77
  abstraction, 81
  advantages of, 78
  archiving and auditing, 80
  binding, 94, 109–110

Index

common styles, 81–82
    graph, 85–90
    hierarchical, 90–92
    tabular, 82–85
data typing, 105–108
identification of, 98–99
    existing schemes for, 100
    future possibilities, 101–103
    in searches, 146
interoperability of, 80–81
markup issues in, 93
    non-XML content, 95–97
    whitespace handling, 93–95
platform and storage independence, 78–79
resources for, 81
reusability of, 79
self-documentation, 79
summary, 111
transactions, 103–105
verification, 79–80
Data interchange format (DIF), 78–79
Data-oriented XML, 93
Database metadata in searches, 37
DataPower, 188
DCMI (Dublin Core Metadata Initiative), 15, 149–150
DCOM (Distributed Component Object Model), 121
De facto vs. *de jure* standards, 26–27
Denormalized documents, 71
Department of Defense (DoD) networking model, 136
Diagrams, UML, 25
Dictionaries, 74–75
DIF (data interchange format), 78–79
Direct mapping to programming interfaces, 110

Disruptive technologies, 33, 40
Distributed Component Object Model (DCOM), 121
Distributed computing, 131
DocBook specification, 13
    interoperability with, 151
    for Linux, 25
    for master documents, 54
    words in, 145
Document Object Model (DOM)
    for parsing, 190–191
    programming bindings for, 22
    tree-based, 180, 185, 192
    W3C working group for, 13
Document type definitions (DTDs), 23
    costs of, 46
    external, referencing, 189–190
    for searching, 159–161
    top-levels of, 75
    validation, 27–28
Documents, XML, 51–53
    change markup in, 62–66
    client-side XML, 69
    content management in, 74–75
    custom publishing, 56
    hybrid data publishing, 55–56
    idioms, 72–74
    knowledge preservation in, 58–59
    layout control for, 61–62
    looseleaf publishing, 66–67
    multiple text flows in, 67–69
    people limitations in, 60–61
    reusability of, 57, 70–72
    single-source publishing, 53–54
    summary, 76
DoD (Department of Defense) networking model, 136
DOM (Document Object Model)
    for parsing, 190–191
    programming bindings for, 22

DOM (Document Object Model) (*cont.*)
    tree-based, 180, 185, 192
    W3C working group for, 13
DOM-like interfaces, 190–191
    pipelines in, 197
    for XSLT, 194
Domain names, 102–103
Down conversions with legacy information, 177
DTDs. *See* Document type definitions (DTDs)
Dublin Core
    for consistency and compatibility, 29
    for RDF data, 156
    with Semantic Web, 164
Dublin Core Metadata Initiative (DCMI), 15, 149–150
Duplicated parsing, 196–197
Durability in ACID test, 104

ebXML
    as B2B initiative, 135
    development of, 14
EDI (electronic data interchange), 14, 134–135
8-bit ASCII encoding, 197
Element content, 95
Element names, repetition of, 188
Emacs LISP language, 70
Embeddable specifications, 19–21
Emergency phone service, 5
Empty tags, 63
Encoding, 189, 197–198
End users in search process, 161
Enterprise resource planning (ERP), 176
Entities in relationships, 87
Enumerated values, 106
ERP (enterprise resource planning), 176

Event-based interfaces, 190–191
Everything-is-a-string philosophy, 98
Excel spreadsheet
    as standard, 78
    tabular style for, 82
    XML format for, 24
Expressions, XPath, 193
Extensibility
    in networking, 114–115
    in XML projects, 44–46
Extensible Business Reporting Language (XBRL) format, 80
Extensible Hypertext Markup Language (XHTML), 25
    consistency in, 29
    interoperability with, 151
External metadata in searches, 154–159
External references, 189–190

Facades for legacy interfaces, 168–170
Fatal errors, 115
Fear, uncertainty, and doubt (FUD) standards, 7–8
Feed readers and aggregators in RSS, 134
Fielding, Roy, 119
Financial-planning software, 133
Firewalls, 117
Flexibility in switching, 139
Footnotes, text flow in, 68
Format level, interoperability in, 5
Formats vs. protocols, 113
Formatting
    change markup, 62–66
    as information, 58–59
    vs. meaning, 54
Forward compatibility, 44–46
FoxPro, 78
Frustration problem, 41
FTP, plaintext with, 185, 187

Index

FUD (fear, uncertainty, and doubt) standards, 7–8
Full-text searches, 37, 143
Fully normalized data, 86–90

Generalized Markup Language (GML), 51
GET headers and requests
    in HTTP, 137–138
    in SOAP, 123
Global identifiers, 100–102
Globus Toolkit, 132
GML (Generalized Markup Language), 51
Gnumeric spreadsheet, XML format for, 24
Goldfarb, Charles, 51
Google search engine, 143–144
Granularity
    in in-line markup, 153
    in legacy information mismatches, 174–175
Graph style, 85–90
Graphic Communications Association, 14
Grid computing, 131–132
Growth in legacy information, 176

Hardware acceleration, 117, 188
Hardware support in performance, 187–188
Headers in HTTP, 137–138
Health Level Seven (HL7), 17
Heuristics in legacy information conversions, 177
Hierarchical style, 90–92
Holman, Ken, 23, 195
Homographs in searches, 144
HTML (Hypertext Markup Language)
    converting XML to, 38
    development of, 12
    extensibility of, 115
    forms and scripts with, 9
    meta elements in, 149–150

    for online documentation, 53
    SGML inspiration for, 52
    vs. XML, 78
HTTP (Hypertext Transfer Protocol)
    extensibility of, 115
    GET headers in, 137–138
    library problems with, 10
    plaintext with, 185, 188
    specifications for, 12
    support for, 113
    for transport, 34
Human intelligence in search process, 161
Human-readable format, 170–172
Hybrid data publishing, 55–56
Hypertext Markup Language. *See* HTML (Hypertext Markup Language)
Hypertext Transfer Protocol. *See* HTTP (Hypertext Transfer Protocol)
HyTime specification, 157

IANA (Internet Assigned Numbers Authority), 101
IBM databases, XML support for, 36
ICANN (International Corporation for Assigned Names and Numbers), 101
ICAO (International Civil Aviation Organization) airport identifiers, 101
ICE (Information and Content Exchange), 15, 38, 134
IDEAlliance, 14–15
Identification of data, 98–99
    existing schemes for, 100
    future possibilities, 101–103
    in searches, 146
Idioms, 72–74
IETF (Internet Engineering Task Force), 12
Ignorable whitespace, 95
In-line markup, 151–154

Independence, platform and storage, 78–79
Indexes
    in in-line markup, 152
    in structural searches, 37
Influence in XML projects, 42–44
Information and Content Exchange (ICE), 15, 38, 134
Information exchange, 91
Information publishing, 91
Inheritance relationships in searches, 163–164
Intelligence in search process, 161–162
Interface designers in search process, 161
Interfaces, legacy, 168–170
Internal text entities, 71
Internalization and size, 198–199
International Civil Aviation Organization (ICAO) airport identifiers, 101
International Corporation for Assigned Names and Numbers (ICANN), 101
International Organization for Standardization (ISO), 11–12
International Press Telecommunication Council (IPTC), 17
International Standard Book Number (ISBN), 100
Internationalization in networking, 114
Internet, interoperability in, 5
Internet Assigned Numbers Authority (IANA), 101
Internet Engineering Task Force (IETF), 12
Internet Explorer, XSLT support in, 22
Internet Protocol (IP), 115
Internet worm, 9
Interoperability
    of data, 80–81
    in searches, 150–151
    standards for, 4–6
Interprocess communications (IPC), 121
Inventory information, 109–110

Invited experts, 13
IP (Internet Protocol), 115
IPC (interprocess communications), 121
IPTC (International Press Telecommunication Council), 17
ISBN (International Standard Book Number), 100
ISO (International Organization for Standardization), 11–12
ISO-8859 encoding, 198
ISO Latin 1 alphabet, 197
Isolation in ACID test, 103–104

Java language
    memory leaks with, 10
    for server-side development, 9
JavaDoc system, 71
Jazz standards, 3
JSPs (JavaServer Pages), 9
Just-in-time rendering, 38

Keys
    for identification, 99
    for relational databases, 85
keywords meta element, 150
Knowledge preservation in documents, 58–59
Knuth, Donald, 71
KOffice spreadsheet, XML format for, 24
Koine (Greek dialect), 167–168

Language codes, 11, 100
LaTeX markup, 51–52
Layer-8 protocols, 138
Layering in networking, 136–138
Layout control for documents, 61–62
Layout designers, costs of, 47
Legacy information, 167
    advantages of XML for, 168
    analysis of, 173–174

Index

bloat in, 175–176
code reduction in, 172
conversion strategies for, 177–182
granularity mismatches in, 174–175
growth and versioning in, 176
interfaces, 168–170
metadata with, 182–184
network effect in, 172–173
summary, 184
transparency for, 170–172
virtual XML for, 180–182
LEPs (lists of effective pages), 66–67
Libraries
    HTML, 10
    reading XML with, 110
    for reuse, 6
Life cycles of XML projects, 33–35
LISP language, 70
Lists of effective pages (LEPs), 66–67
Literate programming, 71
Logical format for data, 79
Looseleaf publishing, 66–67
Loosely-coupled data, 79
Lorie, Ray, 51

MAC (medium access control) addresses, 101
Magna Carta, 5
Markup budgets in XML projects, 46–47
Markup issues
    change markup, 62–63
        custom publishing issues in, 65–66
        problems from, 63–65
    non-XML content, 95–97
    in searches, 151
        external metadata, 154–159
        in-line markup, 151–154
    whitespace handling, 93–95
Marshaling, 116

Mathematical equations, support for, 96
Mathematical Markup Language (MathML), 19–20
Meaning vs. formatting, 54
Measurement units, identification codes for, 100
Medium access control (MAC) addresses, 101
Megginson, David, 15–16
Memory leaks, 10
meta element, 149–150
Metadata
    as commodities, 158
    external, 154–159
    with legacy information, 182–184
    in searches, 37, 154–159
Microsoft Excel
    as standard, 78
    tabular style for, 82
    XML format for, 24
Microsoft Networks (MSN), 5
Microsoft Visual SourceSafe, 36, 74
MIF for printing, 73
Mixed content, 52, 95
Mixed conversions with legacy information, 177
Monocultures from standards, 8–9
Morris Internet worm, 9
Mosher, Ed, 51
Mozilla Project, 17
    XML support in, 69
    XSLT support in, 22
MSN (Microsoft Networks), 5
Multiple text flows in documents, 67–69

Namespaces, 18
    in compatibility, 46
    consistency in, 28
    for embedded specifications, 19–20
    for global identifiers, 102

Namespaces (*cont.*)
    for naming collisions, 115
    in searches, 159–164
Namespaces Recommendation, 18
Network effect
    in legacy information, 172–173
    in transportation standards, 4–5
Networking, 113–114
    advantages of, 114
    for compatibility, 115–116
    disadvantages of, 117
    extensibility in, 114–115
    internationalization in, 114
    layering in, 136–138
    performance of, 117
    resources for, 116
    security for, 117–118
    states in, 118
    styles, 118–120
        asynchronous, 119, 126–127
        grid computing, 131–132
        miscellaneous, 134–135
        RPC, 121–126
        syndication, 132–134
        Web Services, 127–131
    summary, 139–140
    switching and routing in, 138–139
    transparency in, 114
New Testament, 167
News Industry Text Format (NITF), 144–146
NewsML
    identification codes in, 99
    interoperability of data in, 80
    for referencing external objects, 97
    standardized metaformat in, 157
    for syndication, 134
    for transport, 38
Newspapers, text flow in, 68–69
911 phone service, 5
NITF (News Industry Text Format), 144–146
Non-XML content, 95–97
Normalized data, 86–90

OASIS (Organization for Advancement of Structured Information Standards), 13–14
    ad hoc groups, 15–16
    IDEAlliance, 14–15
    RosettaNet, 15
    specialist groups, 16–17
    WS-I, 14
Object-oriented programming, 71
OGSA (Open Grid Services Architecture), 131–132
OGSI (Open Grid Services Infrastructure), 131–132
One-way conversions with legacy information, 178
Opaque names, searching documents with, 160–161
Open Grid Services Architecture (OGSA), 131–132
Open Grid Services Infrastructure (OGSI), 131–132
Open Office spreadsheet, XML format for, 24
Open Systems Interconnection (OSI) model, 136–137
Oracle databases, XML support for, 36
Organization for Advancement of Structured Information Standards. *See* OASIS (Organization for Advancement of Structured Information Standards)
OSI (Open Systems Interconnection) model, 136–137
Overwork problem, 41
OWL (Web Ontology Language), 164
Oxford English Dictionary, 74

Packets, HTTP, 138
Parsers and parsing
    duplicated, 196–197
    external references with, 190–191
    in in-line markup, 152
    performance of, 188, 190–191
    SAX for, 180–181
    security of, 117–118
    Unicode support by, 197
Pattern matching in legacy information conversions, 177
PDF format for printing, 73
Pecking order in XML projects, 42–43
People limitations, 60–61
Performance, 185
    encoding in, 189
    external references in, 189–190
    of networking, 117
    parsing interfaces in, 190–191
    of pipelines, 196–197
    of queries, 191–194
    repetition in, 188–189
    size in, 197–199
    software and hardware support in, 187–188
    space efficiency in, 186
    summary, 199–200
    with transformations, 194–196
Photographs, external metadata for, 157–158
Physical data format, 79
Phytophthora infestans, 9
Pipeline performance, 196–197
Plaintext, 187–188
    performance with, 185
    for transparency, 170–172
Planning XML projects, 33
    components in, 33–35
    creation stage, 35
    forward compatibility and extensibility in, 44–46
    markup budgets in, 46–47
    pitfalls in, 38
    rendering stage, 38
    resistance to change in, 40–41
    search and retrieval, 36–37
    social side of, 42–44
    storage and archiving stage, 36
    summary, 47
    technology in, 44–47
    transformation stage, 37–38
    transport stage, 38
    unrealistic expectations in, 39–40
    unspoken expectations in, 39
Platform independence, 78–79
Polling in RSS, 134
POP3, plaintext with, 185
Port types in WSDL, 128
Postel, John, 115
PostScript language
    as de facto standard, 26
    for printing, 73
Potato blight, 9
Primary keys for identification, 99
Printing, 73
PRISM (Publishing Requirements for Industry Standard Metadata), 15, 29
Processing instructions, 63–64
Processing pipelines, 196–197
Profiles, WS-I, 14
Programmers in search process, 161
Programming interfaces, direct mapping to, 110
Property inheritance in RDF, 163–164
Protocol level, interoperability in, 5
Protocols
    vs. content, 136–137
    vs. formats, 113
Proximity searches, 148

Publish/subscribe networking style, 119–120, 132–134
Publishing Requirements for Industry Standard Metadata (PRISM), 15, 29
Punctuation, 58–59

Queries
    performance of, 191–194
    WSDL, 128

Railroad system standards, 4–5, 7
Random access
    for queries, 193
    for references, 89
    in SAX-like interfaces, 191
    in XSLT, 194–195
Raw tables, 83–84
RDDL (Resource Directory Description Language), 15–16
RDF (Resource Description Framework)
    data representation in, 29
    for data sharing, 78
    embedded data in, 21
    for normalized data, 89
    property inheritance in, 163–164
    schema languages for, 23
    in searches, 156, 159
    Semantic Web with, 162
    specifications for, 10
    standardized metaformat in, 157
    whitespace handling in, 94
Reactivity, 188
Readability of data, 84–85, 89
References, external
    binary, 96
    DTDs, 189–190
Regions, identification codes for, 100
Relational databases, 85
Relationships, 87, 163

RelaxNG schema language
    development of, 14
    external references with, 190
    schema, 23
Remote Method Invocation (RMI), 121
Remote procedure calls (RPC), 121–122
    with REST, 122–124
    with SOAP client, 123–126
    vs. syndication, 132–133
Rendering stage in XML projects, 34, 38
Repeatable information, 86
Repetition in performance and size, 188–189
Representational state transfer (REST) networking
    characteristics of, 119–120
    RPC with, 122–124
Request/response networking style, 119–120
Resistance to change, 40–41
Resource Description Framework. *See* RDF (Resource Description Framework)
Resource Directory Description Language (RDDL), 15–16
Resources
    for data, 81
    for networking, 116
Responses in WSDL, 128
REST (Representational state transfer) networking
    characteristics of, 119–120
    RPC with, 122–124
Reusability
    data, 79
    documents, 57, 70–72
    standards for, 4, 6
Reuters, 38
Rival management in XML projects, 43–44
RMI (Remote Method Invocation), 121
Robustness Principle, 115
Roman Empire, 167
RosettaNet, 15, 135

Round-trip conversions with legacy
information, 178–179
Routing in networking, 138–139
RPC (remote procedure calls), 121–122
    with REST, 122–124
    with SOAP client, 124–126
    vs. syndication, 132–133
RSS, 15–16
    consistency in, 29
    and syndication, 134
    for transport, 38
    for web logs, 25
RTF format for printing, 73

SAI (Standards Australia International), 11
Sarvega, 188
SAX (Simple API for XML) and SAX-like
interfaces, 16
    as de facto standard, 26
    development of, 15–16
    for parsing, 180–181, 190–191
    pipelines in, 197
Scalable Vector Graphics (SVG)
    development of, 19
    support for, 96
Schemas, 107–108
    for data identification, 100
    in searches, 159–164
    as stylesheets, 23
Screen-based formats, 73
Search stage in XML projects, 34, 36–37
Searching, 143
    context in, 143–145
    correlation in, 145–147
    interoperability in, 150–151
    markup considerations in, 151
        external metadata, 154–159
        in-line markup, 151–154
    namespaces, schemas, and Semantic Web
in, 159–164
    summary, 164–165
    trust in, 149–150
    usability in, 147–149
Security for networking, 117–118
Self-documentation, 79
Self-labeling data, 172
Semantic Web project
    with RDF, 21, 25, 28
    in searching, 162–164
Session states in networking, 118
SGML (Standard Generalized Markup
Language), 11–12, 51–53
SGML Open, 13
Sharing information, 45, 78
Shift-JIS encoding, 197
Simple API for XML (SAX) and SAX-like
interfaces, 16
    development of, 15–16
    for parsing, 180–181, 190–191
    programming bindings for, 22
Simple Mail Transfer Protocol (SMTP), 126
    attacks on, 9
    plaintext with, 185, 187
Simple Object Access Protocol (SOAP)
    with REST, 123–124
    RPC with, 124–126
Single-source publishing
    characteristics of, 53–54
    vs. idioms, 73
Size, 185
    compression in, 199
    external references in, 189–190
    and internalization, 198–199
    repetition in, 188–189
    space efficiency in, 186
    summary, 199–200
    Unicode and character size, 197–198
SMTP (Simple Mail Transfer Protocol), 126
    attacks on, 9
    plaintext with, 185, 187

SOAP (Simple Object Access Protocol)
    with REST, 123–124
    RPC with, 124–126
Social side of XML projects, 42–44
Software components for reuse, 6
Software support in performance, 187–188
Solicit/response method, 131
Space efficiency, 186
Specifications vs. standards, 3
Spelling, 60–61
Splitting markup, 64
Spreadsheets
    RPC model for, 133
    standards for, 78
    tabular style for, 82
    XML format for, 24
SQL for searches, 34
Square peg problems for standards, 9
Standard Generalized Markup Language (SGML), 11–12, 51–53
Standard structures for metadata markup, 157
Standards, 3
    advantages of, 4
        abstraction, 6–7
        interoperability, 4–6
        reuse, 6
    consistency and compatibility in, 27–29
    de facto vs. de jure, 26–27
    disadvantages of, 7–8
        abstraction, 10
        FUD, 8
        monocultures, 8–9
        square pegs, 9
    organizations for, 10
        ISO, 11–12
        OASIS, 13–17
        W3C, 12–13
    summary, 29–31

XML-related specifications, 17–18
    application specifications, 24–25
    core specifications, 18
    embeddable, 19–21
    utility specifications, 21–24
Standards Australia International (SAI), 11
Star Office, XML format for, 24
Stateless protocols, 118
States in networking, 118
Stephenson, George, 4
Stock quotes, syndication for, 132–133
Storage and archiving stage in XML projects, 34, 36
Storage independence, 78–79
Streaming APIs, 22
Strings
    efficiency of, 105
    everything-is-a-string philosophy, 98
Structural searching, 37
Structural transformations, XSLT for, 194
Structured programming, 71
Style sheets, 12
    costs of, 46
    as filters, 23
    linking, 20
    XML support in, 69
Styles, networking, 118–120
    asynchronous, 119, 126–127
    grid computing, 131–132
    miscellaneous, 134–135
    RPC, 121–126
    syndication, 132–134
    Web Services, 127–131
Subsets in searches, 147
Supersets in searches, 147
SVG (Scalable Vector Graphics)
    development of, 19
    support for, 96
Switching in networking, 138–139

Index

Synchronous networking, 119
Syndication in networking, 132–134
Synonyms in searches, 147
System integraters in search process, 161

Tabular style, 82–85
TCP (Transmission Control Protocol), 115
Technical committee (TC), 14
Technology in XML projects, 44–47
TEI. *See* Text Encoding Initiative (TEI)
TELNET, plaintext with, 185, 187
TeX language, 51
TeXInfo, 54
Text Encoding Initiative (TEI), 17, 25
  consistency in, 29
  interoperability with, 151
  words in, 145
Tracking changes in markup, 65
Training, 47, 60–61
Transactions, 103–105
Transformation pipeline, 37
Transformation stage in XML projects, 37–38
Transformations
  in hybrid data publishing, 55–56
  performance with, 194–196
  XSL. *See* XSL Transformations (XSLT)
Translators for legacy interfaces, 168
Transmission Control Protocol (TCP), 115
Transparency of information, 107
  for legacy information, 170–172
  in networking, 114
Transport stage in XML projects, 34, 38
Transportation system standards, 4–5
Tree-based APIs, 22
Tree-based DOM, 180, 185, 192
Tree-based interfaces, 190–191
TROFF language, 51, 54

Trust
  in searches, 149–150
  in Semantic Web, 164
Two-phase commits, 105
type field, 106

U.S. Patent and Trademark Office (USPTO), 17
UCS-4 encoding, 189
UDDI (Universal Description, Discovery, and Integration of Web Services), 131
UML (Unified Modeling Language), 25
UN/EDIFACT, 135
Unicast networking, 119
Unicode encoding
  for internationalization, 114
  ISO specification, 11
  size of, 197–198
  UCS-4, 189
Unified Modeling Language (UML), 25
Uniform Code Council, 100
Uniform resource identifiers (URIs), 101
Uniform resource name (URNs), 102
unit attribute, 147
United Nations Centre for Trade Facilitation and Electronic Business (UN-CEFACT), 14
Units of measure, identification codes for, 100
Universal Description, Discovery, and Integration of Web Services (UDDI), 131
Universal product codes (UPCs), 100
Untyped XML data, 106–107
Up conversions with legacy information, 177
UPCs (universal product codes), 100
URIs (uniform resource identifiers), 101

URLs
    RESTful, 124
    vs. URNs, 102
URNs (uniform resource name), 102
Usability in searches, 147–149
User control in XML projects, 42
User training, 47, 60–61
USPTO (U.S. Patent and Trademark Office), 17
UTF-8 encoding, 189, 197–198
UTF-16 encoding, 189, 197–198
Utility specifications, 21–24

Validation
    data, 79–80
    DTDs, 27–28
Vector graphics (SVG)
    development of, 19
    support for, 96
Verification of data, 79–80
version attribute, 46
Versioning in legacy information, 176
Video clips, metadata for, 183–184
Virtual Reality Markup Language (VRML), 9
Virtual XML, 180–182
VisiCalc spreadsheet, 82
Visual SourceSafe, 36, 74
Vocabulary in searches, 148
VRML (Virtual Reality Markup Language), 9

W3C (World Wide Web Consortium), 8, 12–13
    for namespace identifiers, 102
    Semantic Web project, 25
Web browser, XSLT for, 22
web logs, 16, 25
Web Ontology Language (OWL), 164

Web pages in relationships, 87
Web Services, 14
    specifications for, 10
    working with, 127–131
Web Services Definition Language (WSDL), 128–131
Web Services Interoperability Organization (WS-I), 14
Web Services Reliable Messaging (WSRM), 14
Web Services Security (WSS), 14
Whitespace
    in formatting, 58–59
    handling, 93–95
Workload management in XML projects, 43
World Wide Web Consortium (W3C), 8, 12–13
    for namespace identifiers, 102
    Semantic Web project, 25
Wrapping interfaces, 173, 184
WS-I (Web Services Interoperability Organization), 14
WSDL (Web Services Definition Language), 128–131
WSRM (Web Services Reliable Messaging), 14
WSS (Web Services Security), 14
WYSIWYG systems, 40

XBRL (Extensible Business Reporting Language) format, 80
XBRL International, 17
XForms, 21
XHTML (Extensible Hypertext Markup Language), 25
    consistency in, 29
    interoperability with, 151
XLink, 20
    consistency in, 28

Index

for referencing external objects, 97
W3C working group for, 13
XML support in, 69
XMI (XML Metadata Interchange), 25
XML applications, 16
XML Applications and Initiatives page, 25
XML Encryption, 21, 24
XML Entity Catalog specification, 24
XML Information Set, 19
xml:lang attribute, 19
XML Linking Language. *See* XLink
XML Metadata Interchange (XMI), 25
XML Namespaces, 18
   consistency in, 28
   for embedded specifications, 19–20
   for global identifiers, 102
XML Pointer Language, 20–21
   W3C working group for, 13
   XML support in, 69
XML Recommendation, 18
XML Schema language, 14, 107–108
   external references with, 190
   specification for, 23
XML Signature, 21, 24
xml:space attribute, 19, 94–95
XML Stylesheet Language (XSLT)
   consistency in, 29
   for rendering, 34
   W3C working group for, 13

XML Topic Maps (XTM), 25
   for data sharing, 78
   standardized metaformat in, 157
   whitespace handling in, 94
XPath language
   for content switching, 139
   for queries, 192–193
   random access in, 194
   structural searching in, 37
XPOINTER language, 20–21
   W3C working group for, 13
   XML support in, 69
XQuery
   consistency in, 28
   development of, 22–23
   structural searching in, 37
XSL Transformations (XSLT)
   characteristics, 22
   limitations of, 9
   performance with, 185, 188, 194–195
   XML support in, 69
XSLT. *See* XML Stylesheet Language (XSLT); XSL Transformations (XSLT)
XTM (XML Topic Maps), 25
   for data sharing, 78
   standardized metaformat in, 157
   whitespace handling in, 94

informIT

www.informit.com

YOUR GUIDE TO IT REFERENCE

Articles

Keep your edge with thousands of free articles, in-depth features, interviews, and IT reference recommendations – all written by experts you know and trust.

Online Books

Answers in an instant from **InformIT Online Book's** 600+ fully searchable on line books. For a limited time, you can get your first 14 days **free**.

Catalog

Review online sample chapters, author biographies and customer rankings and choose exactly the right book from a selection of over 5,000 titles.

Wouldn't it be great

if the world's leading technical publishers joined forces to deliver their best tech books in a common digital reference platform?

They have. Introducing
InformIT Online Books
powered by Safari.

Specific answers to specific questions.
InformIT Online Books' powerful search engine gives you relevance-ranked results in a matter of seconds.

Immediate results.
With InformIT Online Books, you can select the book you want and view the chapter or section you need immediately.

Cut, paste and annotate.
Paste code to save time and eliminate typographical errors. Make notes on the material you find useful and choose whether or not to share them with your work group.

Customized for your enterprise.
Customize a library for you, your department or your entire organization. You only pay for what you need.

Get your first 14 days FREE!

For a limited time, InformIT Online Books is offering its members a 10 book subscription risk-free for 14 days. Visit **http://www.informit.com/onlinebooks** for details.

informit.com/onlinebooks

InformIT Online Books

Register Your Book

at www.awprofessional.com/register

You may be eligible to receive:

- Advance notice of forthcoming editions of the book
- Related book recommendations
- Chapter excerpts and supplements of forthcoming titles
- Information about special contests and promotions throughout the year
- Notices and reminders about author appearances, tradeshows, and online chats with special guests

Contact us

If you are interested in writing a book or reviewing manuscripts prior to publication, please write to us at:

Editorial Department
Addison-Wesley Professional
75 Arlington Street, Suite 300
Boston, MA 02116 USA
Email: AWPro@aw.com

Visit us on the Web: http://www.awprofessional.com